T0327268

For years, I've taught students and church members that the Bible is a missionary text and Christian history is a missionary story. Ed Smithers believes the same thing, and in *Christian Mission: A Concise Global History*, he offers a winsome, accessible, and edifying introduction to the story of Christian mission. This book is ideal for both classroom use and church reading groups, and my prayer is that it will inspire many readers to join God in his mission to rescue sinners from every nation, tribe, people, and language (Rev. 7:9).

Nathan A. Finn, Provost and Dean of the University Faculty, North Greenville University

The church is a community that lives by the Biblical narrative. The church remembers, rehearses, and lives by the story which the Bible tells. But the church is also nourished by the stories of the growth and progress of the church—from the early intimate communities to the global church of today. Edward Smither's retelling of these stories—his overview of Christian mission spanning more than 21 centuries—serves as guidance and encouragement. He presents a concise and dense retelling of one of the most compelling stories ever.

Nelus Niemandt, Head of the Department Religion Studies, Faculty of Theology, University of Pretoria, South Africa.

Dr. Ed Smither has made a tremendously helpful contribution by providing us with a thorough, yet accessible overview in *Christian Mission: A Concise Global History*. Building on broader exhaustive histories, Smither has focused on a chronology of evangelical mission, missionaries, movements, and missiological insights. Perhaps most importantly, this text emphasizes God's mission being accomplished by ordinary Christians from around the world who came to understand their purpose in their newfound identity. After teaching Introduction to Christian Missions for over a decade, I have finally found a supplementary text that conveys our faith's historical developments in such a way as to call this generation up into God's great mission to reconcile the world to himself.

George G. Robinson IV, Associate Professor of Missions & Evangelism, Headrick Chair of World Missions, Southeastern Baptist Theological Seminary

Ed Smither brings to us—in his own inimitable way—a concise and balanced history of Christian missions. He offers concision (which is important because the history of God's movement among the peoples of the world is so vast, but he so helpfully streamlines and organizes it for the reader in one volume that is eminently accessible) with balance (offering a well-rounded view of missions being from everywhere to everyone, not just from the West to the rest)—and it reads well. It is far from boring! This reads like the best of Kenneth Scott Latourette's *A History of the Expansion of Christianity* and Philip Jenkins' *The Lost History of Christianity*. Smither is a messenger of the Good News to remember all that God has done in the past, which gives us confidence for the present and hope for the future.

Allen Yeh, Associate Professor of Intercultural Studies & Missiology, Biola University, Cook School of Intercultural Studies

I am most delighted to recommend Ed Smither's *Christian Mission* to you. Historical study is extremely important to church health, yet often overlooked. Ask church members about mission history, and they will talk about the New Testament, something that took place with a man named Luther, and Billy Graham's preaching. Beyond these matters, uncertainty exists. Where the Church is ignorant to her history, there her health suffers. Smither has summarized some of the most important aspects of 2000 years of gospel advancement so that the Body of Christ may grow in health and clarity of thought. Important names, places, acts, and events are addressed in a scholarly, well written, and easy-to-understand format. This is the place to begin if you are interested in knowing what occurred as the gospel moved from Jerusalem to the uttermost parts. Keep this book close, for you will return to it again and again.

J. D. Payne, Associate Professor of Christian Ministry, Samford University

Edward Smither's *Christian Mission* is a notable book that brings history to life in a way that is amiable, effortlessly explaining a global mission history, without condescension, of challenging issues such as mission in the Protestant Reformation, all framed within political and social contexts that use vivid imagery of key people and strategies.

Rev. Robert L. Gallagher, Professor of Intercultural Studies and Director of Intercultural Studies Programs, Wheaton College

Christian Mission

Christian
Mission

A CONCISE
GLOBAL HISTORY

EDWARD L. SMITHER

LEXHAM PRESS

Christian Mission: A Concise Global History

Lexham Press, 1313 Commercial St., Bellingham, WA 98225
LexhamPress.com

Print ISBN 9781683592402
Digital ISBN 9781683592419

Lexham Editorial Team: Todd Hains, Erin Mangum, and Claire Vandervelde
Cover Design: Eleazar Ruiz
Typesetting: Scribe Inc.

23 24 25 26 27 28 29 / US / 12 11 10 9 8 7 6 5 4 3 2

Contents

For Mike Barnett (1952–2015)

Acknowledgments

I would like to thank a number of people who have encouraged or challenged me in the process of completing this project:

Students in my one-semester history of mission course over the last decade who've been great conversation partners and ultimately provided the environment to write this book.

Colleagues in the Evangelical Missiological Society and Evangelical Theological Society who've listened to and offered feedback on research—much of which has found its way into these pages.

Ruth Buchanan, beta-reader extraordinaire, who read every word of this manuscript, exhorting me to the active voice, helping to undangle modifiers, and coaching me toward producing a readable book.

Todd Hains, my capital E editor at Lexham. Thanks for going the extra mile to help this work become accessible, relevant, and accurate. Thanks especially for the pushback on mission in the Protestant Reformation. You, your emojis, and gifs, and excessive use of the word *ain't* made this project a lot of fun.

My leadership at Columbia International University who encourage me and offer space to research and write.

My teammates in CIU's College of Intercultural Studies who've sat at coffee and/or lunch, allowing me to think out loud about ideas and themes that made it into the book.

My wife Shawn and my kids who love me and have accepted the fact that my main hobby (besides road biking) is reading, writing, and trying to figure things out.

Abbreviations

ANF	*Ante-Nicene Fathers*
b.	born
c.	circa
d.	died
NPNF²	*Nicene and Post-Nicene Fathers*, Series 2
r.	reigned

Introduction

George Liele (c. 1750–1820) was America's first cross-cultural missionary. He arrived on the shores of Jamaica in 1783 to live, work, and ultimately pioneer Baptist mission work on the island. Born a slave in Virginia, Liele received his freedom and began to pursue ministry, planting churches in South Carolina and Georgia. Fearing that he would be enslaved again, Liele sold himself as an indentured servant to Jamaica. After paying off this debt, he farmed and worked in Jamaica's transportation industry. He never received a salary for pastoral ministry or mission work. The Jamaican Baptist Union, which today consists of 337 congregations and forty thousand believers, is indebted to the work of this bivocational church planter who came to their land as a missionary because he was fleeing slavery in his own.

This book is about the George Lieles in history—innovators in mission who sacrificially went to the nations to make known the gospel of Christ. I will narrate a global history of Christian mission by examining the geographic, political, and social contexts of mission and highlighting the key people, strategies, and outcomes of global mission. I emphasize *global*. The gospel has never been possessed by just one culture or region of the world; throughout history it has flowed from everywhere to everyone.

MISSION IS ABOUT SENDING

The word *mission* is used today in a plethora of contexts. Diplomats, fighter pilots, and some elementary school teachers refer to their work as a mission. Virtually every business, from auto-parts distributors to fast-food restaurants, possesses an articulated mission statement. When a word is used so often, fatigue can set in and obscure its meaning altogether.

Christian mission is no exception. Stephen Neill, a twentieth-century Anglican bishop and historian of mission, warned, "If everything is mission, nothing is mission."[1]

So what do we mean by Christian mission? *Mission* simply means sending. The first instance of sending in Scripture occurs just after the fall when the living God, acting as the first responder, moves toward the fallen couple and poses the haunting question, "Where are you?" (Gen 3:9). From there, God covers their nakedness and shame with animal skins—a sacrifice that prefigured the redeeming work that Christ would accomplish at the cross. God is a missionary God. Unsurprisingly, the narrative of Scripture abounds with God's initiative to send people and groups of people—Abraham, Israel, prophets, Jesus, and the church—to announce his ways, his Messiah, and his message of redemption and reconciliation. Thus, evangelical theologians and missiologists correctly refer to *mission* as the mission of God.[2]

What then distinguishes *Christian* mission from the good work of the Red Cross or the United Nations? One aspect is motivation. Since humankind's greatest needs are spiritual, the central task in mission is proclaiming Christ—his death, burial, and resurrection. The Lord commanded the church to make disciples, and this involves proclaiming Jesus and inviting sinners to follow him (evangelism), teaching new believers all that Jesus commanded about faith and practice (discipleship), and gathering believers into worshiping communities (church planting). From the Scriptures, we see that mission occurs not only in word (proclaiming the gospel, teaching, starting churches) but also in deed (caring for real human needs). In the midst of an earthly mission largely composed of preaching and teaching, Jesus took time to heal the sick, feed the poor, and denounce social injustice. So while a Red Cross worker and a Christian missionary might work side by side in disaster relief, the missionary's work must involve sharing the gospel.

---

1. Stephen Neill, *Salvation Tomorrow: The Originality of Jesus Christ and the World's Religions* (Cambridge: Lutterworth, 1976), 17.

2. See Christopher Wright, *The Mission of God: Unlocking the Bible's Grand Narrative* (Downers Grove, IL: IVP Academic, 2006); Mike Barnett, ed., *Discovering the Mission of God: Best Missional Practices for the Twenty-First Century* (Downers Grove, IL: IVP Academic, 2012); William Larkin and Joel Williams, eds., *Mission in the New Testament: An Evangelical Approach* (Maryknoll, NY: Orbis, 1998).

Growing up, I assumed that mission work occurred in Haiti or Africa because that's where the missionaries I knew lived. Going to make disciples of all nations meant getting a passport, a visa, and shots before boarding a plane to travel far away to minister in Jesus' name. While mission definitely involves crossing borders, *the greatest boundary that a missionary navigates is the one between faith and nonfaith.* This is true of my encounter with a Muslim friend in Tunisia, a Chinese doctoral student in my North American city, and with my North American next-door neighbor.

While mission can be a monocultural experience, Scripture resounds with the admonition to "Declare his glory among the nations, his marvelous deeds among all peoples" (Ps 96:3). The scope or arena of God's mission is the whole earth and among all cultural groups. The mission of God in Scripture is framed by God blessing Abram to be a blessing in order that all of the families of the earth would be blessed (Gen 12:1–3). In Galatians, Paul interpreted this blessing as the gospel itself: "Scripture foresaw that God would justify the Gentiles by faith, and announced the gospel in advance to Abraham: 'All nations will be blessed through you'" (Gal 3:8). In Christian mission we must cross boundaries of faith and nonfaith and go to the nations. While a Brazilian pastor faithfully ministers in his church and engages in mission in his community, he still has a responsibility to go about his work in light of the nations—to lead his church in praying for the nations, to send members of his church as missionaries, or to minister to immigrants from the nations in his community.

Finally, is mission just the work of missionaries? Of course, this assumes we know who a missionary is and what they do! Though I'll more thoroughly define the identity and activity of missionaries through the historical narrative in this book, for now we can affirm that all believers in Christ have some role to play in God's mission. Many will go in an official capacity as full-time vocational missionaries. Others will immigrate abroad for work, study, or even because of displacement and will make disciples and start churches in the process. Some will welcome the nations—international students, immigrants, refugees—and minister in word and in deed in their own communities. Finally, others will pray, give financially, and serve as advocates for unevangelized peoples. God is a missionary God and invites his people to participate in his mission. No one is off the hook.

THE VALUE OF MISSION HISTORY

What value do we find in studying the history of mission? First, examining history in general enriches the human experience as we gain an accurate understanding of the past by grasping contexts, causes, changes, and complex developments.[3] Second, historian Justo González correctly says that church history is in fact mission history. To appreciate the church's story through the ages—beyond the history of buildings, traditions, and doctrine—we must evaluate how the gospel has spread across social and cultural boundaries and how the church has taken root among people groups. Grasping the history of Christianity shapes the global church's consciousness and contributes to a healthy Christian memory. Although a faithful appraisal of mission history will reveal the weaknesses and mistakes of missionaries and even embarrassing developments, it ultimately points to the faithfulness of a missionary God. Finally, practically speaking, modern mission practitioners who evaluate mission history can learn from the mistakes and the innovations of the past—practices that ought to be rightly abandoned as well as other approaches that might be recovered or emulated today.

LITERATURE

A number of authors have written surveys on mission history.[4] I am indebted to their work, and my project builds on their scholarship. Some scholars have strongly emphasized the period of modern missions; however, they only offer brief surveys of mission in the early church period.[5] Other surveys have now become dated and only span until the mid- to late

---

3. See John Fea, *Why Study History? Reflecting on the Importance of the Past* (Grand Rapids: Baker, 2013).

4. See Stephen Neill, *A History of Christian Missions* (London: Penguin, 1990); Ruth A. Tucker, *From Jerusalem to Irian Jaya: A Biographical History of Christian Mission* (Grand Rapids: Zondervan, 2004); J. Herbert Kane, *A Concise History of the Christian World Mission: A Panoramic View of Missions from Pentecost to the Present* (Grand Rapids: Baker, 1982); Jacques A. Blocher and Jacques Blandenier, *The Evangelization of the World: A History of Christian Missions* (Pasadena, CA: William Carey Library, 2012); Dana Robert, *Christian Mission: How Christianity Became a World Religion* (Oxford: Wiley-Blackwell, 2009); and Carlos F. Cardoza-Orlandi and Justo L. González, *To All Nations from All Nations: A History of the Christian Missionary Movement* (Nashville: Abingdon, 2013).

5. See Neill, *History of Christian Missions*; Tucker, *From Jerusalem to Irian Jaya*.

twentieth century.[6] Some authors have compiled surveys for a broader ecumenical audience, examining mainline Protestant, Orthodox, and Roman Catholic mission work in the modern era, which is broader than my focus.[7] Finally, some works are organized more thematically, and others take a biographical approach.[8] Though my study includes both themes and biographies, I will take a broader, chronological, and contextual approach. I want to produce a global history of Christian mission that will celebrate how the gospel has gone from everywhere to everyone. I want to offer a balanced study of mission in the often-neglected patristic and medieval periods while also giving attention to the modern period. I also want to highlight twenty-first-century evangelical mission efforts from the Global South or majority world.

LIMITATIONS

Given the broad nature of this book, there are some necessary limitations. First, compared to other world Christianity surveys, my examination of Christianity in nineteenth- and twentieth-century Oceania, Africa, Asia, and Latin America, for example, will be more representative than exhaustive. Second, I will only briefly discuss political and social history in each period and region in order to show the context for missionary approaches and innovation. Third, although at times some theological controversies may be discussed, I do not intend to thoroughly explore historical theology. Finally, in light of the breadth of global mission efforts since 1800, I will only focus on Protestant evangelical mission work from the nineteenth century onward. Certainly, Roman Catholic and Eastern Orthodox missionaries have engaged in God-honoring mission work during this period; however, given the scope of the book and the predominantly evangelical audience, I have made the difficult choice to focus only on evangelical mission.

---

6. See Neill, *History of Christian Missions*; Kane, *Concise History of the Christian World Mission*; Blocher and Blandenier, *Evangelization of the World*.

7. See Neill, *History of Christian Missions*; Cardoza-Orlandi and González, *To All Nations from All Nations*.

8. See Robert, *Christian Mission*; Tucker, *From Jerusalem to Irian Jaya*.

In this book, evangelicals are characterized by the "Bebbington quadrilateral."[9] First, conversion is necessary. One must be "born again" through faith in the death, burial, and resurrection of the Lord Jesus Christ (John 3:1–8). Second, Scripture is the final authority for Christian belief and practice. Third, Christians experience a victorious life of faith. Though Christians will never realize a state of sinless perfection, the ongoing spiritual growth through the indwelling presence and work of the Holy Spirit in the life of the believer is expected. For this reason, Christians practice spiritual disciplines to grow spiritually (for example, corporate worship, prayer, Bible study). Fourth, Christians must live out their faith. Compelled by the love of Christ, Christians actively engage in service and witness, including participating in the mission of God (2 Cor 5:14). Though some Roman Catholics, Eastern Orthodox, and mainline Protestant Christians may self-identify as evangelical given these attributes, this study will still be limited to missionary efforts from evangelical Protestant churches.

METHODOLOGY AND OVERVIEW

I will frame each chapter posing the following questions. (1) *When and where?* Taking a chronological approach, we will examine how the church expanded geographically around the world. (2) *Who and what?* Here we will consider innovative missionaries and mission movements as well as their approaches to mission. (3) Finally, *What were the key trends, themes, and paradigm shifts in mission thought and practice?* In this section we will evaluate both strengths and shortcomings in each period.

Following a chronological and geographical focus, I have framed the book in six major chapters followed by a brief epilogue. In chapter 1, "Mission in the Early Church," we begin at the end of the first century and examine mission through the patristic era until the middle of the eighth century. We will journey west, exploring mission through the regions of the Roman Empire, as well as east, from Syria through central Asia and ultimately China. We will experience climates both favorable and hostile to Christianity. We will see how the church sorted through what it means to be on mission when

---

9. See David Bebbington, *Evangelicalism in Modern Britain: 1730s to 1980s* (London: Routledge, 1988).

church and state became more united following the fourth-century conversion of the Emperor Constantine (274–337). During this period, very few "full-time" missionaries existed; instead, most were bivocational. This included missionary-bishops, missionary-teachers, missionary-monks, and also anonymous missionaries—those who witnessed to Christ and planted churches without self-identifying as missionaries.

In chapter 2, "Mission in the Medieval Church," we explore how the church engaged in mission from the mid-eighth century until the eve of the Protestant Reformation. We will observe the gospel's expansion into the remainder of Western Europe, Eastern Europe and Russia, Scandinavia, and across central and east Asia. During this time, the key missionaries continued to be bishops and monks; however, we will also note the rise of the mendicant monastic orders (Franciscans, Dominicans, and others) and their innovation in mission. To be sure, ministering in an age of fully orbed Christendom made the idea of mission confusing. But missionaries, committed to the biblical approach of making disciples, continued to serve in contexts of violence among the Vikings, Muslims, and Mongols.

In chapter 3, "Mission in the Early Modern Church," we will focus on the period of 1500 to 1800. As the Spanish and Portuguese empires, and later others, pursued global expansion in the sixteenth century, Christian missionaries accompanied explorers and conquistadores. This fusion of mission and empire certainly bred confusion; however, we will observe examples of biblically authentic mission as Roman Catholic missionaries carried the gospel to Asia, the Americas, and Africa. While the mendicant orders continued to minister across the globe, the most significant Catholic missionary movement began in the sixteenth century with the Society of Jesus. From 1500 to 1800, the work of global mission was still largely a Roman Catholic affair. Unfortunately, the vision and efforts of the magisterial reformers did not translate into a viable global mission movement. Despite flickers of Protestant foreign mission work, the first Protestant global missionary movement did not develop until the Moravians emerged in 1727.

In chapter 4, "The Great Century," we discuss the nineteenth century of evangelical Protestant mission efforts. This era began when a bivocational English pastor named William Carey (1761–1834) emphasized a fresh reading of the Great Commission (Matt 28:18–20). He concluded that the church was God's means for accomplishing mission in every generation. Driven by the voluntary principle, Carey and others founded mission societies that mobilized and sent laborers to Asia, Africa, the Americas, and Oceania.

Chapter 5, "The Global Century," captures the twentieth century of Christian mission. The twentieth century was marked by violence and turbulence—including two world wars and numerous regional conflicts, the rise and influence of communism, and multiple genocides. It also spelled the end of colonialism in much of Africa and parts of Asia. Despite these upheavals, the gospel spread undaunted in the Americas, Africa, and Asia. At the same time, however, Europe became progressively post-Christian. While during the nineteenth century Great Britain had been the leading mission-sending country, during the twentieth the United States led the charge. Mission organizations continued to be formed during the twentieth century, including a number emerging in the Global South.

In chapter 6, "Mission from the Majority World," we encounter the missional reversal of the twenty-first century. At the beginning of the twentieth century, missionaries were primarily being sent from the West to the rest of the world; however, by the late twentieth century, Brazilian, Nigerian, Korean, Indian, and Chinese believers were engaging in cross-cultural mission. Global South Christianity emerged. The majority of the world's Christians reside in Africa, Asia, and Latin America, and the demographic of the global mission movement began to reflect this. In this chapter, we will explore the development of missionary movements from the non-Western world. Finally, we will evaluate mission in the context of global migration and diaspora.

In a final epilogue, we will discuss the future of global mission in light of what we have learned form the past, teasing out the overarching themes of missionary identity, suffering, indigenous churches, and mission from everywhere to everyone.

FURTHER READING

Barnett, Mike, ed. *Discovering the Mission of God: Best Missional Practices for the Twenty-First Century*. Downers Grove, IL: IVP Academic, 2012.

————. "The Missing Key to the Future of Evangelical Mission." In *MissionShift: Global Issues in the Third Millennium*, edited by Ed Stetzer and David Hesselgrave, 223–23. Nashville: B&H Academic, 2010.

Bebbington, David. *Evangelicalism in Modern Britain: 1730s to 1980s*. London: Routledge, 1988.

Blocher, Jacques A., and Jacques Blandenier. *The Evangelization of the World: A History of Christian Missions*. Pasadena, CA: William Carey Library, 2012.

Cardoza-Orlandi, Carlos F., and Justo González. *To All Nations from All Nations: A History of the Christian Missionary Movement*. Nashville: Abingdon, 2013.

Escobar, Samuel. *The New Global Mission: The Gospel from Everywhere to Everyone*. Downers Grove, IL: IVP Academic, 2003.

Fea, John. *Why Study History? Reflecting on the Importance of the Past*. Grand Rapids: Baker, 2013.

Kane, J. Herbert. *A Concise History of the Christian World Mission: A Panoramic View of Missions from Pentecost to the Present*. Grand Rapids: Baker, 1982.

Larkin, William, and Joel Williams, eds. *Mission in the New Testament: An Evangelical Approach*. Maryknoll, NY: Orbis, 1998.

Latourette, Kenneth Scott. *A History of the Expansion of Christianity: The First Five Centuries*. New York: Harper & Brothers, 1937. Reprint, Grand Rapids: Zondervan, 1970.

Neill, Stephen. *A History of Christian Missions*. London: Penguin, 1990.

————. *Salvation Tomorrow: The Originality of Jesus Christ and the World's Religions*. Cambridge: Lutterworth, 1976.

Ott, Craig, ed. *The Mission of the Church: Five Views in Conversation*. Grand Rapids: Baker Academic, 2016.

Pierson, Paul. *The Dynamics of Christian Mission: History through a Missiological Perspective*. Pasadena, CA: William Carey International University Press, 2009.

Robert, Dana. *Christian Mission: How Christianity Became a World Religion*. Oxford: Wiley-Blackwell, 2009.

Wright, Christopher. *The Mission of God: Unlocking the Bible's Grand Narrative*. Downers Grove, IL: IVP Academic, 2006.

1
Mission in the Early Church (100–750)

The New Testament is a missionary story. Capturing the life, earthly ministry, and passion of our Lord, the Gospels offer an up-close look at Jesus, the Sent One. In the book of Acts, Luke chronicles the church on mission as it crossed the geographical and cultural boundaries of Jerusalem, Judea, and Samaria, toward the ends of the earth (Acts 1:8). The rest of the New Testament writings—letters from Paul and other apostles to young churches—were also forged in a context of mission. On one hand, mission is the impetus for the New Testament writings; on the other, the New Testament (along with the Old) serves as a record of God's mission.

Luke remembers the birth of the church on the day of Pentecost and lists some of the people groups who were present, hearing and believing the good news: "Parthians, Medes and Elamites; residents of Mesopotamia, Judea and Cappadocia, Pontus and Asia, Phrygia and Pamphylia, Egypt and the parts of Libya near Cyrene; visitors from Rome (both Jews and converts to Judaism); Cretans and Arabs" (Acts 2:9–11). Churches emerged in these regions in the late first and early second centuries, in part because of the witness of these Pentecost worshipers who returned home and shared what they had experienced in Jerusalem.

The Christian community Antioch of Syria was planted in the first century. It quickly became the sending church for Paul and his companions (Acts 11:19–27; 13:1–3). Paul and his co-laborers proclaimed the gospel on the islands of Cyprus, Malta, and Crete; in Asia Minor and Asia between Tarsus and Macedonia; in Greece, Italy, and Rome; and probably as far as Spain. About half of the book of Acts focuses on Paul's ends-of-the-earth mission, which largely flowed westward from Antioch.

In this opening chapter, we will follow in the footsteps of Paul and the early Pentecost believers and examine where the gospel spread and how it took root in the first eight and a half centuries. We'll begin by journeying west and describing the church's missionary encounter within the Roman Empire. We'll also consider several places of mission (Ireland, Scotland, Germania) on the fringes of the empire. Then we'll continue east and explore how the Christian movement expanded east from Syria across Asia toward China.

ROMAN EMPIRE

CONDITIONS

A number of contextual realities facilitated the mission of the church in the first-century Roman world.[1] Structurally, finely engineered and well-maintained Roman roads enabled evangelists such as Paul to travel easily within a network of cities in the empire. Politically, in the first century the Roman Empire experienced its famed *Pax Romana* or period of peace. Although Roman emperors were at times toppled, and foreign armies positioned themselves around the outskirts of the empire, overall Rome knew an unprecedented period of peace. Along with good roads, this meant that early Christians could travel safely, cover vast amounts of territory, and encounter diverse cultural groups all within the boundaries of the empire.

Although the Roman Empire was made up of many diverse cultural groups, the Greek language united the empire linguistically. While this lingua franca facilitated oral communication for conducting business and preaching, common, everyday Greek (*koine*) also served as the language for the New Testament Scriptures. So, the teachings of an Aramaic-speaking Messiah were translated and rendered in Greek for maximum transmission around the Roman world. Paul, a native Cilician speaker from Tarsus (Asia Minor), wrote a letter in Greek that was read by Latin speakers in Rome. This widespread use of Greek in the empire proved to be a strategic vehicle for spreading the gospel.

---

1. See Michael Green, *Evangelism in the Early Church* (Grand Rapids: Eerdmans, 1970; rev. ed., 2003), 29–49.

Greek philosophy and religions also provided a bridge of understanding for Christian teaching. The two greatest Greek philosophers, Plato (d. 348 BC) and Aristotle (c. 384–322 BC), were avowed monotheists who were quite critical of polytheism. Greek mystery religions, which were assimilated into Greek and Roman paganism, raised questions about forgiveness, cleansing, unity with the divine, and immortality. The early Christians' gospel provided a response to these questions. As Christianity took root in this Greco-Roman milieu, most early Christian thinkers, including Justin Martyr (d. 165) and Origen of Alexandria (185–254), constructed their theologies within Greek philosophical frameworks.

A final factor that aided the spread of the gospel in Rome was the presence and spiritual influence of the Jews, who comprised about 7 percent of the Roman population. This figure included ethnic Jews, who had been dispersed throughout the empire, and also Hellenistic Jews, who had joined the faith through conversion. Jewish belief in one God, its emphasis on a Messiah, and its value on Scriptures and worship gatherings provided a logical foundation for Christian preaching. Michael Green aptly notes, "The Christian faith grew best and fastest on Jewish soil, or at least soil that had been prepared by Judaism."[2]

ROMANS AND CHRISTIANS

The Romans accused the Christians of general impiety toward pagan belief and practice. In failing to honor the many deities of the Roman pantheon, which often included the emperor, Christians were accused of atheism—worshiping a god that they could not see. The Romans believed that this lack of devotion would anger the gods, who would then remove their protection from Rome. On this point, Tertullian of Carthage (c. 160–c. 220) remarked: "They think the Christians the cause of every public disaster, of every affliction with which the people are visited. If the Tiber rises as high as the city walls, if the Nile does not send its waters up over the fields, if the heavens give no rain, if there is an earthquake, if there is famine or pestilence, straightway the cry is, 'Away with the Christians to the lion!'"[3] Though sarcastic, Tertullian's remarks capture the motivations

---

2. Green, *Evangelism in the Early Church*, 49.

3. Tertullian, *Apology* 40 (ANF 3:48).

Figure 1. Map of the Roman Empire c. 116

The Roman Empire AD 117
AT ITS GREATEST TERRITORIAL EXTENT

SARMATIA

REGNUM
BOSPORI

DACIA

IBERIA

MOESIA
INFERIOR

MOESIA
SUPERIOR

PONTUS EUXINUS

ARMENIA

THRACIA Byzantium

BITHYNIA ET PONTUS

MACEDONIA

REGNUM PARTHICUM

EPIRUS

GALATIA

CAPPADOCIA

ASIA

ACHAIA

ASSYRIA

Athenae

CILICIA

MESOPOTAMIA

Antiochia

LYCIA ET
PAMPHYLIA

SYRIA

CYPRUS

MARE
INTERNUM

CRETA

IUDAEA

ARABIA PETRAEA

Hierosolyma

ARABIA

CYRENAICA

Alexandria

AEGYPTUS

of pagan mobs and some emperors whose religion was tied to the empire's economic, political, and military health. In the mind-set of many Romans, being Roman meant honoring the gods of the Roman pantheon. And not doing this was considered dangerous impiety.

Building on this religious underpinning, the Roman government condemned Christianity in a legal sense for being an unlawful sect (*religio illicita*). This was due to both the church's exclusive faith claims about Christ and the rejection of the Roman pantheon's plurality of gods. Again, because Christians worshiped a god they could not see, the Romans considered them atheists. Because of Roman misunderstandings about the Eucharist and agape feasts, they also charged the Christians with cannibalism and sexual immorality. Finally, Christians were deemed unlawful because they were a new religion. Though the Jews were not always appreciated, they never received this illegal status because of their antiquity.

The early church endured sporadic periods of discrimination and suffering from its beginnings until the early fourth century.[4] Beginning around 64, Emperor Nero (r. 54–68) persecuted Christians in Rome, while Domitian (r. 81–96) did the same toward the end of the first century. This pattern of discrimination, which at times included violence, continued until just before Constantine came to power in the early fourth century.

Most anti-Christian actions were carried out on a local level. In many cases, angry pagan mobs initiated proceedings against Christians before local governors, frustrated at the so-called Christian impiety that divided families and threatened society. Because most Roman governors oversaw vast territories, they often made hasty judgments largely in the interest of maintaining order. This scenario describes the famous trials of Polycarp in Smyrna in 156 and the martyrs of Lyons in 177. It also provides a context for understanding the Bithynian (Asia Minor) governor Pliny's (r. 111–113) appeal in 112 to Emperor Trajan (r. 98–117) for advice in dealing with accused Christians. His questions included: Should people be treated

---

4. See Robert L. Wilken, *The First Thousand Years: A Global History of Christianity* (New Haven, CT: Yale University Press, 2012), 65–71; Candida Moss, *Ancient Christian Martyrdom: Diverse Practices, Theologies, and Traditions* (New Haven, CT: Yale University Press, 2012), 12; George Kalantzis, *Caesar and the Lamb: Early Christian Attitudes on War and Military Service* (Eugene, OR: Wipf & Stock, 2012), 11, 25, 149; W. H. C. Frend, *Martyrdom and Persecution in the Early Church* (Cambridge: Lutterworth, 2008), 238–42, 285–323, 351–92; and Wilken, *The Christians as the Romans Saw Them* (New Haven, CT: Yale University Press, 2003).

differently according to age? Does recanting constitute a pardon? Is merely professing to be a Christian a crime? Trajan famously responded: "You have adopted the proper course . . . in your examination of the cases of those who were accused to you as Christians, for indeed nothing can be laid down as a general ruling involving something like a set form of procedure. They are not to be sought out; but if they are accused and convicted, they must be punished."[5] If Christians were not to be pursued, how could they be convicted and punished? Trajan's crafty, ambiguous response, which became the official imperial policy for a century and a half, contributed to further mob-instigated discrimination and violence.

Though anti-Christian actions occurred largely on a local level, some Roman emperors took action against the church from the highest level. In 202, Septimius Severus (r. 193–211), the first Roman emperor from Africa, enacted a law forbidding conversion to Judaism and Christianity. Later, in 249, Decius (r. 249–251) launched an empire-wide campaign to revive traditional Roman religion. Part of his strategy included rooting out anti-Roman, atheistic sects such as the Christians. In 249, the government issued an initial decree, ordering all church leaders to offer sacrifices to the Roman deities and to lead their congregations to do the same. The following year, administrators were dispatched to every Roman province to enforce an order for a universal sacrifice to the Roman gods. Many Christians obeyed the order and received a certificate (libellus) for being sacrificati ("sacrificers"). Some managed to secure a certificate by bribing the officials, while others, including some church leaders, refused altogether and paid with their lives. The Decian persecution ended in 251, when the emperor was killed in battle.

Beginning in 257, Valerian (r. 253–260) initiated a similar campaign. The government initially demanded a sacrifice from all Roman citizens and particularly targeted church leaders. Christian worship assemblies and funerals were also banned. Unhappy with the response, the emperor ordered the execution of resistant clergy and laymen, confiscated church members' property, and purged the Roman Senate of all Christians. In 260, Valerian was killed in battle against the Persians, and the following year,

---

5. Trajan, *Letter* 10.97 (trans. James Stevenson, *The New Eusebius: Documents Illustrative of the Church to AD 337* [London: SPCK, 1957], 16).

his son and successor, Gallienus (r. 260–268), issued an edict of toleration, beginning forty years of peace for Christians in the empire.

Also desiring to revive Roman paganism, in 303 Emperor Diocletian (r. 284–305) launched what has been called the Great Persecution. In the first of four edicts, the government ordered churches closed, banned worship services, seized Scriptures, and targeted influential Christians in society. In the second edict, clergy were forced to sacrifice or face imprisonment; in the third, they were threatened with torture and execution. In a final act, all citizens in the empire were commanded to sacrifice or face death. Ironically, in this last stage, some members of Diocletian's family and his counselors—professing Christians—were arrested and executed. Following Diocletian's abdication in 305, Galerius (r. 305–311) continued suppressing Christians in the eastern part of the empire until 311. Constantius (r. 293–306), the western emperor and Constantine's father, chose not to enforce the suppressing edicts in his domain.

CONSTANTINE AND IMPERIAL CHRISTIANITY

Christianity in Rome took a drastic turn on the eve of Constantine's battle with Maxentius at Milvian Bridge in 312.[6] According to conflicting reports from Eusebius (263–339) and Lactantius (240–320), Constantine saw a sign in the sky (either the *chi-rho labarum* symbol or a cross), which he interpreted as a promise for victory in battle. Emerging victorious, Constantine embraced the god of the Christians, though he put off baptism until shortly before his death in 337.

Initially granting peace to the Christians 312, Constantine elevated the movement to favored status in 324 once he gained complete control of the empire. Some of the benefits extended to the church included tax-exempt status for clergy as well as funds to construct new church buildings and to carry out church ministry. Although Christians had already been meeting for worship on the first day of the week since the first century, Constantine supported this practice by closing the markets on Sunday.

---

6. See Eusebius, *Life of Constantine* 1.28–31; *Church History* 9.9; Lactantius, *On the Manner in Which the Persecutors Died* 44; also Glen Thompson, "From Sinner to Saint? Seeking a Consistent Constantine," in *Rethinking Constantine: History, Theology, Legacy*, ed. Edward L. Smither (Eugene, OR: Pickwick, 2014), 5–25; and Smither, "Did the Rise of Constantine Mean the End of Christian Mission?," in Smither, *Rethinking Constantine*, 130–45.

Christians also began to occupy important roles in government and society, and bishops were given a prominent status. Concerned about unity in the church, Constantine waded into the Donatist (314) and Arian (325) controversies, gathering the bishops involved and sponsoring theological reflection toward resolving the issues. Though Christianity was not declared the official Roman religion until Emperor Theodosius I's (r. 379–395) late fourth-century legislation, Constantine's conversion set into motion a pattern in which kings converted and greatly influenced their subjects to do the same. It also signaled the birth of Christendom—the union of church and state.

This paradigm shift in church and state relations, in which the church increasingly had access to wealth and even power, influenced thoughts about and approaches to Christian mission. At times, some church and state leaders regarded compulsion and even violence as acceptable "missionary" methods. The worst example of this was when Charlemagne (742–814) marched into Saxony in the late eighth century, declared the Saxons enemies of the church, and ordered them to convert or face the sword. Despite such troubling developments, the rise of Constantine and the continual development of Christendom did not signal the end of authentic Christian mission. Our study will show many other examples of bishops, monks, and even political leaders who engaged in mission by proclaiming Christ and making disciples.

CURRENTS OF THOUGHT

As the Christian movement spread in the Roman Empire, it encountered various philosophies and religions apart from Roman paganism.[7] In the second and third centuries, Gnosticism posed many challenges to Christian thought. Though scholars today struggle to formulate a comprehensive definition for the philosophy, they do agree on certain foundational

---

7. See J. Kevin Coyle, "Mani, Manicheism," in *Augustine through the Ages: An Encyclopedia*, ed. Allen Fitzgerald (Grand Rapids: Eerdmans, 1999), 520–25; Ben Quash and Michael Ward, eds., *Heresies and How to Avoid Them: Why It Matters What Christians Believe* (Peabody, MA: Hendrickson, 2007); J. N. D. Kelly, *Early Christian Doctrines* (New York: HarperCollins, 1978); and Smither, "Augustine, Missionary to Heretics? An Appraisal of Augustine's Missional Engagement with the Donatists," in *A Uniquely African Controversy: Studies on Donatist Christianity*, ed. A. Dupont, M. A. Gaumer, and M. Lamberigts, Late Antique History and Religion 9 (Leuven: Peeters, 2015), 269–88.

principles; namely that Gnosticism generally viewed creation and matter in a negative light and taught that redemption came through a secret knowledge (*gnosis*) that liberated the spirit from the body.

Manichaeism, a mix of Gnosticism, Zoroastrianism (a Persian religion focusing on wisdom and a dualistic view of the world), and neo-Platonic thought that was largely concerned with the problem of evil, had followers from North Africa to China. Led by ascetic intellectuals, the movement appealed to young thinkers such as Augustine of Hippo (354-430) who were disillusioned with the church.

In addition to these philosophical challenges from outside the church, early Christian leaders and missionaries dealt with heresy within the church. Correctly articulating the doctrine of Christ (Christology) proved to be one of the greatest points of contention. In the first three centuries, the church responded to the heresy of docetism—that Jesus was a mere phantom and only appeared (*dokeo*) to have a human body. Later controversies included adoptionism (Jesus being adopted as the Son of God and taking on divinity at his baptism) and subordinationism (that Jesus was less than the Father). In the fourth century, Apollinarius (c. 310-c. 390) emphasized Jesus's divinity to such an extent that he denied the Lord's human will and nature. Finally, in the midst of a theological battle with Cyril of Alexandria (c. 376-444), Nestorius (c. 386-c. 451) taught that there were two Jesuses—one divine and one human. The Council of Chalcedon (451) refuted Nestorius's aberrant Christology. The gathered church leaders affirmed one Christ who was both fully human and fully divine.

Adoptionist and subordinationist thinking continued into the fourth century as church leaders sought to understand and articulate how the Father, Son, and Holy Spirit—particularly the Father and the Son—related together in essence and action. Alexandrian Presbyter Arius (c. 250-336) taught that since the Father was eternal and uncreated and the Son was created by the Father, then Jesus was necessarily subordinate to the Father. Though the Council of Nicaea (325) affirmed that the Father and Son share the same essence (*homoousios*), the Arian controversy raged on for most of the fourth century. The official Nicene position was challenged by two groups: the homoians (the Father and Son have a *similar* essence), and, to a lesser extent the anomoians, (the Father and Son are entirely *different*). Though this issue was largely debated within the church, some missionaries such as homoian missionary-bishop Ulfilas (c. 311–c. 383) preached an Arian gospel among the Goths in the fourth century.

In the fourth and fifth centuries, the church also wrestled with the doctrines of grace (free will, the effects of the fall, and original sin) through the Pelagian controversy. Pelagius (c. 354–c. 420/440) asserted that humanity did not have a sinful nature and that perfection was possible and even obligatory. Augustine thoroughly answered Pelagius's claims in a number of books, letters, and church councils. During the same period Augustine engaged the Donatists for instigating division within the African church. Regarding their schism as a form of heresy, Augustine considered this faction as a type of mission field.

PALESTINE AND SYRIA

Following Paul's first-century ministry, Christian mission continued to flow westward from Jerusalem and Antioch within Rome. Palestine, despite being the heartland of Christ's earthly ministry, remained largely non-Christian until the reign of Constantine and many missionaries focused on reaching the Jews. In neighboring Phoenicia, a strong church emerged in the city of Tyre; however, Christian communities remained largely Greek speaking and were confined to the cities.

Antioch of Syria was evangelized in the first century amid suffering. It is remembered as the place where followers of Jesus were first called Christians—a pejorative term given by the pagan majority (Acts 11:26). Antioch was also the sending church for Paul, Barnabas, and their companions (13:1–3). A cosmopolitan center shaped by Jewish, Hellenistic, and Roman influences, it became an important locale for biblical interpretation and for sending intercultural missionaries toward the West and the East.

In the late first and early second century, Bishop Ignatius (d. 110) pastored the Antioch church and strengthened the office of bishop in the Asian churches. Ignatius engaged both pagans and heretical Christians, particularly docetists, with the gospel. Following his arrest, Ignatius was transported to Rome, where he witnessed to Christ through martyrdom. On the journey to Rome, he penned seven letters to the culturally diverse churches in Asia and Rome, admonishing them to unity, sound doctrine, and a faithful witness to the pagan majority.

ASIA AND ASIA MINOR

Asia and Asia Minor saw a great deal of mission activity in the latter half of the first century. Since Paul was a native of the province of Cilicia, it's not surprising that he preached and planted churches in the region. His employers and ministry colaborers, Priscilla and Aquila, were originally from Pontus and perhaps embraced the gospel there before conducting business and engaging in mission in Rome and Corinth (Acts 18:1–3). The earliest non-Christian witness to the Christian movement in the region comes in Pliny's famous letter to Trajan in 112 in which he spoke of "many [Christians] in every period of life, on every level of society, of both sexes . . . in towns and villages and scattered throughout the countryside."[8] These observations indicate that the church was becoming a transformational movement, welcoming diverse members and bridging social, economic, and generational barriers.

In addition to leading the church at Smyrna, Bishop Polycarp (d. 156) labored to evangelize pagans and gnostics. Able to relate to both the lower classes and members of the royal court, he proclaimed the gospel through discussion and debate. Polycarp's most significant opportunity to witness unto Christ also came through his martyrdom. After being arrested and placed on trial for leading an atheistic sect, the aging bishop refused to deny his faith and famously declared, "For eighty-six years I have been his servant, and he has done me no wrong. How can I blaspheme my king who saved me?"[9]

Originally from Palestine, Justin Martyr (d. 165) was a trained philosopher who taught in Ephesus and later Rome. Employing the language of Greek philosophy, Justin communicated through public debates and written treatises, directing his message to Jews, pagan intellectuals, and Christian heretics. Around 135, Justin debated Jewish thinker Trypho in Ephesus, which was later published as the *Dialogue with Trypho*. Part of the exchange included Justin recounting his own journey to faith in Christ. Relating his experiences in various schools of Greek philosophy, Justin's conversion story reached its climax when he met an elderly man by the

---

8. Trajan, *Letter* 10.96 (trans. Stevenson, *New Eusebius*, 16).

9. Martyrdom of Polycarp 9 (trans. Holmes, *The Apostolic Fathers in English* [Grand Rapids: Baker, 2006], 150).

seashore who challenged his assumptions about Plato and introduced him to the Hebrew prophets and the Messiah. After believing in Christ, Justin declared himself to be a true philosopher.

Already communicating biblical ideas in the language of Greek philosophy, Justin also borrowed one existing form of Roman communication to make his point. In crafting his *First Apology*, in which he defended the church against the charges of atheism and cannibalism while also clarifying what Christians believed and how they worshiped, Justin employed the Roman *biblidion* (court petition) template to make his case. Paul Parvis explains, "What Justin did was to hijack this normal Roman administrative procedure and turn it into a vehicle for articulating and disseminating the message of the gospel."[10]

While his writings defended the church and confronted the Roman government for treating Christians unjustly, Justin intended his apologetic writings to be uniquely missional. Near the end of his *First Apology*, Justin reminded his pagan audience, "We do not hate you but we wish to convert you."[11] Despite these intentions, following a debate with a pagan opponent in Rome around 165, Justin was arrested and put to death, joining Polycarp in martyrdom.

While studying in Palestinian Caesarea, Gregory Thaumaturgus (c. 213–270) embraced the gospel through the witness of his professor, Origen of Alexandria. Returning home, where he intended to pursue a monastic lifestyle, Gregory was ordained as bishop of Neo-Caesarea in Pontus in 240. In addition to serving as bishop, Gregory is also remembered for evangelizing Pontus, employing a diverse mission strategy. He put his command of philosophy, mathematics, and law to work by communicating with pagan intellectuals. He also reached others, including the poor, through healing, exorcising demons, and preaching Scripture. Describing the significance of Gregory's ministry with some exaggeration, Basil of Caesarea (c. 329–c. 379) claimed that when Gregory arrived in Pontus as bishop there were just seventeen Christians, but when he died, only seventeen pagans remained.[12]

---

10. Paul Parvis, "Justin Martyr," in *Early Christian Thinkers: The Lives and Legacies of Twelve Key Figures*, ed. Paul Foster (Downers Grove, IL: IVP Academic, 2010), 6–7.

11. Justin, *First Apology* 57.2 (ANF 1:86).

12. Basil, *On the Holy Spirit* 74; *Letter* 28.

After a few years of living as a monk, Basil himself was set apart by the church at Caesarea as a reader, presbyter, and finally a bishop. Though ordained, Basil remained in his monastic calling and joined a growing number of fourth-century church leaders who served as monk-bishops.[13]

Because of Caesarea's strategic location on Roman roads that connected trading centers such as Constantinople and Syria, it had become an important city and Roman administrative center by the fourth century. With diverse peoples from Asia Minor, Armenia, Syria, Persia, and the northern Gothic regions regularly passing through, it became a significant intercultural crossroads. On the other hand, because of an earthquake and famine that hit the area around 368, many Cappadocians faced poverty and near-starvation.

As bishop of Caesarea, Basil made preaching his priority—both to train believers and to evangelize nonbelievers. His preaching also included a prophetic discourse against the injustices occurring in Caesarea, particularly slavery and the exploitation of the poor. Basil also actively cared for the needs of the poor in Cappadocia, including opening the storehouses of grain and distributing food to the poor and hungry. Later, he established the *basileas* ("new city"), a complex at the edge of Caesarea that included a home for the poor, a hospital, an early form of a job-training center, a food bank and distribution center, and a hospitality house for travelers. Basil's ministry also included mission to heresy. Along with Gregory of Nazianzus (c. 329–390) and Gregory of Nyssa (c. 335–c. 395), Basil preached and wrote against the Arian heresy, which plagued the church in the fourth century. He was also the earliest Christian theologian to write a stand-alone treatise on the doctrine of the Holy Spirit.

ROME

Though the church at Rome became the largest community of Christians in the western Roman Empire by the third century, the church's origins remain a mystery. The first likely evidence of Christianity in the city comes from the historian Suetonius, who recorded that Emperor Claudius dealt

---

13. See Edward L. Smither, "Basil of Caesarea: An Early Christian Model of Urban Mission," in *Reaching the City: Reflections on Mission for the Twenty-First Century*, ed. Gary Fujino et al. (Pasadena, CA: William Carey Library, 2012), 77–95.

with an uprising of the followers of *Chrestus* (perhaps a misspelling of *Christos* or "Christ") around the year 50. For most of the second century, the church continued as a Greek-speaking community, an indication that the movement had largely taken hold among the lower classes. This changed in 189, when Bishop Victor (d. 199) introduced Latin as the church's liturgical language.

By the middle of the third century, as many as thirty thousand Christians may have been in the city, worshiping in a network of house churches. This figure is extrapolated from the number of church leaders being financially supported by the church. Eusebius recorded that, in addition to Bishop Cornelius (d. 253), the mid-third-century Roman church was served by "forty-six presbyters, seven deacons, seven sub-deacons, forty-two acolytes, fifty-two exorcists, readers and doorkeepers."[14] At the same time, over one hundred bishop-led churches existed in greater Italy.

The prominence of the Roman church and its bishop began to increase in the fourth century for at least two reasons. First, since the church was regarded as the apostolic see due to its alleged connection to Peter, it gained increasing theological importance. Second, once Constantine moved the seat of the empire to Constantinople in 330, a significant power vacuum was left in Rome that was ultimately filled by the Roman bishop. As the church and state union continued following Theodosius's late fourth-century legislation, over time the bishop of Rome went from being the leader of a church in a single city to the vicar of Christ on earth.

Known for his deep spirituality and administrative efficiency, Gregory the Great (540–604) is considered one of the greatest popes in church history. Originally a Roman state official, Gregory left that career to pursue an ascetic calling. In 578, he began serving as a deacon and was tasked with distributing material aid throughout the city—a ministry that exposed him to the Romans' great spiritual and material needs. A decline in agricultural productivity coupled with a plague brought on by the flooding of the Tiber River created many social and economic problems in the city. In addition, the neighboring Lombards' attack on the Italian countryside in 586 left the Romans living in constant fear of another invasion. In 590, Gregory became the first monk in church history to serve as the bishop of Rome. Convinced

---

14. Eusebius, *Church History* 6.43.11 (NPNF[2] 1:288).

that the ascetic life should include contemplation (prayer, worship) as well as activism (service, ministry), Gregory's monastic theology compelled him to engage in mission in Rome, Italy, and beyond.[15]

GAUL AND SPAIN

Historical evidence for the origins of the church in Gaul and Spain is also quite limited. Though some traditions claim that Paul's disciple Crescens (2 Tim 4:10) ministered in the region, Christian merchants and other immigrants from Syria, Asia, and Asia Minor most likely brought the gospel. Indeed, Irenaeus (c. 115–200), who served as bishop of Lyons, was initially set apart to minister to a congregation of Greek-speaking immigrants in the city. Further, many of the martyrs of Lyons who suffered in 177 were not of Gallic origin. As the church expanded, bishops were appointed in Cologne and Mainz by 185, while other churches launched in Arles, Rouen, Bordeaux, and Paris by the fourth century. Though it's difficult to confirm whether Paul ministered in Spain, both Tertullian and Cyprian (195–258) refer to Spanish churches in their third-century writings. Finally, the acts of the fourth-century Council of Elvira list some thirty-six Spanish churches.

Irenaeus labored as a missionary-bishop in southern Gaul in the latter half of the second century. A native Greek speaker ministering in a largely Latin-speaking region, Irenaeus also made it a point to learn the local Gallic dialect in order to preach in the pagan villages around Lyons. This ministry was, of course, in addition to his responsibilities as a bishop.

Irenaeus labored in an environment greatly plagued by gnostic thought. Through key writings such as *Against All Heresies* and *Demonstration of the Apostolic Teaching*, he defended the gospel both in Gaul and at Rome. Attacking Gnosticism for its most general claims against creation, Irenaeus took a fourfold approach in responding to the heresy. First, he carefully detailed the tenets of gnostic thinking, a skill he had developed from spending nearly twenty years studying in gnostic schools. Second, he attacked Gnosticism's baseless and mythological foundations. Third, he challenged its claim to a historical relationship to Jesus. Finally, he polemicized against

---

15. See Edward L. Smither, *Missionary Monks: An Introduction to the History and Theology of Missionary Monasticism* (Eugene, OR: Cascade Books, 2016), 83–84.

the gnostics' attempts to interpret Christian Scripture. Proclaiming the gospel to the gnostics—the God who creates is the God who redeems—he appealed to the authority of Scripture, apostolic authority, and an inherited Trinitarian doctrine of God.[16]

Martin of Tours (c. 316–397) was another innovative fourth-century missionary-bishop. Originally from Pannonia (modern Hungary), Martin experienced a dramatic conversion while serving as a soldier in the Roman army. After, he became a monk and established monasteries in Milan and Gaul and on the Italian island of Gallinaria. In 372, Martin was rather forcibly ordained as the bishop of Tours, and like a number of other fourth-century bishops, he combined the vocations of monk and bishop. From this position, he evangelized the pagan populations of Gaul through confronting pagan practices, destroying pagan temples, performing healings and other miracles, and demonstrating a holy life. Martin's mission field was also within the church as he, along with his mentor Hilary of Poitiers (c. 315–c. 367), defended the Gallic church against the Arian heresy.[17]

With the baptism of the Frankish king Clovis (c. 466–511) in 496, the Christendom paradigm began to shape Christianity in Gaul. Apparently, Clovis ordered many of his troops to be baptized along with him, which surely influenced the Franks to follow their king's faith. This tendency continued through the eighth century as Frankish leaders such as Charles Martel (c. 686–741), Pepin the Short (c. 714–768), and Charlemagne strengthened the union between the state and church.

Though Irenaeus, Martin of Tours, and others evangelized Gaul, and established churches existed, Irish monk Columban (c. 543–615) arrived in 590 with a mission to bring renewal to the church. After gaining favor with the Frankish king, Columban and his monks established a monastery in an old abandoned military fort at Anegray. Later, he opened additional monasteries at Luxeuil and Fontaines. By the end of his life, he'd built a monastic network of over sixty communities. Though Columban's charisma helped attract new monks to his communities, it also led to conflicts with others, including other bishops and church leaders. After initially receiving favor

---

16. Irenaeus, *Against All Heresies* 1.8, 23–27; see Edward L. Smither, *Mission in the Early Church: Themes and Reflections* (Eugene, OR: Cascade Books, 2014), 85–86.

17. See Smither, *Missionary Monks*, 42–50.

from a Gallic monarch to enter the region, he struggled to maintain good relationships with political leaders. Ultimately, Columban was expelled from Burgundy by the monarch Brunhilda (543–613) for refusing to bless her illegitimate grandchildren. Escorted from the kingdom, he traveled through Gaul to what is now Switzerland before arriving in Italy, where he dreamed of preaching to the Arian-leaning Lombards. Eventually he established a final monastery at Bobbio in northern Italy, where he remained for the rest of his life.

Columban's mission approaches included engaging political leaders—both seeking favor at the outset of his ministry and also staying in contact with them. The Irish monk was also an itinerant preacher, reaching out to Franks, Swabians, and Slavs. Columban's biographer reported that miracles often accompanied his preaching, especially healings and exorcisms. Like Martin, Columban openly confronted paganism and occasionally physically destroyed idols and sacred places. Finally, Columban proclaimed the gospel to heretics, particularly the Arian Lombards in Italy.

BRITAIN

Some legends claim that Paul and even Joseph of Arimathea evangelized Britain in the first century. Tertullian mentions the presence of Christians in the region by the early third century, though he gives no indication of how the church started. The earliest concrete evidence for a British church comes from the acts of the Council of Arles (314), in which bishops from London and York participated. Since the organizers paid the bishops' way to Arles, it appears that the early fourth-century British church was impoverished. By 400, the Briton people of Roman Britain appear to have been evangelized; however, their Anglo-Saxon neighbors, with whom they often clashed, remained largely neglected until the late sixth century.

Around 596, several years after he became bishop of Rome, Gregory the Great sent Augustine of Canterbury (d. 604) and a group of about forty monks on a mission to reach the Anglo-Saxons. It was the first cross-cultural mission effort in church history initiated by a Roman bishop. After traveling over land through Gaul, the monks were greeted upon their arrival in England by King Ethelbert of Kent (r. 589–616). It comes as little surprise that after having been married to a Christian wife for thirty years and apparently unmoved by the gospel, Ethelbert did not respond immediately to the monks' message. However, the king allowed them to build a church and establish a mission base at Canterbury, giving them freedom to preach among his subjects. According to Gregory, in the first year of ministry, over ten thousand Anglo-Saxons were baptized. Eventually Ethelbert embraced the gospel for himself.

Like other early Christian missionaries, the monks began their work by approaching a political leader, preaching the gospel to him, seeking his favor, and receiving permission to minister to his subjects. The monks gained credibility in their preaching through their exemplary lives and apparent working of miracles. Finally, they demonstrated sensitivity by contextualizing the gospel in English forms. In particular, they transformed existing pagan temples into houses of Christian worship and adapted a pagan cattle festival into a thanksgiving feast.[18]

Around 635, King Oswald of Northumbria (r. 634-642) returned from exile to reclaim his throne. Having spent nearly twenty years in exile at Iona, where he was converted, the restored king invited Christian missionaries to come teach the Northumbrians. The Celtic monks at Iona responded by sending Aiden (d. 651). According to Bede, the king gave him space to set up a monastery and base for ministry on the island of Lindisfarne. Despite this favor, Aiden ministered in a turbulent context, including Oswald being killed in battle by the pagan King Penda (d. 655) of neighboring Mercia, which increased the Germanic pagan influences in Northumbria. Aiden's approach to mission included collaborating with political leaders such as Oswald, itinerant preaching, at times performing miracles, and caring for the poor and disenfranchised.[19]

EGYPT

Prior to the lives and ministries of Clement (c. 150-c. 215) and Origen, little is known about the early Egyptian church. Clement, Eusebius, and Jerome (c. 347-420) advanced the traditional claim that Mark the Evangelist was the pioneer missionary to Egypt.[20] Church leaders in Alexandria labored to teach their congregations Christian orthodoxy in a strongly gnostic

---

18. Smither, *Missionary Monks*, 82–92.

19. Smither, *Missionary Monks*, 73-76.

20. See Thomas C. Oden, *The African Memory of Mark: Reassessing Early Church Tradition* (Downers Grove, IL: IVP Academic, 2011).

environment. In the late second century, Pantaenus (d. 200), a missionary-philosopher who also ministered in India, launched a catechetical (discipleship) school to meet this challenge. Later, Clement and Origen directed this famous school.

During his lifetime, Origen numbered among the greatest thinkers in the world—among both Christians and non-Christians. In addition to writing biblical commentaries and other works, he engaged in mission to intellectuals, employing philosophy and apologetics. Around 178, Celsus, an Egyptian Platonic philosopher, had written *On True Doctrine*, attacking Christians for preying on the simple and uneducated. Despite showing some familiarity with the New Testament, Celsus claimed that Jesus was a magician and that the church was a secret and illegal society. The biggest problem Celsus had with Christianity was its exclusive nature—divine ways being revealed through a particular people. Though Origen wrote *Against Celsus* some seventy years later, the work was still relevant because many philosophically minded opponents of Christianity continued to share Celsus's sentiments. Origen replied to these critics as a Christian Platonist. He "plundered the Egyptians" and appropriated their philosophical framework to demonstrate that Christianity was indeed rational. Though acknowledging the superiority of the Scriptures (divine philosophy) to Greek philosophy, he argued that the general knowledge of the divine played an important role in leading one to a divine philosophy. Robert Wilken summarizes Origen's abilities to engage Egyptian intellectual culture this way: "When [he] began to write, even philosophers knew he was someone to be reckoned with."[21]

Following in the footsteps of Pantaenus, who served as a missionary philosopher in India, Origen also ministered in a cross-cultural environment. After a number of years of leading the Alexandrian school and confronting the gnostic heresies in Egypt, Origen migrated to Palestinian Caesarea, where he established a school and taught theology and philosophy. Through teaching philosophy while thinking Christianly, Origen led some students to faith in Christ, including Gregory Thaumaturgus.[22]

The early translation of Scripture into the Coptic language was also an outcome of mission in Egypt. Though Greek was the primary language

---

21. Wilken, *First Thousand Years*, 55.
22. See Smither, *Mission in the Early Church*, 11, 39, 81–82.

of Egypt's Hellenized urban centers and its churches, Coptic was widely spoken in towns and villages in the early church period. Reflecting the Christian transformation happening among the Copts, the Coptic alphabet and language were created to distinguish a Christian worldview from the prevailing Egyptian paganism. By the third century, the first translations of Scriptures began to appear in Coptic, supporting the Egyptian church's liturgical assemblies and teaching ministry. Later, these translations went through revision, and the Coptic church adopted the Bohairic dialect (one of six Coptic dialects) as the standard language for its Scriptures. Bruce Metzger comments on the legacy of the Coptic Scriptures: "The dialect survived as the ecclesiastical and liturgical language of the Coptic Church, even after Arabic had been adopted as the speech of everyday life."[23] Because of the Coptic Scriptures, Egyptian Christianity continued to survive even after Arabic became the dominant language and Islam the majority religion.[24]

Egyptian monasticism, led by innovative abbots such as Antony (251-356) and Pachomius (c. 290-c. 346), also emerged within a Coptic Christian context. In addition to influencing early Christian theology and practice, Egyptian monasticism indirectly encouraged mission as monks served alongside bishops in local evangelism, while others were ordained to church ministry.

Apart from Origen, the greatest Egyptian theologian in the early church period was Athanasius of Alexandria (c. 296-373). While serving as bishop of Alexandria for forty-five years, Athanasius also evangelized heretics, particularly as he defended the church against Arian teaching.

NORTH AFRICA

The region of the Roman Empire where Christianity flourished most strongly was North Africa. What makes this growth even more significant is that we know almost nothing about the origins of the African church. We have no record of early missionaries or church planters—only the emergence of a vibrant church in the late second and early third

---

23. Bruce M. Metzger, *The Bible in Translation: Ancient and English Versions* (Grand Rapids: Baker Academic, 2001), 36–37.

24. See Smither, *Mission in the Early Church*, 100–101.

century.[25] To explore this further, let's consider a timeline of North African Christianity working backward from the mid-third to the early second century.

In 220, Bishop Agrippinus of Carthage presided over a church council attended by seventy bishops from a single African province (Proconsular Africa). Since there were seventy churches in one African province and many more in the rest of Roman Africa, this signified much growth in the early third-century church. Even more remarkable, this council occurred just forty years after the first literary reference to Christianity in Africa—the account of the martyrs of Scilli condemned at Carthage in 180. Interestingly, a majority of these twelve martyrs (seven men and five women) bore indigenous African (Punic-Berber) names, indicating that the church had penetrated the African interior, evidence that Christianity was surely present in North Africa well before 180. Further, archaeologists have dated the catacombs of Hadrumetum (modern Sousse), which contain at least fifteen thousand graves of second- to fourth-century Christians, to the mid-second century. Though Carthage was probably the first African city the gospel reached, French archaeologist Paul Monceaux discovered Christian graves in Jewish cemeteries in Cyrene that date to the beginning of the second century.[26] So the origins of African church are quite early (early second century), and the missionaries who brought the gospel are strikingly anonymous. These early evangelists were most likely made up of merchants, colonists, and even soldiers whose work brought them to Africa.[27]

The first written records of African Christianity—the trial of the Scillitan martyrs—were what François Decret calls "testimonies of blood."[28] The African church story was marked by discrimination and suffering in the second and third centuries. The most famous account of African martyrdom involved two young women named Perpetua and Felicitas.

---

25. See Stephen Neill, *A History of Christian Missions* (London: Penguin, 1990), 34; also François Decret, *Early Christianity in North Africa*, trans. Edward L. Smither (Eugene, OR: Cascade, 2009), 10.

26. See Kenneth Scott Latourette, *A History of the Expansion of Christianity: The First Five Centuries* (New York: Harper & Brothers, 1937; repr., Grand Rapids: Zondervan, 1970), 1:92.

27. See Smither, *Mission in the Early Church*, 45–46.

28. Decret, *Early Christianity in North Africa*, 10.

The women were initially arrested along with three other men when they embraced Christianity—an affront to Emperor Severus's decree of 202. Perpetua came from a wealthy, well-known Carthaginian family, and Felicitas was her servant. Though they hailed from disparate economic backgrounds, they had one thing in common: they were both young mothers. At the time of their arrest, Perpetua was nursing a newborn, while Felicitas gave birth to a child in prison. On March 7, 203, the two women were marched into the Carthage Amphitheatre and torn apart by wild beasts.

While many Roman spectators were surely moved by the moral conviction of Christians unwilling to deny their faith even in the face of death, some African Christians gave a public witness when brought to trial or the place of execution. During his trial, Speratus, one of the Scillitan martyrs, declared: "I do not recognize the empire of this world. Rather, I serve that God whom no man has seen, nor can see, with these eyes." Prior to his execution in Carthage, Cyprian stated: "I am a Christian and a bishop. I recognize no other gods but the one true God who made heaven and earth, and the sea, and that that is in them."[29] This environment of suffering and witness offers a fitting context for Tertullian's late second-century declaration: "The blood of the martyrs is seed [for the Christians]."[30]

As the gospel permeated Africa, especially in the urban areas, the earliest translations of the Latin Scriptures began to crop up, first appearing near the end of the second century. Rather than appointing an official team of translators, members of African worship gatherings directly produced the Old Latin Bible. The Greek Scriptures were read aloud during the liturgy and then simultaneously translated into Latin. As these translations were captured in writing, revised, and circulated, the Old Latin Bible became what Bruce Metzger calls a "living creation, constantly growing."[31] Since the first Latin Scriptures developed organically in this environment of worship and discipleship, the immediate hunger for the Word of God trumped the need for precision. Although this account is inspiring, all was

---

29. Passion of the Scillitan Martyrs; Acts of Cyprian 1, 3.

30. Tertullian, *Apology* 50 (ANF 3:55).

31. Metzger, *Bible in Translation*, 30; see Smither, *Mission in the Early Church*, 45–46, 53–54, 95–99.

not well. African pastors such as Augustine freely expressed their frustration with the various versions of the Old Latin Bible.

In the late fourth century, after Latin had become the language of worship for most of the church in the western Roman Empire, Bishop Damasus of Rome (c. 304–384) tasked Jerome with revising the Latin Gospels. Though initially reluctant to take on the project, Jerome spent over twenty years developing a fresh translation of the Old and New Testaments. This work became known as the Latin Vulgate. His greatest innovation in the task was translating the Old Testament directly from the original Hebrew instead of the Greek Septuagint, as the Old Latin Bible translators had done. Though a logical decision in the eyes of the modern reader, Jerome's Hebrew verity value was controversial to many early Christians who believed that the Septuagint was inspired.

As the North African church grew, a number of influential theologians shaped its development. Tertullian, the father of Latin Christian literature, defended Christian thought in a largely pagan environment while also contributing some early thoughts on the meaning of the Trinity. Cyprian made a lasting impression on how the church thought about pastoral leadership and ecclesiology. Along with his theological works on the Trinity and the doctrines of grace, Augustine also served as a missionary of sorts to heretics, defending the church against Manichean, Donatist, and Pelagian teaching.

IRELAND AND SCOTLAND

Despite its geographical proximity to Roman Britain, Ireland was never part of the Roman Empire. In the fifth century, however, a Roman British missionary-bishop, Patrick (c. 389–c. 461), labored to evangelize the nation. Captured by the Irish as a teenager, Patrick spent six years among this Celtic people as a slave, clarifying his own commitment to Christ while also learning the Irish language and culture. After escaping captivity and returning home to Roman Britain, Patrick reported in his *Confessions* that he received a vision calling him back to the Irish. Eventually, Bishop Celestine (d. 432) of Rome set him apart as a missionary bishop for all of Ireland.

Believing that he was ministering in the last days and literally at the ends of the earth, Patrick's first steps in the Irish mission were to approach tribal leaders, seek their protection and favor, and ask permission to proclaim the gospel among their people. After thirty years of ministry (c. 432–c. 461), Patrick had evangelized much of Ireland, establishing new churches and monasteries. With no towns to speak of in Ireland prior to Patrick's mission, the monastic communities (and their structures) filled that void and became the first towns. Though bishops existed in the Irish church, monastic abbots became the primary leaders. Because of Patrick's ministry, the Irish church became a hub for reaching other parts of Europe.[32]

The most famous Irish missionary monk was Columba (521–597), remembered as the apostle of Scotland. Summarizing his call and work, the Venerable Bede (672–735) wrote:

> [In 565], there came from Ireland to Britain a priest and abbot named Columba, a true monk in life no less than habit; he came to Britain to preach the word of God to the kingdoms of the northern Picts. . . . Columba came to Britain when Bridius [Brute] . . . a most power-ful king, had been ruling over them for over eight years. Columba turned them to the faith of Christ by his words and example and so received the island of Iona from them in order to establish a monastery there.[33]

If Bede is correct, Columba first sought the favor of King Brute, who was apparently converted to the gospel, and allowed Columba and his monks to begin a monastery at Iona. Brute also granted them the freedom to evan-gelize the Pictish peoples throughout the Scottish highlands.

One particular approach to mission that the Iona monks adopted was engaging the visual culture of the Pictish people. Art historians have long been intrigued with Pictish Insular art, which included stone art, metal works, and also book art. While the Picts had traditionally constructed stone monuments to commemorate military victories and other important events in their history, once the gospel took root among them, the primary focus of stone art became publicly displaying the cross.

32. Smither, *Mission in the Early Church*, 51–63.

33. Bede, *Ecclesiastical History of the English People* 3.4, ed. Judith McClure and Roger Collins (Oxford: Oxford University Press, 2009), 114–15.

While the Picts allowed their arts forms to be transformed for Christian purposes, Columba and his monks also seemed deliberate about adopting them to proclaim the gospel. Indeed, Insular stone crosses communicated the essence of the gospel—the death, burial, and resurrection of Christ. Later, other crosses communicated more detailed biblical narrative. For example, St. Martin's cross, a large eighth-century stonework, which stands to this day at Iona, contains a number of Bible stories. At the center of the cross, Mary is depicted holding the newborn Christ. Stories of Daniel in the lions' den, Abraham raising his sword to sacrifice Isaac, David fighting Goliath, and David playing music are also carved into the cross. Stone crosses like that at St. Martin's functioned as a visual form of catechism and Bible study for visitors to Iona.

The Iona monks further communicated the gospel visually through developing the famous Book of Kells in the late eighth century. Though the book only contains the four Gospels in Latin, it weighs in at eight hundred pages due to its intricate artwork: the beautiful calligraphy, stone art images, and many illustrations—including many New Testament Bible stories. Though small and portable enough to be carried on mission trips around Pictland, the Book of Kells probably largely remained at Iona. As visitors arrived on the island and participated in liturgical assemblies, the visual themes conveyed in the book (the person and work of Christ, the cross, other Eucharistic imagery) offered instruction for new believers. Since the Book of Kells connected with the Pictish visual imagination and oral memory, these Bible stories and truths were probably circulated orally throughout Pictland.[34]

GERMANIA

The Goths were a Germanic people who originated from north of the Danube River on the fringe of the Roman Empire. Eventually, they divided into two distinct groups: the Visigoths (western Goths) and the Ostrogoths (eastern), who lived in what is now Hungary. While the Ostrogoths enjoyed a peaceful relationship with the eastern Roman Empire at Constantinople, the Visigoths are remembered in history for sacking the city of Rome in

---

34. See Smither, *Mission in the Early Church*, 40, 118–22.

the early fifth century and taking control of much of the western empire, including North Africa, for a century.

The Visigoths probably first encountered the gospel when they expanded into Moesia and Dacia (modern Romania and Bulgaria), where they met Christians. Christian slaves, captured from Cappadocia, also witnessed among them. However, the moderate Arian, Ulfilas, became the most celebrated missionary to this Germanic people. Born to Gothic and Cappadocian parents, Ulfilas grew up around Constantinople. In 340, Eusebius of Nicomedia (d. 341), another Arian bishop, set Ulfilas apart as bishop for the Goths.

Ulfilas also labored to develop a Gothic alphabet in order to make Scripture available to the Goths. Committed to a word-for-word, literal translation, he purposefully omitted Kings and Samuel from the Old Testament because he feared that the Visigoths, known for their warring ways, would find new inspiration for violence from these books. Following the Goth's fifth-century conquest of Rome, their language became widely spoken throughout what is now Europe, which should have increased the circulation of the Gothic Scriptures. However, with the Byzantine resurgence in the following century, the Gothic language largely died out as a vernacular, and the Gothic Scriptures had little influence on the church in the region.[35]

Another Germanic people, the Frisians, were evangelized in the eighth century by the English monks Willibrord (c. 658–737) and Boniface (c. 680–754). After serving with Willibrord for a year in 719, Boniface was set apart by Bishop Gregory II (669–731) of Rome as a missionary envoy to the Frisians. Later, in 722, Gregory II set him apart as a missionary bishop for all of Germany. Similar to Patrick's appointment in Ireland, Boniface was made a bishop for a region and people where churches had not yet been established. Boniface took a vow of allegiance to the pope and committed to propagating a Roman form of Christianity among the Germanic peoples.

The most celebrated account of Boniface's ministry among the Frisians came in 724, when he confronted pagan ritual and belief head-on by cutting down the sacred oak tree of Thor in the town of Geismar:

---

35. Smither, *Mission in the Early Church*, 102–3.

Boniface in their presence attempted to cut down, at a place called Geismar, a certain oak of extraordinary size called in the old tongue of the pagans the Oak of [Thor]. Taking his courage in his hands (for a great crowd of pagans stood by watching and bitterly cursing in their hearts the enemy of the gods), he cut the first notch. But when he had made a superficial cut, suddenly, the oak's vast bulk, shaken by a mighty blast of wind from above crashed to the ground shivering its topmost branches into fragments in its fall. As if by the express will of God (for the brethren present had done nothing to cause it) the oak burst asunder into four parts, each part having a trunk of equal length. At the sight of this extraordinary spectacle the heathens who had been cursing ceased to revile and began, on the contrary, to believe and bless the Lord. Thereupon the holy bishop took counsel with the brethren, built an oratory from the timber of the oak and dedicated it to Saint Peter the Apostle.[36]

As he continued to serve, his leadership recognized Boniface's gifts as an administrator. From 737 to 747, the Roman bishop tasked him with organizing and reforming the existing German and Frankish churches. However, driven by a missionary zeal to reach unbaptized German pagans, Boniface, now in his seventies, headed back to the Frisians in 753. In the midst of this new work of preaching, baptizing, and teaching, Boniface and his companions were attacked by an angry mob and martyred in 754.

Like other early Christian missionaries, Boniface first made contact with German leaders and preached Christ to them, while also seeking their favor to preach among their people. Boniface also connected with Frankish Christian political leaders, including Charles Martel and Pepin, who provided military protection as he preached among the Frisians. Despite this protection, Boniface's mission work relied more on building relationships with local people and preaching. As observed in the account at Geismar, a key element of his preaching involved confronting paganism. Boniface followed up evangelism among the Frisians through teaching, catechesis, and the

---

36. Willibald, *Life of Boniface* 6, trans. C. H. Talbot, in *The Anglo-Saxon Missionaries in Germany, Being the Lives of SS. Willibrord, Boniface, Leoba and Lebuin Together with the Hodoepericon of St. Willibald and a Selection from the Correspondence of St. Boniface* (London: Sheed and Ward, 1954).

establishment of new churches. Finally, Boniface involved teams of monks in his work and was one of the first to recruit women to serve in mission.[37]

THE EAST

Unfortunately, the trend among Western students of church and mission history is to focus so much on early Christianity in the Roman Empire that they overlook what was going on in the rest of the world.[38] And yet, in the first eight centuries of the church, the gospel traveled much farther east than it did west. In the same year (635) that Aiden began ministering in Northumbria, Church of the East missionary monks were proclaiming the gospel to the emperor of China.

In this section, with our starting point once again at Antioch, we explore the expansion of the gospel east outside the Roman Empire. Our journey will take us through the horn of Africa, the Middle East, central Asia, and all the way to China. Eastern Christians also endured discrimination and suffering, especially Persian believers who were persecuted by Zoroastrian kings even after Constantine had come to power in Rome. Along the Silk Road through central Asia, the church remained on mission in Zoroastrian, Hindu, Buddhist, and Taoist contexts. By the beginning of the seventh century, the church in the Middle East and parts of Asia struggled to exist in an environment dominated by Islam. Because the eastern world outside Rome was not as unified culturally or politically, some background detail will be offered in each regional section.

EDESSA

From Antioch, the gospel spread eastward to the kingdom of Osrhoene and its capital, Edessa. In the opening chapter of his *Church History*, Eusebius claimed that Edessa's King Abgar V (d. c. 40) corresponded with Jesus, inviting the Lord to come and heal him.[39] Though this account lacks historical

---

37. See Smither, *Missionary Monks*, 93–106.

38. See Phillip Jenkins, *Lost History of Christianity: The Thousand-Year Golden Age of the Church in the Middle East, Africa, and Asia—and How It Died* (New York: HarperOne, 2009); also Samuel Moffett, *A History of Christianity in Asia*, vol. 1, Beginnings to 1500 (New York: HarperCollins, 1992).

39. Eusebius, *Church History* 1.13.

support, it does indicate that the Edessans were thinking about Jesus and the Christian faith from a very early period. Before Osrhoene was annexed by the Roman Empire in the early third century, the church at Edessa was nurtured by the Antioch church in the second century until a bishop was set apart around 200.

Since the church was planted in this Syriac-speaking region, it became necessary to translate the Scriptures into the local language. Though it's not clear whether Latin or Syriac was the earliest Bible translation, the Old Syriac New Testament emerged in the late second century. The most celebrated portion of the Syriac Scriptures was Tatian's (c. 110–c. 180) *Diatessaron*, a harmony of the four Gospels. Tatian's project marked the first time that the four Gospels were bound together in a single volume. In the fourth century, the Old Syriac Scriptures went through a revision, which resulted in the Peshitta ("clear") text. Also in the fourth century, the first translations of the Syriac Old Testament appeared. Though some New Testament books (2 Peter; 2–3 John; Revelation) were not considered canonical, by the sixth century the Syrian church, concurring with the broader catholic church, revised the Peshitta and included all twenty-seven New Testament books in its final publication. In addition to serving the needs of the Syriac-speaking church, the Syriac Scripture project influenced the translation structure for the Armenian, Georgian, and Arabic Bibles.[40]

In the fourth century, the church in Edessa grew in part through the ministry of Ephraem the Syrian (306–373). The most famous theologian of the fourth-century Syriac church, Ephraem articulated theology in the form of hymns and poetry. Originally from Persia, Ephraem spent the last decade of his life caring for the Edessa's poor, especially those afflicted by famine and the plague. His ministry included organizing food drives for the hungry, starting a hospital, and comforting the sick and dying through his theologically rich hymns. In this midst of the courageous service, Ephraem himself fell ill and died in 373.

---

40. See Smither, *Mission in the Early Church*, 93–95.

MESOPOTAMIA, PERSIA, AND ARABIA

The Christian movement in Mesopotamia and Persia probably spread from Edessa in the second and third centuries through merchants and Christians who had been captured by the Persians. By 225, some twenty churches existed in the Tigris-Euphrates Valley bordering Persia. One of these communities converted a house into a small church building around 232 at Dura-Europos on the Tigris River—one of the earliest excavated church structures from the early Christian period.

The primary church movement that flourished in the region was the Church of the East, which was composed of Syrian and Persian Christians living between Edessa and Nisibis in the border region between the Roman and Persian empires.[41] Their spiritual leader was the patriarch of Seleucia-Ctesiphon. Following the emergence of the Sassanid Empire in Persia in 225, the Church of the East took on more of a Persian identity. By 285, the first Persian bishop was set apart, and by the beginning of the fifth century, there was a recognizable network of churches and bishops in the region. Christianity did not, however, gain official acceptance in Persia. Despite enjoying a brief period of toleration in 409, for much of the fourth, fifth, and sixth centuries, the church was discriminated against and at times persecuted by the Zoroastrian-dominated government. Persian Christians were often associated with the hated Romans, who had, of course, embraced Christianity as an imperial religion in the fourth century. In response to a letter from Emperor Constantine in 315 requesting that Persian Christians be protected, Shah Shapur II (r. 309-379) did the opposite and launched a brutal persecution against the Persian believers. Such discrimination and pressure led many Persian believers to leave their homeland and immigrate to places such as Arabia.

The Church of the East developed its own rich theological tradition and opened theological schools in Edessa and later Nisibis. Although the church rejected the formula of Chalcedon (451), this rejection was not due to solidarity with Nestorius and his aberrant Christology. Rather, the church

---

41. See Wilhelm Baum and Dietmar W. Winkler, *The Church of the East: A Concise History* (London: Routledge, 2000); also Samuel N. C. Lieu and Ken Parry, "Deep into Asia," in *Early Christianity in Contexts: An Exploration across Cultures and Continents*, ed. William Tabbernee (Grand Rapids: Baker Academic, 2014), 143-80.

Figure 2. Map of the Church of the East at its height (c. 800–1200)

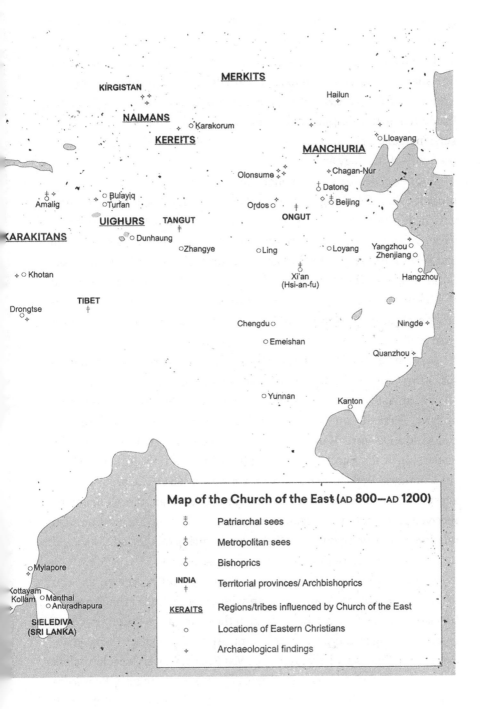

MERKITS

KIRGISTAN

Hailun

NAIMANS
Karakorum

KEREITS

MANCHURIA

Olonsume ·Chagan-Nur

Datong

Bulayiq
Amalig Turfan Ordos Beijing

UIGHURS **TANGUT** **ONGUT**

KARAKITANS Dunhaung

Zhangye Ling Loyang Yangzhou
Zhenjiang

Khotan Xi'an Hangzhou
(Hsi-an-fu)

TIBET
Drongtse

Chengdu Ningde

Emeishan

Quanzhou

Yunnan Kanton

Mylapore

Kottayam Manthai
Kollam Anuradhapura

SIELEDIVA
(SRI LANKA)

Map of the Church of the East (AD 800—AD 1200)

⚲	Patriarchal sees
⚲	Metropolitan sees
⚲	Bishoprics
INDIA ‡	Territorial provinces/ Archbishoprics
KERAITS	Regions/tribes influenced by Church of the East
o	Locations of Eastern Christians
⬧	Archaeological findings

opposed the very Greek manner in which the formula was articulated and that alienated the more Semitic-minded Eastern Christians.

In fourth-century Persia, monasticism developed in part as a means for Christians to pursue safe communities in light of the discrimination they experienced from the Zoroastrian majority and leaders such as Shapur II. In addition to training monks and others in theology and pastoral ministry, Persian monasteries also gave instruction in medicine and often integrated the study of theology and medicine.

In one sense, the gospel penetrated Arabia very early because Paul preached there following his conversion (Gal 1:15-17). Despite this, we know very little about Christianity in Arabia before the fourth century. Arabs were probably most exposed to the gospel through the witness of Roman and Persian believers. The first known churches emerged in what is now Qatar, while another bishop who ministered to Bedouin Arabs attended the Council of Nicaea (325). Finally, a number of fourth-century Arab monarchs embraced Christianity and invited missionaries to come and teach their people.

Muhammad (570-632), the prophet of Islam, was born in Mecca. Within just a few years of his death, the Arab-Muslim empire gained control of all of Arabia. By the middle of the eighth century, Muslims controlled all of Syria, Persia, Egypt, and North Africa, and had expanded to India, central Asia, and China. Many Arab Christians converted to Islam under the leadership of the rightly guided caliphs of Medina (632-661) and during the Ummayad Dynasty (661-750), which was based at Damascus. Others accepted *dhimmi* status. In exchange for paying a tax, these Christians received protection and freedom to continue worshiping. Though Christian mission diminished greatly in Muslim lands during this period, we should note some accounts of Christian-Muslim engagement.

Yanah ibn Mansur ibn Sarjun (c. 650-749), better known as John of Damascus, was an Arab Christian who grew up under the Umayyad Dynasty. Like his father, John worked in the court of the caliph (leader of Islam), serving as a type of accountant. Around 726, after thirty years of service in Damascus, he retired to the Mar Saba monastery near Jerusalem. During this period, John wrote his most famous work, *Fount of Knowledge*. In part two of the book, he discusses a group of heresies—one of which was Islam, or what he calls "the Heresy of the Ishmaelites." In particular,

John criticizes Muhammad for teaching that God has no son, while also castigating the movement for its practice of polygamy. In defense of historic, Nicene Christianity, John argues that Jesus was the inseparable Word and Spirit of God and that the Godhead should be understood as the mutual indwelling of the Father, Son, and Holy Spirit. Although his approach was polemical, John's theological and apologetic method paved the way for other evangelists to Muslims such as Timothy of Baghdad (727–823) and Theodore Abu Qurrah (c. 750–c. 823).[42]

INDIA

The most famous apostle-missionary account in early Christianity was Thomas's alleged first-century mission to India. We say *alleged* because the main literary source presenting the mission is the third-century apocryphal work the Acts of Thomas, which tells a rather fanciful tale of Thomas going to prison after building a spiritual palace for a certain King Gundaphar. Despite the credibility issues with the Acts, other evidence actually offers some support for Thomas's work. These include the discovery of Roman coins from the period in southern India—an indication of trade between India and the Roman Empire—and archaeological evidence confirming that King Gundaphar (r. c. 20–40) lived. Finally, when the Portuguese reached India in 1500, they encountered a community of one hundred thousand Christians in southern India who traced their spiritual lineage to the doubting apostle.

Pantaenus, known mostly for directing the Alexandrian catechetical school, also served as a missionary to India. Eusebius wrote: "[Pantaenus] displayed such zeal for the divine word that he was appointed as a herald of the gospel of Christ to the nations in the East, and was sent as far as India."[43] Though specific details about his ministry are lacking, he was apparently sent by Bishop Demetrius of Alexandria (d. 232) to teach philosophy and the Bible in India.

In the third century, the Church of the East expanded from Persia and also had a presence in India. The Indian church related administratively to the Persian church and experienced communion with the global

---

42. See Smither, *Mission in the Early Church*, 23, 88–89; also Smither, *Missionary Monks*, 138–47.

43. Eusebius, *Church History* 10.1–4 (NPNF² 1:225).

church. Bishop John of Persia (d. 345) attended the Council of Nicaea (325) and signed the Nicene Creed on behalf of the churches of Persia and India.[44]

ETHIOPIA

The most reliable accounts for the Ethiopian church's origins date to the early fourth century. Two youths from Tyre, Frumentius and Aedesius, were traveling with their teacher down the Red Sea when their ship was attacked, and they were sold into slavery. Gaining favor with the authorities and allowed to go free, Frumentius (d. c. 383) eventually returned to Ethiopia, where he apparently led the royal family to faith in Christ, started new churches, and ordained priests. In 347, Athanasius of Alexandria set apart Frumentius as bishop for the Ethiopian church.

Following Frumentius and Aedesius's mission, the Ethiopic alphabet was fully developed, which paved the way for the Bible to be translated into Ethiopic or Ge'ez. Though translation work may have begun as early as the fourth century during the brothers' mission, it was certainly underway by the fifth century. Since the translators were either unaware of or unmoved by Jerome's value of Hebrew verity, they based their Old Testament translation on the Greek Septuagint text. Interestingly, the Ethiopic Scriptures consisted of eighty-one books—nine additional apocryphal books that were rejected by the Western catholic church. Finally, though Amharic is the national language of Ethiopia today, Ethiopic remains the scriptural and liturgical language of the ancient Ethiopian Orthodox Church.[45]

ARMENIA

According to the Armenian historian Agathangelos, Gregory the Illuminator (c. 240-332) came from Asia Minor to serve the Armenian king. Because he refused to make sacrifices to an Armenian goddess and because his father was apparently an enemy of King Trdat (r. 287-330), Gregory was tortured and thrown in prison for some thirteen years. The chronicler reported that Trdat, along with his household and servants, became afflicted by demons and fell ill. In desperation, they summoned Gregory to pray for them. Experiencing healing and liberation from demonic oppression,

---

44. See Smither, *Mission in the Early Church*, 30-31, 38-39.
45. See Smither, *Mission in the Early Church*, 14, 105-6.

Trdat granted Gregory the freedom to proclaim the gospel among the Armenians. Along with the royal household and Armenian nobility, Trdat embraced Christianity and was baptized. Taking it one step further, the king declared Christianity the new national religion in 301, ordering the baptism of some four million Armenians. To place these events in a global context, they took place a decade before Constantine's reported conversion and nearly a century before Theodosius declared Christianity as the official religion of the Roman Empire.

As the Armenian church grew over the next century, Bishop Daniel, a native of Syria, first recognized the need for the Armenian Scriptures. Borrowing letters from Aramaic, Daniel made an initial unsuccessful attempt at developing an Armenian alphabet. In the early fifth century, Armenian Bishop Sahak (d. 439) revived the project and enlisted a monk named Mesrob (362–440) as his scribe as well as Persian scholars who served as language consultants.

Mesrob and his team began work on the Armenian New Testament in 406 and completed it by 410. By 414, they had also completed the Old Testament. Scholars remain divided over whether the Armenians worked from the Syriac or Greek Bible as a basis for their translation. Interestingly, the first Old Testament book they translated was Proverbs, revealing that the Armenian church likely had an affinity for biblical wisdom literature. The Armenian Scriptures also included some Old and New Testament apocryphal books that the greater catholic church rejected as noncanonical.[46]

CENTRAL ASIA AND CHINA

Continuing from Seleucia-Ctesiphon in Persia, a crossroads to the East on the Silk Road route, Christian merchants and Church of the East missionary monks spread the gospel through central Asia toward China in the seventh and eighth centuries. Because of this continual witness, over time, the Syriac word for *merchant* became synonymous with *missionary*.

Through establishing some 150 monasteries and starting new churches in the major cities along the Silk Road, the Church of the East represented the most vital expression of Christianity east of Antioch following the rise of Islam. Though the Silk Road environment could at times

---

46. See Smither, *Mission in the Early Church*, 13, 103–4.

be dangerous and was populated with merchants and traders intent on making money, the Eastern monks lived very simply: their possessions amounted to coats, sacred books, and walking sticks. Upon establishing a new monastery, the monks invited the local population to take part in the community's physical labor, which led to new relationships and opportunities to share the gospel.

Overall, the monks took a holistic approach to ministry, which included showing hospitality, setting up schools, and offering medical care. Many monasteries functioned as small hospitals and became known to the local communities as healing places. Other monasteries, particularly those established in western China, contained significant libraries with medical and philosophy books, biblical commentaries, sacred biographies of saints and martyrs, and copies of Scripture itself.

In the early seventh century, China came under control of the powerful T'ang dynasty, which brought more stability in the region and encouraged traders, merchants, and others to visit the Far East. Although Confucianism was the state religion, around 631, Emperor T'ai Tsung (r. 626-649) began to show religious tolerance and welcomed Manichean and Buddhist missionaries into China. In this environment of spiritual openness, Church of the East missionary bishop Alopen arrived in 635 preaching *Jang Jiao* ("the luminous religion of Syria")—a clear Christian message with a focus on the Trinity.

Alopen and his team of largely Persian monks had been set apart for the mission by Bishop Ishoyahb II (d. 645) of Balad (modern Iraq). This Persian bishop was also responsible for sending missionaries and setting apart new church leaders in Hulwan (modern Iran), Herat (Afghanistan), Samarkand (Uzbekistan), India, and other regions of China. The Chinese emperor welcomed the monks and apparently began to study the Christian faith himself. An educated man with an interest in learning, T'ai Tsung seemed especially interested in the fact that the missionaries had Scriptures, which he invited the monks to translate into Chinese. After three years, the emperor issued an edict giving Alopen and his team freedom to proclaim the gospel in China, while effectively sponsoring their work by giving them land to build a monastery in the imperial capital.

The Church of the East monks connected with Buddhist adherents and monks because of their shared ascetic values and practices. Though the

Christian monks did not serve the Chinese through education or libraries as they did in central Asia, their education level gave them common ground to relate to and converse with the Buddhist monks.

Quite adept at speaking Chinese, the Eastern monks translated the entire New Testament, some of the Old Testament, and some liturgical manuals into Chinese. They also produced a body of Chinese Christian literature, which grew to some five hundred works by the year 1000. These books seemed to connect well with the educated Chinese. For some works, the Christian monks formed the texts in the Buddhist genre of sutras. They also contextualized some biblical ideas with their choice of vocabulary. For example, they referred to divinity in general as "Buddha" and the Holy Spirit as a "pure wind," and they chose a very local Chinese term for God.

The monks also contextualized Christianity by constructing lotus-style crosses that connected with Buddhist values. Despite the pure motives of these missional efforts, the Church of the East monks probably went too far and identified too closely with Chinese Buddhism. Later, when China later came under Taoist leadership in the ninth century, Christianity was still viewed as a foreign religion and was suppressed alongside Buddhism.[47]

SUMMARY

So far in our survey, we have taken a broad sweep of the world—both the West and the East, the Roman and non-Roman worlds—and observed the spread of the Christian movement. Let's now summarize some significant aspects of early Christian mission, including the identities and activities of missionaries.

WHO WERE THE EARLY CHURCH MISSIONARIES?

According to the author of the Didache (early second century), Origen, and Eusebius of Caesarea, the early church communities sent unnamed, itinerant evangelists to travel and cross cultures to proclaim the gospel. Origen notes: "Some of them, accordingly, have made it their business to itinerate not only through cities, but even villages and country houses, that

---

47. See Smither, *Missionary Monks*, 138–47.

they might make converts to God."[48] These early Christian missionaries were anonymous, bivocational, church-centered, cross-cultural laborers for the gospel.

Anonymous Laborers

Though some operated as vocational evangelists, one remarkable element of early Christianity was its anonymous missionary element. It is intriguing that the two largest church communities in the western Roman Empire, Rome and Carthage, had anonymous origins. Observing this phenomenon, Henri Irénée Marrou writes: "The whole church considered itself to be involved in mission and to have a missionary duty, and every believer was a witness, felt called to the work of evangelization."[49] This spirit of early Christian mission seems best captured in the anonymous Letter to Diognetus:

> For Christians are no different from other people in terms of their country, language or customs. Nowhere do they inhabit cities of their own, or live life out of the ordinary. . . . They inhabit both Greek and barbarian cities according to the lot assigned to each. . . . They participate in all things as citizens. . . . They live in their respective countries, but only as resident aliens; they participate in all things as citizens, and they endure all things as foreigners. They marry like everyone else and have children, but they do not expose them once they are born. They share their meals but not their sexual partners. They are found in the flesh but do not live according to the flesh. They live on earth but participate in the life of heaven.[50]

---

48. Origen, *Against Celsus* 3.9 (cited in Eckhard Schnabel, *Early Christian Mission: Paul and the Early Church* [Downers Grove, IL: IVP Academic, 2004], 2:1528).

49. Henri Irénée Marrou, "L'expansion missionaire dans l'empire romain et hors de l'empire au cours des cinq premiers siècles," in *Histoires Universelles des Missions Catholiques I*, ed. S. Delacroix et al. (Paris: Libraire Grunds, 1957), 50, cited in Jacques A. Blocher and Jacques Blandenier, *The Evangelization of the World: A History of Christian Missions* (Pasadena, CA: William Carey Library, 2012), 40; see also Neill, *History of Christian Missions*, 24.

50. Letter to Diognetus 5.1-6 (cited in Schnabel, *Early Christian Mission*, 2:1566).

Bivocational Laborers

This ownership for mission was also evident by the number of bivocational missionaries in the early church—those who witnessed unto Christ while occupied with other work. For instance, philosophers and teachers such as Justin Martyr and Origen taught philosophy and directed schools while also engaging in cross-cultural witness. Likewise, a number of bishops, those set apart to lead established congregations, engaged in missionary work. In Gaul, Irenaeus reached out as an apologist to gnostics and also learned Gaelic in order to preach in rural villages in addition to leading the church at Lyons. Similarly, Martin of Tours was an itinerant preacher and cared for the poor in addition to his responsibilities as bishop of Tours. Finally, monks comprised the most significant group of early Christian bivocational missionaries. In our survey we have observed the work of Basil of Caesarea in Asia Minor, Columba and the monks of Iona in Scotland, and the Church of the East missionary monks in central Asia and China.[51]

Church-Centered Laborers

Early Christian mission was inextricably linked to the local and universal church.[52] Though strategies changed over time and church forms looked different, a time never came when there was a churchless Christianity.

Figure 3. Early mosaic of a North African church structure (Photo by Edward L. Smither)

---

51. See Smither, *Mission in the Early Church*, 32–39.
52. See Smither, *Mission in the Early Church*, 149–63.

The church was both a powerful means for mission and the most visible outcome of mission. In the first century, mission occurred through a deliberate house-to-house approach, and the *oikos* (household) structure facilitated an organic church, especially during periods when Christians were unable to exist as a legitimate organization. Even after peace was given to the church in the fourth century, mission flowed from the church and back to the church in the absence of any structured mission societies. Because evangelism, catechesis, and baptism ministries were located in the context of the church, this solidified a church-focused mission. The phenomenon of church art showed that nonbelievers could embrace the gospel through seeing the gospel visually in basilicas built after the fourth century.

The church provided authority, sponsorship, and support for mission activity. Patrick, Boniface, and Alopen were all set apart for their work by mission-minded bishops. Bishops such as Gregory the Great, Ishoyahb II, and Timothy of Baghdad retained authority over their missionaries and also offered pastoral care and guidance. Finally, that authority was shared as these noted bishops ordained missionary bishops in order to establish new churches with leaders.

Cross-Cultural Laborers

While surveying mission over a broad period of time and vast geographical territory, it might be easy to lose sight of the fact that early Christian missionaries were cross-cultural boundaries. For example, Alopen and the Church of the East monks learned a new language and culture to minister in China. Martin of Tours, a native of Pannonia (Hungary), was an immigrant missionary monk to the peoples of fourth-century Gaul. Though Basil of Caesarea did not physically go on preaching journeys, he welcomed the nations and peoples on the move who passed through his home region of Asia Minor. Finally, missionaries such as Justin, Irenaeus, and John of Damascus crossed frontiers of worldview and belief to proclaim the gospel.

WHAT DID THE EARLY CHURCH MISSIONARIES DO?

As early Christian bishops, monks, teachers, and others engaged in mission, a number of prominent practices developed. Early Christian missionaries suffered, evangelized, contextualized the gospel, translated the Bible, and ministered in word and deed. While we celebrate the virtues of early church missionaries, we must also honestly describe their flaws and practices.

Suffered

Suffering shaped the story of early Christian mission, especially in the period prior to Constantine's rule. Though no responsible student of history would claim that Christians were unceasingly persecuted in the centuries prior to Constantine, it is difficult to deny the accounts of the churches in places such as Lyons, Carthage, Alexandria, and Rome. A survey of various accounts of persecution and martyrdom, including the words and actions of those who suffered, shows that in an indirect manner, suffering helped spread the gospel.[53] Though early Christians did not adopt suffering as a deliberate missionary strategy, the reality of discrimination and persecution created an environment and opportunity for witness. The public context of persecution allowed Christians the opportunity to witness verbally about their faith and to clarify and defend the gospel. In some cases, some bystanders apparently embraced the gospel because of the persecution they witnessed. In other contexts, non-Christian observers sympathized with suffering Christians—an influence that seemed to lay further groundwork for the growth of the church. Persecution against Christians also resulted in apologetics, written treatises that defended and articulated Christian belief. Finally, suffering served to invigorate the church and its mission through the death of martyrs. As they were memorialized on feast days, mentioned in sermons, remembered in sacred biographies (*vitae*), and honored through the construction of churches, Christian martyrs strengthened the witness of the church.

However, during this period Christianity went from a suppressed cult to one sanctioned by kings and kingdoms. The relationship between power and mission proved problematic; some Christian missionaries wielded worldly power against others. Beginning with the conversions of Trdat of Armenia and the Roman emperor Constantine, a developing state-church union was put into motion that led some Christian monarchs to believe they could use position or force to spread the faith. While the Frankish kings Clovis, Pepin, and Charlemagne resorted to compulsion and violence,

---

53. See Smither, *Mission in the Early Church*, 49–73.

some missionaries, including Willibrord and Boniface, did not refuse this state power or protection. Boniface had the courage to cut down the sacred oak at Geismar in part because he enjoyed Frankish military protection. Though some missionaries followed behind politically forced conversions with authentic evangelism and discipleship, this did not erase the unfortunate connection between political power and the gospel in the minds of these newly Christianized peoples and their neighbors.

Evangelized

Evangelism was central to early Christian mission.[54] As shown in the Letter to Diognetus, many Christians verbally witnessed about their faith in the marketplace and in their spheres of influence. Philosophers such as Justin, Pantaenus, and Origen focused on proclaiming Christ to intellectuals, while Gregory the Enlightener, Patrick of Ireland, and Columba engaged political leaders with the Christian message. Others focused their attention on evangelizing heretics. Augustine of Hippo reached out to the schismatic Donatists, and John of Damascus sought to evangelize the "heretics" of his day—Muslims. Finally, some early Christian leaders—including Justin in his *Dialogue with Trypho* and Augustine in his *Confessions*—shared public, recorded testimonies of how they were converted for the benefit of a broader audience.

Contextualized

How to contextualize the gospel in diverse contexts was a key challenge for this period.[55] Missionaries had to be conversant with ideas and forms of communication, through redeeming sacred space and preexisting festivals, by connecting with visual culture, and by understanding the culture of the marketplace. Through these approaches, the gospel began to take root among many peoples and in many areas. This demonstrated that Christianity was a faith that could be at home in a given culture while also bringing transformation to that culture.

Unfortunately, some sending churches poorly distinguished between gospel and culture. In some cases, missionaries conflated their own culture

---

54. See Smither, *Mission in the Early Church*, 74–90.
55. See Smither, *Mission in the Early Church*, 109–26.

with the gospel, imposing their own traditions and ways on their host cultures. This was most apparent in post-sixth-century mission efforts originating from Rome. Augustine of Canterbury and Boniface made allegiances to the Roman bishop to propagate cultural Roman forms in their respective church-planting efforts in England and Germany. While this hindered local forms of Christianity from flourishing, it also resulted in conflict on the mission field between church leaders from different traditions such as the Celts and Romans. Cultural hegemony hinders and harms going to the nations with the gospel of Jesus. Missionaries come as servants, not conquerors.

In contrast to the cultural hegemony of some—such as those who destroyed pagan temples and sacred places—some missionaries took contextualization too far. They insufficiently distinguished their hosts' culture from the gospel. For example, when Augustine of Canterbury transformed English pagan temples into church buildings, he probably opened the door to accommodating paganism in Christian worship. In China, Church of the East monks probably went too far in communicating Christianity in Buddhist forms—constructing lotus-style crosses, writing literature in the sutra format, and in some of the language choices they made to communicate Christian ideas. As shown, during the ninth-century Taoist suppression of Buddhism, Christianity was not seen as that distinct and was suppressed alongside Buddhism. While the gospel sets out to be *at home* in every culture and also *pilgrim* to every culture, the early history of contextualization reveals this delicate tension and the difficult choices that cross-cultural missionaries needed to make.

Translated the Bible

Early Christian mission emphasized translating the Scripture into the vernacular—the heart language—of evangelized peoples.[56] Once churches were established, many congregations worshiped in a regional trade language, and Christians, who were fluent in another language, benefited from Scripture or Christian literature through that medium. As the gospel moved across social and cultural boundaries, what Lamin Sanneh has termed the "vernacular principle" prevailed. Asserting that translation into

---

56. See Smither, *Mission in the Early Church*, 91–108.

local languages clarifies the Christian message for a given people, Sanneh notes: "Scriptural translation rested on the assumption that the vernacular has a primary affinity with the gospel, the point being conceded by the adoption of indigenous terms and concepts for the central categories of the Bible."[57] In the early Christian period, these languages included Syriac, Latin, Coptic, Gothic, Armenian, Georgian, and Ethiopic.

Nevertheless, the church needed to translate Scripture into other local languages in the region, including Punic and Libyan. African cities, such as Carthage and Hippo, had no other way of accessing Scripture except through the Old Latin Bible. Although Roman Christianity seemed to grow fastest in North Africa in the first three centuries, it also died out the quickest in the seventh century with the rise of Islam. Without Scripture in the local languages, Christianity failed to take root in much of North Africa. The North African church could have learned from the Egyptian (Coptic) and Ethiopian (Ethiopic, Ge'ez) churches that developed Scripture in their local languages and continued to survive after the arrival of Islam.

Ministered in Word and Deed

Ministry in both word (proclamation) and deed (caring for real human needs) marked early Christian mission.[58] Mission was not limited to proclamation alone, nor did it ever become gospel-less humanitarian aid. Preaching and acting compassionately were quite integrated and intuitive. Though the gospel remained unchanged—a message centered on the death, burial, and resurrection of Christ and supported by the rule of faith and early Christian creeds—deed ministry varied and evolved according to context. Such ministries involved caring for the poor, hungry, imprisoned, enslaved, and otherwise marginalized. However, it was also apparent in ministries of healing and casting out evil spirits.

FURTHER READING

Baum, Wilhelm, and Dietmar W. Winkler. *The Church of the East: A Concise History*. London: Routledge, 2000.

---

57. Lamin Sanneh, *Translating the Message: The Missionary Impact on Culture* (Maryknoll, NY: Orbis, 2009), 166.

58. See Smither, *Mission in the Early Church*, 127–47.

Bede. *Ecclesiastical History of the English People.* Edited by Judith McClure and Roger Collins. Oxford: Oxford University Press, 2009.

Blocher, Jacques A., and Jacques Blandenier. *The Evangelization of the World: A History of Christian Missions.* Pasadena, CA: William Carey Library, 2012.

Coyle, J. Kevin. "Mani, Manicheism." In *Augustine through the Ages: An Encyclopedia*, edited by Allen Fitzgerald, 520–25. Grand Rapids: Eerdmans, 1999.

Decret, François. *Early Christianity in North Africa.* Translated by Edward L. Smither. Eugene, OR: Cascade, 2009.

Eusebius. *Church History, Life of Constantine. NPNF².* Peabody, MA: Hendrickson, 1994.

Frend, W. H. C. *Martyrdom and Persecution in the Early Church.* Cambridge: Lutterworth, 2008.

Green, Michael. *Evangelism in the Early Church.* Grand Rapids: Eerdmans, 1970. Rev. ed., 2003.

Holmes, Michael W. *The Apostolic Fathers in English.* Grand Rapids: Baker, 2006.

Irvin, Dale T., and Scott Sunquist. *History of the World Christian Movement*, vol. 1, *Earliest Christianity to 1453.* Maryknoll, NY: Orbis, 2001.

Jenkins, Phillip. *The Lost History of Christianity: The Thousand-Year Golden Age of the Church in the Middle East, Africa, and Asia—and How It Died.* New York: HarperOne, 2009.

Justin. *First Apology. ANF.* Peabody, MA: Hendrickson, 1994.

Kalanztis, George. *Caesar and the Lamb: Early Christian Attitudes on War and Military Service.* Eugene, OR: Wipf & Stock, 2012.

Kelly, J. N. D. *Early Christian Doctrines.* New York: HarperCollins, 1978.

Latourette, Kenneth Scott. *A History of the Expansion of Christianity: The First Five Centuries.* New York: Harper & Brothers, 1937. Reprint, Grand Rapids: Zondervan, 1970.

Lieu, Samuel N. C., and Ken Parry. "Deep into Asia." In *Early Christianity in Contexts: An Exploration across Cultures and Continents*, edited by William Tabbernee, 143–80. Grand Rapids: Baker Academic, 2014.

Marrou, Henri Irénée. "L'expansion dans l'empire romain et hors de l'empire au cours des cinq premiers siècles." In *Histoires Universelles des Missions Catholiques I*, edited by S. Delacroix et al., 33–62. Paris: Libraire Grunds, 1957.

Metzger, Bruce M. *The Bible in Translation: Ancient and English Versions.* Grand Rapids: Baker Academic, 2001.

Moffett, Samuel. *A History of Christianity in Asia*, vol. 1, *Beginnings to 1500.* New York: HarperCollins, 1992.

Moss, Candida. *Ancient Christian Martyrdom: Diverse Practices, Theologies, and Traditions.* New Haven, CT: Yale University Press, 2012.

Neill, Stephen. *A History of Christian Missions.* London: Penguin, 1990.

Oden, Thomas C. *The African Memory of Mark: Reassessing Early Church Tradition.* Downers Grove, IL: IVP Academic, 2011.

Parvis, Paul, "Justin Martyr." In *Early Christian Thinkers: The Lives and Legacies of Twelve Key Figures*, edited by Paul Foster, 1–14. Downers Grove, IL: IVP Academic, 2010.

Quash, Ben, and Michael Ward, eds. *Heresies and How to Avoid Them: Why It Matters What Christians Believe.* Peabody, MA: Hendrickson, 2007.

Sanneh, Lamin. *Translating the Message: The Missionary Impact on Culture.* Maryknoll, NY: Orbis, 2009.

Schnabel, Eckhard. *Early Christian Mission: Paul and the Early Church.* Vol. 2. Downers Grove, IL: IVP Academic, 2004.

Smither, Edward L. "Augustine, Missionary to Heretics? An Appraisal of Augustine's Missional Engagement with the Donatists." In *A Uniquely African Controversy: Studies on Donatist Christianity*, edited by A. Dupont, M. A. Gaumer, and M. Lamberigts, 269–88. Late Antique History and Religion 9. Leuven: Peeters, 2015.

———. "Basil of Caesarea: An Early Christian Model of Urban Mission." In *Reaching the City: Reflections on Mission for the Twenty-First Century*, edited by Gary Fujino et al., 77–95. Pasadena, CA: William Carey Library, 2012.

———. "Did the Rise of Constantine Mean the End of Christian Mission?" In *Rethinking Constantine: History, Theology, Legacy*, edited by Edward L. Smither, 130–45. Eugene, OR: Pickwick, 2014.

———. *Mission in the Early Church: Themes and Reflections.* Eugene, OR: Cascade Books, 2014.

———. *Missionary Monks: An Introduction to the History and Theology of Missionary Monasticism.* Eugene, OR: Cascade Books, 2016.

Stevenson, James. *The New Eusebius: Documents Illustrative of the Church to AD 337.* London: SPCK, 1957.

Tertullian. *Apology.* ANF. Peabody, MA: Hendrickson, 1994.

Thompson, Glen. "From Sinner to Saint? Seeking a Consistent Constantine." In *Rethinking Constantine: History, Theology, Legacy*, edited by Edward L. Smither, 5–25. Eugene, OR: Pickwick, 2014.

Wilken, Robert L. *The Christians as the Romans Saw Them.* New Haven, CT: Yale University Press, 2003.

———. *The First Thousand Years: A Global History of Christianity.* New Haven, CT: Yale University Press, 2012.

Willibald. *Life of Boniface.* Translated by C. H. Talbot. In *The Anglo-Saxon Missionaries in Germany, Being the Lives of SS. Willibrord, Boniface, Leoba and Lebuin Together with the Hodoepericon of St. Willibald and a Selection from the Correspondence of St. Boniface.* London: Sheed and Ward, 1954.

2
Mission in the Medieval Church (750–1500)

The period between AD 500 and 1000 has been referred to as the Dark Ages. For Western European peoples, this time was dark because of the decline of the Roman Empire and because of more frequent encounters with Goths, Muslims, and later Vikings, whom they regarded as barbaric, uncivilized hordes. From a Protestant perspective, the entire medieval period was dark theologically because extrabiblical doctrines (such as purgatory) continually crept into the life and practice of the church. The Western Roman Catholic Church also faced challenges with corruption, as some church leaders used their positions to gain wealth and political power, while other so-called celibate priests and even popes were fathering illegitimate children.

But was this period of church and mission history completely dark? Had the church completely lost its missionary impulse? In this chapter, we will explore how, despite these challenges, the church engaged in mission during the medieval period from AD 750 until the eve of the Protestant Reformation. Specifically, we will focus on how the gospel continued to expand to the rest of Western Europe, while reaching new regions such as Scandinavia, Eastern Europe and Russia, the Middle East, North Africa, and central Asia. The key missionaries continued to be bishops and monks, but we will also discuss the rise of the mendicant monastic orders and their innovation in mission. To be sure, ministering in an age of fully orbed Christendom—in which the church and state were united, and each exerted a strong influence on the other—certainly made the idea of mission confusing. However, missionaries—committed to the biblical approach of making disciples—continued to engage heretics and

Muslims and serve in contexts of violence among the Vikings, Muslims, and Mongols.

WESTERN EUROPE

The most significant missionary monastic orders of the Middle Ages—the mendicants—emerged in the thirteenth century as a direct response to Western Europe's new cash economy that encouraged profit and exploitation. Rejecting riches, greed, and power, the mendicants embraced poverty and humility, striving to earn a living through begging for alms. They also experienced a renewed apostolic vision and a commitment to Christian mission. The two most significant orders included the Franciscans, who will we discuss later, and the Dominicans. The Dominicans focused much of their energy on Western Europe before spreading out into other parts of the world.

DOMINICANS

Also known as the Friar Preachers or the Black Friars, the Dominicans received this latter distinction because their members wore a black coat over a white habit. Castilian priest Dominic de Guzman (c. 1170–1221) founded the order in the early thirteenth century. While accompanying his bishop on a trip to Denmark in 1203, Dominic encountered a deacon in the Cathar or Albigensian church in France. Manichean in their thinking, the Cathars held to a dualistic view of God (a good spiritual side but an evil material one). They also condemned marriage and sexual relations, and opposed water baptism and the Eucharist. The Cathars believed that purification came through the imposition of hands and reception of the Holy Spirit. Dominic was able to reach this Cathar deacon and lead him back to Christian orthodoxy, which led to his vision for the new order. For the Dominicans, their mission was a mission to heresy—crossing barriers from Christian orthodoxy to unsound doctrine.

In 1206, Dominic established an initial monastic and mission base at Prouille (modern France), which served as a place of rest for itinerant ministers preaching against heresy and also as a refuge for Cathar women who had turned to the Catholic Church. The same year, the bishop of Toulouse invited Dominic to establish a base for training preachers. He gave the friars a house to live in and supported them with tithes from the church.

Dominic also began sending many of his monks to study theology at the cathedral school to train for the Cathar ministry.

At the Fourth Lateran Council (1215) at Rome, the council gave the Friar Preachers permission to preach but required that they live off church tithes instead of begging. In 1216, the following year, the pope issued a bull officially recognizing the Dominicans and sent a letter to all Latin-speaking bishops ordering them to welcome the Friars' work.

Dominic's vision for global mission apparently developed early and was probably first influenced by the missionary zeal that he encountered in the church at Lund (Sweden). Shortly after the Fourth Lateran Council, Dominic established chapters (monastic mission bases) in France, Italy, and Spain. Later he established similar works in England, Germany, Denmark, Hungary, Poland, Greece, and Jerusalem. Dominic set up his personal base at Bologna and regularly traveled and visited his preachers in the field.[1]

The Dominicans took a multifaceted approach to mission in Europe. Preaching was, of course, foundational to their work. To support this strategy, Dominican leaders developed a number of preaching manuals and resources including Humbert of Romans' *The Instruction of Preachers*, Thomas Waleys' *The Art of Preaching*, as well as Bible concordances and books on the lives of saints. The Friars were also trained in the art of speaking.

Because of their commitment to answering heresy, the Dominicans regarded academic theological studies as vital to their training. Hugh of Saint-Cher (1200-1263) perhaps put it best when he wrote, "First the bow is bent in study, then the arrow is released in preaching."[2] Dominic began to send his preachers to university towns such as Paris, Bologna, and Oxford to enroll as theology students. As the order expanded, new Dominican houses emerged with their own theological schools, equipped with professors who taught Scripture, theology, and philosophy. Some of these houses affiliated with existing European universities.

---

1. See Greg Peters, *The Story of Monasticism: Retrieving an Ancient Tradition for Contemporary Spirituality* (Grand Rapids: Baker Academic, 2015), 172-75, 183; Simon Tugwell, ed., *Early Dominicans: Selected Writings* (Mahwah, NJ: Paulist Press, 1982), 9-12, 14-16, 26-31; C. H. Lawrence, *The Friars: The Impact of the Early Mendicant Movement on Western Society* (London: Longman, 1994), 8, 17, 65-80, 202.

2. Hugh of St. Cher, *Postilla super Genesim* (Gen 9:13) cited in Peters, *Story of Monasticism*, 178.

The most famous Dominican friar, who exemplified academic study in theology and philosophy for the purpose of combating heresy, was Thomas Aquinas (1226–1274). Having been raised by Benedictine monks at Monte Cassino, Aquinas was attracted to the Dominicans during his university studies at Naples. He pursued advanced theological studies in Paris and later taught in the universities at Paris, Cologne, and Rome. His greatest work, *Summa Theologica*, served as a theological resource for his Dominican colleagues and the greater church.[3]

Finally, Dominic saw voluntary poverty as an important means for reaching heretics. Summarizing Dominic's approach to ministering to the Cathars, Greg Peters writes, "The message is only as believable as the messenger" and they were committed to meeting them "in humility—barefoot and without gold or silver in imitation of the apostles."[4]

SCANDINAVIA

By 793, much of Western Europe had met the Vikings—whether they had wanted to or not. Seeking wealth and swift military victories, these sea-going Scandinavian peoples regularly attacked and pillaged monasteries and other soft targets along the coasts of England, Ireland, and Germany. Naturally, their actions drew the serious attention of European monarchs such as Frankish King Charlemagne and his son Louis the Pious (778–840). Much of the European Christian literature from the ninth to eleventh centuries portrays the Scandinavians as barbaric, pillaging pirates—"Northmen"—who were driven by their Norse pagan beliefs. This Scandinavian paganism resembled what Boniface encountered in Germany among the Frisians. Even within this understandable environment of fear and cultural loathing, some believers participated in Christian mission toward the Scandinavian peoples.

One intriguing example was missionary monk Anskar of Corbie (801–865), who ministered in Denmark and Sweden while also serving as a missionary bishop in the northern regions of the Frankish empire. Raised in a noble Frankish family, Anskar entered the monastery at Corbie

---

3. See Peters, *Story of Monasticism*, 175–77; also Lawrence, *Friars*, 84–88, 127–51.

4. Cited in Peters, *Story of Monasticism*, 174.

at a young age. This monastery, founded by Columban's disciples from Luxeuil two centuries prior, followed a modified Benedictine rule that was surely influenced by Columban's missionary vision. Around 822, Anskar set up a new monastery at Corvey in Saxony, where he started a school.[5]

DENMARK

In 826, following a diplomatic visit with Louis the Pious, exiled Danish King Harald Klak (c. 785–c. 852) was baptized along with his wife and four hundred members of their court. Desiring to regain his kingdom and to forge an alliance with the Franks, Harald's conversion was at least partly politically motivated. When Harald planned his return to Denmark, King Louis urged him to take Christian missionaries with him. Anskar and a group of monks agreed to accompany Harald on the mission.[6]

Anskar and his team began their work in Schleswig in the northernmost region of Denmark. His ministry included public preaching and evangelizing the Danes while also starting a school for children, an extension of his previous work at Corvey. He also constructed a church facility in Schleswig and began to hold services. Anskar was probably granted this freedom because of the tolerance of some Danish kings and because, at this point, revering the Christian God was not considered incompatible with Norse pagan practices. Despite these initial signs of openness to their work, Anskar's team encountered hardship, including the death of a sickly colleague, as well as anti-Christian backlash from local pagans, which forced them to return to Corvey. In the end, King Harald was unable to regain his kingdom, and Anskar was disheartened by the overly political nature of the mission.[7]

---

5. See Rimbert, *Life of Anskar, the Apostle of the North, 801–865*, cited in C. H. Robinson, *Medieval Sourcebook*, 2.

6. See Adam von Bremen, *History of the Archbishops of Hamburg-Bremen* 1.17, trans. Francis Joseph Tschan (New York: Columbia University Press, 1959); also Anders Winroth, *The Conversion of Scandinavia: Vikings, Merchants, and Missionaries in the Remaking of Northern Europe* (New Haven, CT: Yale University Press, 2012), 16, 53, 105–6.

7. See Rimbert, *Life of Anskar* 8; also Preben Meulengracht Sørensen, "Religions Old and New," in *The Oxford Illustrated History of the Vikings*, ed. Peter H. Sawyer (Oxford: Oxford University Press, 1997), 223.

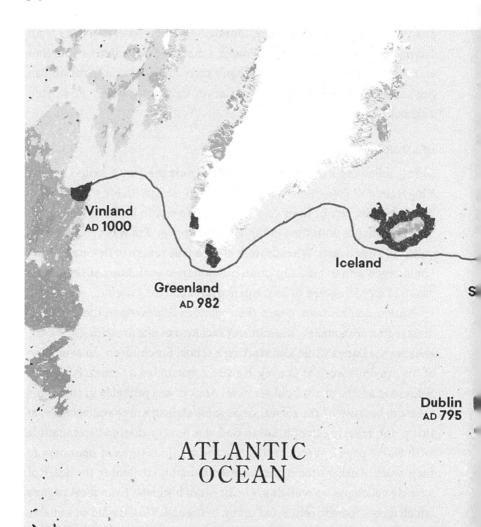

Figure 4. Map of Viking voyages and settlements (c. 800–1000)

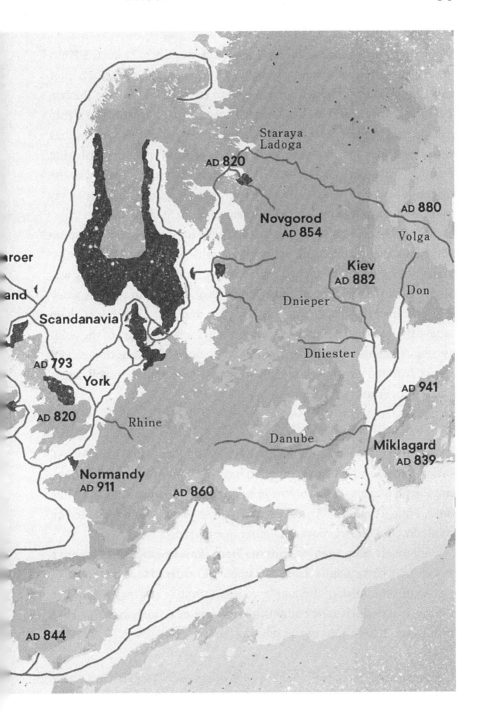

SWEDEN

Around 830, King Bjorn of Sweden sent ambassadors to Louis the Pious requesting Christian teachers be sent to his people. The Frankish monarch once again summoned Anskar to lead the mission. During the trip to Sweden, Anskar and his team experienced further hardship: their ship was attacked by pirates, who robbed them of nearly all of their possessions, including Bibles and liturgical books as well as gifts for the Swedish king. Eventually, the party arrived in Sweden, where they were received by the king and allowed to establish a base of operations, presumably a monastery, on the island of Birka on Lake Mälar near modern Stockholm.

Part of Anskar's strategy in Sweden was to connect with diaspora Christians there, including many slaves who had been taken captive during Viking raids around the region. Part of his Swedish ministry was working for the freedom of those in bondage. In addition to this work, he proclaimed the gospel to Swedish pagans and saw a number of them believe the gospel and be baptized, including some members of the nobility and local government. He also started a church and another school. After a year and a half of successful ministry, Anskar and his colleagues returned to Frankia.[8]

HAMBURG AND BREMEN BASE

Pleased with Anskar's work among the Swedes, the Frankish king appointed Anskar to lead a school and a mission base in Hamburg in 832. This location served as a staging point for mission to Scandinavia. Affirming this move, Pope Gregory IV (r. 827–844) set apart Anskar as a papal legate for the Swedes, Danes, Slavs, and other northern peoples.

Generously supported by Louis the Pious, Anskar established a monastery, church, library, and schools at Hamburg in order to send missionaries to Scandinavia. Anskar also employed an innovative strategy for recruiting new missionaries: he bought the freedom of Danish and Slav boys, training them for ministry and sending them out in mission.[9]

---

8. See Rimbert, *Life of Anskar* 6, 9–11; Peter H. Sawyer, *Kings and Vikings: Scandinavia and Europe AD 700–1100* (New York: Barnes & Noble Books, 1994), 39–40; and Winroth, *Conversion of Scandinavia*, 106.

9. See Adam von Bremen, *History of the Archbishops* 1.15; Rimbert, *Life of Anskar* 15; Sørensen, "Religions Old and New," 202.

Perhaps irritated at Anskar's encroaching ministry, a band of Vikings stormed Hamburg in 845. They razed the church and monastery and destroyed Bibles and other books. Escaping with just the clothes on his back, Anskar witnessed his work at Hamburg come to a grinding halt. Despite this major setback, in 848 the pope made Anskar the archbishop of Bremen, which also included Hamburg as well. From Bremen, Anskar relaunched successful mission efforts to Denmark and Sweden.

Anskar continued his ministry in Scandinavia until his death in 865. During Anskar's lifetime, he saw little lasting fruit among the Vikings. The Scandinavian pagans continually resisted the gospel, and there was a strong reaction to missionaries in Denmark toward the end of Anskar's life. Vikings and pirates continued to pillage and incite violence. Nevertheless, Anskar persevered in the ministry with unparalleled patience. Christianity most clearly took hold in Scandinavia in the tenth and eleventh centuries with the public conversion and baptism of a number of kings, including Knut of Denmark (c. 995-1035), who banned pagan worship and practices in society.[10]

NORWAY, FINLAND, GREENLAND, AND ICELAND

In contrast to the regions affected by Anskar, Christianity entered Norway in a decidedly less missional manner. When the recently baptized, former Viking Olaf Tryggvesson (c. 969-c. 1000) became king of Norway in 995, he essentially coerced the Norwegians into accepting his new faith. His successor, Olaf Haraldson (995-1030), continued to Christianize the country once he came to power. Similarly, upon conquering Finland in 1155, Swedish King Eric IX (1120-1160) forced Christianity on the Finnish people. Baptized in their native Norway, the Viking Erik the Red (950-c. 1003) and his explorer son, Leif Erikson (c. 970-1020), brought Christianity to neighboring Greenland in the eleventh century. By the twelfth century, Greenland's first bishop had been appointed.

The story of Iceland's conversion provides one of the most fascinating accounts in Christian history. In the late ninth century, Irish monks

---

10. See Rimbert, *Life of Anskar* 31-34; Sawyer, *Kings and Vikings*, 9, 135-43; Winroth, *Conversion of Scandinavia*, 27-28, 150-52; Edward L. Smither, *Missionary Monks: An Introduction to the History and Theology of Missionary Monasticism* (Eugene, OR: Cascade Books, 2016), 107-18.

had labored on the volcanic island in the north Atlantic. In the late tenth century, Olaf Tryggvesson dispatched an emissary to Iceland, hoping to coerce them toward baptism as he had done in Norway; however, the Icelanders thoroughly rejected this. Around the year 1000, matters of faith came to a head on the island. Some of the Icelandic chiefs had embraced Christianity, while others remained pagan. Because Iceland had adopted an early parliamentary system, the two major parties were at odds over whether the island people should be governed by Christian or pagan laws. Thorgier Thorkelsson, a pagan law speaker (wise counsel), was tasked with this decision. After a period of reflection, he ruled that Iceland's parliament should accept Christianity and that all of the Icelandic people should be baptized, though pagan dissenters should be free to practice their religion. His decision literally kept civil war from erupting. In the end, Thorgier was also baptized as a Christian. By the middle of the twelfth century, the Icelandic church had set apart its own bishops.[11]

EASTERN EUROPE AND RUSSIA

SLAVIC PEOPLES

In 862, Prince Ratislav of Moravia (d. 870) approached Byzantine Emperor Michael III (r. 842–867), requesting Christian teachers for his people, the Slavs. The Slavs were an Indo-European people occupying what is now Eastern Europe and southern Russia. A cluster of tribes that included Serbs, Croats, and Bulgarians among others, the Slavs generally shared a common language. Spiritually, they were pagan monotheists who gave homage to a supreme being while also venerating other deities.[12]

Ratislav was not asking for pioneer missionaries but rather for Christian teachers to help fortify the Slavs in their Christian faith. Initial evangelization work among the Slavs probably began in the early seventh century when the bishop of Rome sent missionaries to the Slavs. Despite their pagan heritage, the Slavs were rather tolerant toward Christian teachers

---

11. See Stephen Neill, *A History of Christian Missions* (London: Penguin, 1990), 90–92.

12. See Francis Dvornik, *The Slavs: Their Early History and Civilization* (Boston: American Academy of Arts and Sciences, 1956), 42, 47–51, 53–54, 57–59.

and eventually embraced Christianity in the seventh and eighth centuries through the work of Frankish, German, and Greek missionaries.[13]

In response to the Moravian prince's request, the emperor summoned two Greek brothers—Cyril (c. 826-869) and Methodius (815-885)—who were living as monks at the famous Mount Olympus monastery. They were chosen for the mission because of their intellectual abilities and previous diplomatic and mission experience, and because they were already fluent in the Slavic language.[14]

The first step in the mission, begun before the brothers ever set foot in Moravia, was developing a Slavic alphabet in order to translate liturgy and Scripture. Cyril probably led a team of scholars and linguists based at Mount Olympus. Starting with a rough version of the Slavonic alphabet, the team produced a script known as Glagolithic (or Old Slavonic) that was derived from Hebrew, Syriac, Georgian, and other alphabets. Once an alphabet and spiritual vocabulary were in place, they translated portions of the four Gospels for use in the Slavonic liturgy.[15]

Following this initial year of work, Cyril, Methodius, and colleagues left for Moravia in 863. Cyril's primary task was translating the Byzantine liturgy (the Mass, daily office, and Psalter) so that Slavic worship assemblies could begin. Next, the team turned their focus to translating the four Gospels into Slavic. Cyril also trained a group of students selected by Ratislav to learn the Slavic script and religious language in order to serve as indigenous preachers.[16]

The monks encountered great opposition from the German clergy in Moravia who propagated trilingualism—the belief that the only acceptable languages for Christian worship in the world were Latin, Greek, and Hebrew. Following a curious logic and hermeneutic, they argued that since Jesus's title "King of the Jews" had been affixed to the cross in these three languages, only

---

13. See Francis Dvornik, *Byzantine Missions among the Slavs: SS. Constantine-Cyril and Methodius* (New Brunswick, NJ: Rutgers University Press, 1970), 5-6, 9-11, 13-48, 78-79; also A. P. Vlasto, *The Entry of the Slavs into Christendom: An Introduction to the Medieval History of the Slavs* (Cambridge: Cambridge University Press, 1970), 24-26.

14. See *Life of Methodius* 5.

15. See *Life of Cyril* 14; *Life of Methodius* 6; also Anthony-Emil N. Tachioas, *Cyril and Methodius of Thessalonica: The Acculturation of the Slavs* (Crestwood, NY: St. Vladimir's Seminary Press, 2001), 68-73.

16. See Tachioas, *Cyril and Methodius*, 79.

these languages could be used in worship. Cyril was eventually ordered to appear before a church council in Venice to defend his work. However, the pope summoned the brothers to Rome and affirmed their work in cultivating an indigenous Slavic Christianity. Pope Hadrian II (792–872) personally took a copy of the Slavonic Scriptures and blessed them, while also participating in a Slavic liturgical assembly in Rome's famous St. Peter's basilica.[17]

Following Cyril's untimely death at the age of forty-two, Methodius returned to minister among the Slavic peoples. Though he faced continual opposition from German church leaders, he persevered in the Slavic ministry and labored furiously in his final years to complete the Slavic Scriptures and other theological works. Despite this, Slavic Christianity did not immediately flourish in Moravia. However, because many of Cyril and Methodius's followers were monks organized in ascetic communities, they migrated and expanded this indigenous Christian movement into Poland, Bohemia, Croatia, and Russia. Following the baptism of Prince Boris of Bulgaria, his country also embraced Slavic Christianity. In the end, the materials of Slavic Christianity (an alphabet, liturgy, Scriptures, body of Christian literature) helped to shape not only Eastern Orthodox Christianity but also broader Slavic culture.[18]

RUSSIA

Christianity first entered Russia in 957, when Princess Olga of Kiev (r. 945–963) traveled to Constantinople and was baptized. Though she endeavored to propagate her new faith among the Russian people, opposition from the Russian nobility and her own son thwarted her efforts. Olga's grandson Prince Vladimir (r. 980–1015) initiated a renewed interest in Christianity when he came to power. While some leaders in this period had invited Christian missionaries to teach their subjects, Vladimir made the search for a national religion a bit broader. He sent emissaries to the Jewish Khazars (southern Russia), Muslim Bulgars (Bulgaria),

---

17. See *Life of Cyril* 16–17; *Life of Methodius* 6; also Tachioas, *Cyril and Methodius*, 83–86; and Dvornik, *Byzantine Missions*, 129–31.

18. See *Life of Methodius* 15; Dvornik, *Byzantine Missions*, 174–76, 193–245, 272–82; also Tachioas, *Cyril and Methodius*, 97–98, 104, 108–16; Dimitri Obolensky, *Byzantium and the Slavs* (Crestwood, NY: St. Vladimir's Seminary Press, 1994), 210–14; and Smither, *Missionary Monks*, 119–37.

German Roman Catholics, and the Orthodox in Constantinople. Ultimately, Vladimir embraced Orthodox Christianity and invited Greek-speaking bishops to minister among his people, which resulted in a Byzantine style of Christianity in Russia. Over time, the Russian Orthodox Church developed its own liturgy, Scriptures, and indigenous form of Christianity.[19]

MIDDLE EAST AND NORTH AFRICA

Within the first century of Islam's rise and expansion, the Christians of the Middle East, North Africa, and central Asia quickly became religious minorities. Despite this *dhimmi* (minority and taxed) status, some Christians engaged missionally with Muslims. Already we have met John of Damascus, who defended historic Christian teaching while also declaring Islam a Christian heresy. Of course, John wrote his polemical works against Muslims from the security of a monastery in the Syrian desert.

TIMOTHY OF BAGHDAD

Unlike John, Timothy of Baghdad (727–823) encountered Muslims on a very personal level while serving as Church of the East bishop for the city. Timothy began leading the church in Baghdad in 762, a little over a decade after the Abbasid Dynasty established its caliphate (global ruling center for Islam) in the city. The Church of the East was actually eager to establish a presence in the city in order to keep an eye on what the Muslim leaders were doing. Many Christians also served in various roles within the court of the caliph. Ironically, Church of the East Christians enjoyed more freedom under Muslim rule than they had under the recently defeated Byzantine Empire. As a result, Timothy secured permission from the caliph to send missionaries to the formerly Christian lands in central and east Asia. Timothy used the Church of the East monasteries in Persia as training centers where monks studied theology, philosophy, medicine, and linguistics in order to preach, care for physical needs, and translate Scripture. Timothy also set apart bishops for new churches in central Asia, Tibet, and China.[20]

---

19. See Neill, *History of Christian Missions*, 76–77.

20. See Frederick W. Norris, "Timothy I of Baghdad, Catholicos of the East Syrian Church, 780–823: Still a Valuable Model," *International Bulletin of Missionary Research* 30, no. 3 (2006): 133–35; also Smither, *Missionary Monks*, 143–145.

Timothy was also quite involved in local mission to his Muslim neighbors in Baghdad. Trained in theology as well as philosophy, the bishop was well equipped to winsomely respond to the objections Muslim leaders in Baghdad had to the gospel. Although Timothy had discussed Christianity with Caliph Mahdi before, in 781 the caliph offered the bishop protection and a safe space for a two-day open dialogue about their respective faiths. First, the caliph asked: How could God have sexual relations with a woman and father a son? Timothy responded that the Holy Spirit does not have genitals and that the conception of the Son of God was miraculous and spiritual, and therefore unlike any other human conception. Next, the Muslim leader posed: Why do Christians worship three gods? Offering an analogy of the sun (one body with shape, light, and heat), Timothy stayed true to his Nicene convictions while also using the philosophical theology of the Cappadocian fathers to answer this question. Finally, Timothy refrained from attacking the prophet Muhammad; rather, he simply stated that he did not follow Muhammad because the Scriptures did not teach about another prophet.[21]

Timothy's model for engaging Muslims continues to be instructive for the church today. As the leader of a religious minority group in a Muslim majority context, Timothy did not live in isolation; rather, he and the Church of the East Christians lived among and conducted business with their Muslim neighbors. Timothy was wise to dialogue with his Muslim counterparts instead of attacking Islam and its prophet. Finally, since the Muslim caliph's objections to Christianity mirror similar questions posed by modern-day Muslims—on God having a son, on the Trinity, on Muhammad being a prophet—Timothy's responses are useful for modern Christians in their discussions with Muslims.

CRUSADES

Arguably, the darkest period in Christian history was the Crusades (1095-1291). Although Christians, Muslims, and Jews had lived rather peaceably since Muslims first took control of Jerusalem in 637, by the eleventh

---

21. See Norris, "Timothy I of Baghdad," 135-36; also Alphonse Mingana, "The Apology of Timothy the Patriarch before the Caliph Mahdi," in *Woodbrooke Studies* (Cambridge: Heffer, 1928), vol. 2.

century, the so-called Christian kings of Europe united with the pope in a single-minded obsession to take control of the Holy Land. From a religious perspective, Catholics desired access to the Holy Land to go on pilgrimages, which was a form of penance. Politically, the Roman Catholic Church hoped to reunite with the Eastern Orthodox Church following the Great Schism of 1054 since the rival Christian factions now had Muslims as a common enemy.

In 1095, Pope Urban II preached a sermon declaring that it was God's will that the church take up arms to reclaim the Holy Land. This launched a series of four Crusades that spanned nearly two centuries, with battles ranging from the ancient Christian centers of Acre, Nicaea, Antioch, and Edessa all the way to Jerusalem. In the end, although Christian pilgrimages were once more allowed in the Holy Land, Muslims remained in control of Jerusalem, the Eastern and Western churches continued to be divided, and thousands of Christians, Muslims, and Jews had lost their lives.[22] Although Muslims embraced *jihad* as an acceptable means for expanding a Muslim empire, the early church never viewed warfare as a means to expanding the kingdom of God.[23] Instead, at the height of Christendom, the church allowed the political aims of the state to overtake its mission vision, and they embraced their own form of Christian *jihad*.

FRANCISCANS

While much of the church drifted from a New Testament vision for mission during the Crusades, some biblically authentic examples for mission can be observed through the work of missionary monks, particularly the Franciscans.

The Franciscans or Friars Minor ("little brothers") were founded as a direct result of the conversion, vision, and ministry of Francis of Assisi (1182–1226). The son of a wealthy Italian textile merchant, Francis was embroiled in Italy's civil war as a young man. After being captured and imprisoned, Francis

---

22. See Jonathan Riley-Smith, *The Crusades: A History*, 3rd ed. (London: Bloomsbury Academic, 2014).

23. *Jihad* literally means a struggle. For the individual Muslim, there is the spiritual struggle to be pure and obey Allah, which is also known as greater jihad. Lesser jihad refers to the struggle to defend Islam through armed resistance or warfare. In the current discussion, I am using *jihad* in the lesser sense. See William E. Shepard, *Introducing Islam*, 2nd ed. (London: Routledge, 2014), 10.

rethought his life, converted, and eventually became a monk. Striving to imitate Christ through voluntary poverty, preaching, and caring for the poor, Francis quickly attracted a community of brothers (Friars Minor) around him. In 1216, the pope officially recognized the Franciscan order.[24]

From an early point in their history, the Friars Minor engaged in cross-cultural mission work. Particularly burdened to "preach the Christian faith and penance to the Saracens [Muslims]," Francis set sail for the Holy Land in 1212 but never made it because of a shipwreck.[25] Later he attempted to go to Spain and meet with the Muslim leader of Morocco but was prevented by illness. A certain Brother Giles was deployed to work with Muslims, journeying to Spain in 1209, Palestine in 1215, and Tunisia in 1219. Francis's dream of preaching the gospel to Muslims was finally realized in 1219 when he accompanied the Christian armies to Egypt as a chaplain. There he crossed enemy lines to meet with the Egyptian Sultan Malik al-Kamil (c. 1177-1238), proclaiming the Christian message to him.[26]

Francis's mission to Muslims demonstrated two significant mission values. First, his initiative toward Muslims seemed to fulfill a longing that he had for martyrdom. This was his motivation in the initial attempt to sail to the Holy Land in 1212 and also to the Egyptian sultan in 1219. Upon learning of the death of five Friar Minors, who had been sent to Morocco to preach to Muslims, Francis praised their memories and declared that he now truly had five brothers.[27]

Second, though Francis longed for martyrdom, his posture toward Muslims and nonbelievers in general was one of peace. In a section of his *Earlier Rule*, arguably written after Francis's visit to the sultan, he wrote:

All my brothers: Let us pay attention to what the Lord says: Love your enemies and do good to those who hate you, for our Lord Jesus

---

24. See Francis, *The Rule* 6.4; also Lawrence, *Friars*, 34.

25. Thomas of Celano, *Life of Francis* 20.55 (trans. Michael F. Cusato, "Francis and the Franciscan Movement," in *The Cambridge Companion to Saint Francis of Assisi*, ed. Michael J. P. Robson [Cambridge: Cambridge University Press, 2012], 24).

26. See E. Randolph Daniel, "Franciscan Missions," in Robson, *Cambridge Companion to Saint Francis of Assisi*, 241-42; Lawrence, *Friars*, 37-38, 43-46; John Moorman, *A History of the Franciscan Order: From Its Origins to the Year 1517* (Oxford: Clarendon, 1968), 24-25, 30-31, 62-74, 166-69, 227-29.

27. See Robson, "Writings of St. Francis," in Robson, *Cambridge Companion to Saint Francis of Assisi*, 46-47; also Daniel, "Franciscan Missions," 244.

Christ, whose footprints we must follow, called his betrayer a friend and willingly offered himself to his executioners. Our friends, therefore, are all those who unjustly inflict upon us distress and anguish, shame and injury, sorrow and punishment, martyrdom and death. We must love them greatly, for we shall possess eternal life because of what they bring us.[28]

Francis instructed the brothers to serve among Muslims with peace and humility and to avoid arguments and disputes while preaching the gospel. Clearly, Francis illustrated these values during his encounter with the sultan: he refrained from attacking Islam or the prophet Muhammad and focused on proclaiming the gospel and praying for the sultan. Interestingly, Francis received safe passage to the sultan's camp and was returned safely at the conclusion of their discussions.

Though Francis was quite committed to peaceful encounters with Muslims, it would be a mistake to describe his communications with the sultan or others as interfaith dialogue. Instead, he presented a Trinitarian God; an incarnate Christ who was crucified, buried, and risen; and a Holy Spirit who made the virgin birth of Christ possible. Finally, he called his Muslim listeners to repent and believe this message.[29]

RAYMUND LULL

In the generation following Francis's death, Franciscan monks continued to reach out to Muslims; however, some adopted more polemical approaches. The most famous of these was Raymund Lull (1232–1315), a Castilian Franciscan from the island of Majorca. Lull spent nine years learning Arabic, established Franciscan houses as missionary training centers for the Muslim world, and also convinced the pope to make Arabic and Oriental studies part of the curriculum in European universities. After a career in training and mobilization, Lull himself engaged in three short-term

---

28. Francis, *Earlier Rule* 22 (trans. Stephen J. McMichael, "Francis and the Encounter with the Sultan [1219]," in Robson, *Cambridge Companion to Saint Francis of Assisi*, 134).

29. See Francis, *Rule* 3, 11–12; Francis, *Admonitions* 1, 15; also Daniel, "Franciscan Missions," 242–43; McMichael, "Francis and the Encounter with the Sultan," 128–35; and William J. Short, "The *Rule* and the Life of the Friars Minor," in Robson, *Cambridge Companion to Saint Francis of Assisi*, 55, 61.

preaching trips to Algeria and Tunisia in North Africa. Lull's approach was to enter a city and invite Muslim leaders to a public debate over the virtues of Islam and Christianity. A polemicist, Lull did not hesitate to criticize Muhammad in his presentation of the gospel. His first two preaching trips ended abruptly as he was expelled from North Africa. During the third trip, the eighty-three-year-old monk was stoned to death by his Muslim listeners. Though Raymund Lull emulated Francis's vision for martyrdom, he clearly departed from the friar's core value of peaceful engagement.[30]

CENTRAL ASIA

While Christians and Muslims were continuing to fight the Crusades, the Mongol Empire had conquered much of China and central Asia and had even bored inroads into Europe. A number of Christians, including mendicant monks, were killed during Mongol attacks in Eastern Europe. As a result, Pope Innocent IV (1195–1254) sent Italian Franciscan monk John de Piano di Carpini (c. 1180–1252) and his Polish colleague Benedict on an official mission to the Mongol khan in 1246. This two-pronged assignment would prove political and evangelistic.

The friars trekked the rugged terrain of central Asia and arrived at the court of the khan, where they were welcomed in peace and shown hospitality. The men delivered letters from the pope, expressing concern over the Mongols' violence, called for peace, and also announced the Christian message to the khan. Though hospitable, the khan rejected the pope's call for peace and for Christian baptism. While the mission was not very fruitful spiritually, Carpini took careful notes and conducted his own ethnographic survey of the Mongols, which helped the mendicant missionaries who came after him. Also, the friar made the surprising discovery that Church of the East believers lived and worshiped freely among the Mongols.[31]

In 1247, in response to the Mongol leader's initiative toward King Louis of France, the king dispatched Dominican Andre de Longjumeau (d. 1270)

---

30. See E. Allison Peers, *Ramon Lull: A Biography* (London: SPCK, 1929); Samuel M. Zwemer, *Raymund Lull: First Missionary to the Muslims* (New York: Funk and Wagnalls, 1902).

31. See Peter Jackson, "Franciscans as Papal and Royal Envoys to the Tatars (1245–1255)," in Robson, *Cambridge Companion to Saint Francis of Assisi*, 224–26; also Smither, *Missionary Monks*, 148–63.

as an emissary and preacher to the khan. Though the khan continued to show no interest in the gospel, Longjumeau discovered more Eastern Christians, which increased the pope's concern for them and desire to minister to them. As a result, in 1253, Franciscan William of Rubruck (1220–c. 1293) was sent to continue the mission, ministering to diaspora Christians and slaves, and attempting (to no avail) to communicate the gospel to the khan. Like Carpini, Rubruck engaged in ethnographic and linguistic studies in order to better understand the Mongol culture.

Finally, in 1289, Pope Nicolas IV (1227–1292) sent Franciscan John of Montecorvino (1247–1328) all the way to China to reach out to the khan. By this time, the Mongol leader had actually converted to Buddhism; however, he allowed Montecorvino much freedom to preach the gospel among his people. The friar reportedly baptized some six thousand Mongols and started a church, making his mission the most fruitful work in the thirteenth century among this Asian people.[32]

Despite these thirteenth-century efforts from some courageous mendicant missionary monks, by 1300, the Mongols had embraced Islam. Though some Franciscan monks continued to migrate with the Mongols across the central Asian steppe, there was little apparent fruit. By 1362, the Chinese had conquered the Mongols, retaking Peking (Beijing) and killing the last Church of the East bishops in the region.

SUMMARY

Perhaps after reading this account of medieval mission, some might conclude that these actually were Dark Ages. The violent actions of some Christian kings during the Crusades and the compulsive manner by which some monarchs forced Christianity on their subjects contributed to a dark history. However, the Christian story—including the work of mission—is a messy one. Amid political and nationalistic motivations, other missionaries arose with biblical and missional motivations, preserving a remnant of the church during the medieval period.

---

32. See Lawrence, *Friars*, 175, 209–17; Jackson, "Franciscans as Papal and Royal Envoys," 228–36; Daniel, "Franciscan Missions," 246, 253–54; and Smither, *Missionary Monks*, 163–64.

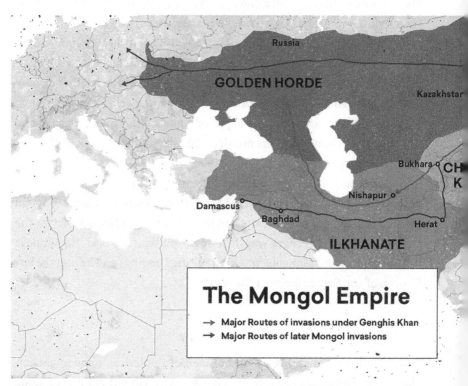

Figure 5. Map of the Mongol Empire

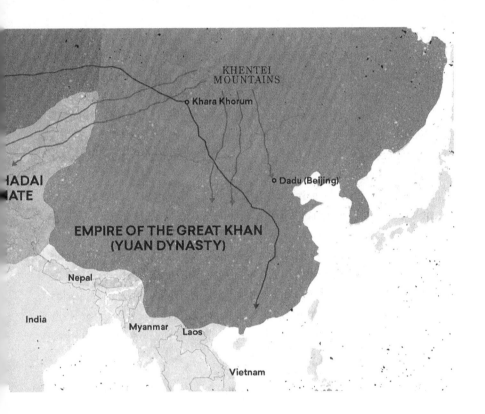

WHO WERE THE EARLY CHURCH MISSIONARIES?

During this period, the vast majority of missionaries were monks. In fact, one of the key reasons for the formation of the mendicant orders—Franciscan, Dominicans, and later Cistercians and others—was to facilitate global mission. Mission-minded bishops such as Timothy of Baghdad and many of the bishops of Rome also participated in and encouraged global mission.

Throughout the medieval mission story, kings and political leaders embraced the gospel, and national conversions followed. In Norway and Finland, leaders forced Christianity on their subjects. In Russia, Prince Vladimir seemed to take a more persuasive approach, and the Russian people followed. The peoples of Iceland were baptized after a parliamentary debate and the declaration of a wise and respected leader. Though the circumstances varied, national conversions initiated by political leaders became common.

Some political leaders, including Ratislav of Moravia, Harald Klak of Denmark, and King Bjorn of Sweden, reached out to other leaders asking for missionaries to come and teach their people. Christian monarchs and emperors such as Louis the Pious and Michael III seemed eager to respond to these requests, sending the likes of Anskar, Cyril, and Methodius to minister cross-culturally. While some monarchs, such as Harald and Ratislav, seemed as interested in political alliances as Christian teaching for their people, their initiative still opened a door for missionary monks to proclaim the gospel and begin churches.

WHAT DID THE EARLY CHURCH MISSIONARIES DO?

Labored in the Context of Christendom

The union of church and state and the church's resulting access to power was never greater than in the medieval period. In some instances, the pope's power enabled otherwise-healthy mission efforts to continue, such as Anskar's work to the north from his base at Hamburg and Bremen. Pope Hadrian II's intervention in Eastern Europe allowed Cyril and Methodius to work toward an indigenous Slavic Christianity against the German trilingualists. Of course, papal involvement also meant that greater Roman influence and control were exerted on these mission fields.

The most horrific expression of Christendom in this period was when the church forsook its mission and launched a holy war against Muslims. The medieval church was never in more need of Raymund Lull's simple and prophetic words: "It seems to me that the conquest of the Holy Land ought . . . to be attempted . . . by love and prayers, and the pouring out of tears and blood."[33]

Ministered in Vulnerability

In contrast to the political and church leaders mentioned, many missionaries during this period served from a posture of vulnerability. Timothy of Baghdad had no access to political power in his ministry to Muslims and to the churches of central and east Asia. While Timothy seemed to enjoy protection as a minority, Anskar, Cyril, Methodius, and Francis carried out their work in clear contexts of violence.

Given the convergence of monasticism and mission in the early church and medieval period, the monks we have encountered cultivated a theology of suffering in mission. Since monasticism emerged as a protest to Christianity's worldly success in the fourth century, monks became the new martyrs. Arguably, the monastic disciplines of prayer, fasting, keeping vigil, and austerity were self-imposed forms of hardship and suffering. The fortitude developed through these spiritual disciples made the monks resilient and capable of persevering in difficult situations. Again, this was true of Askar among the Scandinavian Vikings, Francis among Muslims in Egypt, and the mendicants traveling across the central Asia steppes to meet the Mongol khan. While monks such as Francis of Assisi yearned for martyrdom, others such as Raymund Lull actually achieved it.

Ministered in Word and Deed

Ministering from a posture of vulnerability, the monks we have met preached the gospel in word and in deed. Their ministry of proclamation (evangelism, catechesis, church planting) was naturally integrated with attention to human needs—education, medicine, agriculture, and poverty. Some monks such as Anskar, Cyril, and Methodius also confronted slavery through the course of their ministries. As these monks pushed into the

---

33. Zwemer, *Raymund Lull*, 52–53.

world and founded new monasteries—communities of prayer, study, and service—their way of life together became "cities on a hill" and an attractive, transformative witness to local peoples.

Engaged Other World Religions

While Anskar and other missionaries confronted the Norse paganism through the course of their ministries, during the later medieval period (1000–1500), we observe a more deliberate engagement with adherents to the major world religions. Church of the East missionaries in central Asia and east Asia, and Franciscans among the Mongols, presented the gospel in a Buddhist context.

During this time, many Christian thinkers and theologians were also crafting a response to Islam. Among others, John of Damascus and Dominican theologian Thomas Aquinas (1225–1274) wrote significant polemical works confronting Islamic thought. Raymund Lull introduced Islamic and Oriental studies into the Franciscan monasteries and universities of Europe so that Christians might understand Muslims and be able to evangelize them. While some engaged Muslims from a distance, a number of medieval missionaries maintained very personal ministries with Muslims. Timothy of Baghdad participated in a very open and honest dialogue with the caliph. Leading with a posture of peace, Francis did not withhold any offensive aspect of the gospel in his encounter with the Egyptian sultan. Though quite polemical in his approach, Raymund Lull also demonstrated much love toward Muslims.

Learned Language and Culture

Finally, many of the missionaries in the medieval period showed great commitment to learning the languages and cultures of their host peoples. Raymund Lull dedicated nine years toward mastering Arabic. Many Church of the East monks under Timothy's charge mastered Chinese. Though Cyril and Methodius already spoke Slavic prior to their Eastern European mission, they labored significantly to render it in written form. Finally, in addition to learning some of the Mongol language, John de Piano di Carpini and William of Rubruck took careful notes about Mongol culture and practiced an early form of ethnographic studies.

FURTHER READING

Armstrong, Regis J., and Ignatius C. Brady, eds. and trans. *Francis and Clare: The Complete Works*. New York: Paulist, 1982.

Bremen, Adam von. *History of the Archbishops of Hamburg-Bremen*. Translated by Francis Joseph Tschan. New York: Columbia University Press, 1959.

Cusato, Michael F. "Francis and the Franciscan Movement (1181/2-1226)." In Robson, *Cambridge Companion to Saint Francis of Assisi*, 17-33.

Daniel, E. Randolph. "Franciscan Missions." In Robson, *Cambridge Companion to Saint Francis of Assisi*, 240-57.

Duichev, Ivan, ed. *Kiril and Methodius: Founders of Slavonic Writing; A Collection of Sources and Critical Studies*. New York: Columbia University Press, 1985.

Dvornik, Francis. *Byzantine Missions among the Slavs: SS. Constantine-Cyril and Methodius*. New Brunswick, NJ: Rutgers University Press, 1970.

———. *The Slavs: Their Early History and Civilization*. Boston: American Academy of Arts and Sciences, 1956.

Irvin, Dale T., and Scott Sunquist. *History of the World Christian Movement*, vol. 1, *Earliest Christianity to 1453*. Maryknoll, NY: Orbis, 2001.

Jackson, Peter. "Franciscans as Papal and Royal Envoys to the Tatars (1245-1255)." In Robson, *Cambridge Companion to Saint Francis of Assisi*, 224-39.

Jenkins, Phillip. *The Lost History of Christianity: The Thousand-Year Golden Age of the Church in the Middle East, Africa, and Asia—and How It Died*. New York: HarperOne, 2009.

Lawrence, C. H. *The Friars: The Impact of the Early Mendicant Movement on Western Society*. London: Longman, 1994.

McMichael, Steven J. "Francis and the Encounter with the Sultan (1219)." In Robson, *Cambridge Companion to Saint Francis of Assisi*, 127-42.

Mingana, Alphonse. "The Apology of Timothy the Patriarch before the Caliph Mahdi." In vol. 2 of *Woodbrooke Studies*. Cambridge: Heffer, 1928.

Moffett, Samuel. *A History of Christianity in Asia*, vol. 1, *Beginnings to 1500*. New York: HarperCollins, 1992.

Moorman, John. *A History of the Franciscan Order: From Its Origins to the Year 1517*. Oxford: Clarendon, 1968.

Neill, Stephen. *A History of Christian Missions*. London: Penguin, 1990.

Norris, Frederick W. "Timothy I of Baghdad, Catholicos of the East Syrian Church, 780-823: Still a Valuable Model." *International Bulletin of Missionary Research* 30, no. 3 (2006): 133-36.

Obolensky, Dimitri. *Byzantium and the Slavs*. Crestwood, NY: St. Vladimir's Seminary Press, 1994.

Peers, E. Allison. *Ramon Lull: A Biography*. London: SPCK, 1929.

Peters, Greg. *The Story of Monasticism: Retrieving an Ancient Tradition for Contemporary Spirituality*. Grand Rapids: Baker Academic, 2015.

Riley-Smith, Jonathan. *The Crusades: A History*. 3rd ed. London: Bloomsbury Academic, 2014.

Rimbert. *Life of Askar, the Apostle of the North, 801–865*. Translated by C. H. Robinson. *Medieval Sourcebook*. http://legacy.fordham.edu/halsall/basis/anskar.asp.

Robson, Michael J. P., ed. *The Cambridge Companion to Saint Francis of Assisi*. Cambridge: Cambridge University Press, 2012.

———. *The Franciscans in the Middle Ages*. Suffolk, UK: Boydell, 2009.

———. "The Writings of Francis." In Robson, *Cambridge Companion to Saint Francis of Assisi*, 34–49.

Sawyer, Peter H. *Kings and Vikings: Scandinavia and Europe AD 700–1100*. New York: Barnes & Noble Books, 1994.

———, ed. *The Oxford Illustrated History of the Vikings*. Oxford: Oxford University Press, 1997.

Shepard, William E. *Introducing Islam*. 2nd ed. London: Routledge, 2014.

Short, William J. "The *Rule* and the Life of the Friars Minor." In Robson, *Cambridge Companion to Saint Francis of Assisi*, 50–67.

Smither, Edward L. *Mission in the Early Church: Themes and Reflections*. Eugene, OR: Cascade Books, 2014.

———. *Missionary Monks: An Introduction to the History and Theology of Missionary Monasticism*. Eugene, OR: Cascade Books, 2016.

Sørensen, Preben Meulengracht. "Religions Old and New." In Sawyer, *Oxford Illustrated History of the Vikings*, 19–47.

Tachioas, Anthony-Emil N. *Cyril and Methodius of Thessalonica: The Acculturation of the Slavs*. Crestwood, NY: St. Vladimir's Seminary Press, 2001.

Vlasto, A. P. *The Entry of the Slavs into Christendom: An Introduction to the Medieval History of the Slavs*. Cambridge: Cambridge University Press, 1970.

Wilken, Robert L. *The First Thousand Years: A Global History of Christianity*. New Haven, CT: Yale University Press, 2012.

Winroth, Anders. *The Conversion of Scandinavia: Vikings, Merchants, and Missionaries in the Remaking of Northern Europe*. New Haven, CT: Yale University Press, 2012.

Zwemer, Samuel M. *Raymund Lull: First Missionary to the Muslims*. New York: Funk and Wagnalls, 1902.

3
Mission in the Early Modern Church (1500–1800)

Christian mission efforts in the age of empire were fraught with difficulties, competing interests, and confusion. In some instances, missionaries were caught in the crosshairs of imperial advance; in others, they seemed content to accompany explorers and conquistadores to these new lands.

Given this tension between empire and mission, we will focus on those groups most intent on making disciples of all nations in Asia, Latin America, and Africa. While mendicant monastic groups such as the Franciscans and Dominicans continued their ministries, the most significant Roman Catholic missionary order to emerge in the sixteenth century was the Society of Jesus, or the Jesuits. In the first portion of this chapter, we sketch out the global context of imperial expansion, particularly the growth of the Spanish and Portuguese empires during the sixteenth-century age of discovery.

Between 1500 and 1800, global mission remained largely a Roman Catholic affair. Despite the preaching, writing, and theological clarification of the Protestant magisterial reformers (Luther, Calvin, and Zwingli), their work did not translate into a viable global mission movement in the sixteenth century. Although Protestant mission efforts flickered in North America and Asia in the seventeenth century, no visible Protestant missionary movement can be observed until 1727, when the Moravians emerged. The second portion of this chapter will cover early Protestant missionary efforts.

THE AGE OF DISCOVERY

On the eve of the sixteenth century, with China withdrawing from the world scene, the monarchs of Spain and Portugal began zealously expanding their empires across the globe. As the monarchs took part in what Andrew Walls has described as the "Great European Migration," their motives were political, economic, and spiritual.[1] Global expansion was a new way for these Western nations to extend the medieval Crusades and gain an upper hand on the world of Islam. Western Christian leaders hoped to reconnect with Eastern Christians and gain allies against Muslims. By sending explorers out by sea, the Portuguese and Spanish intended to discover alternative trade routes to the Asian Silk Road and find better markets. As the European nations expanded and even took control of new lands, they also wanted to evangelize the world and bring it under Christendom. For this reason, in 1454, Pope Nicolas V blessed the Spanish and Portuguese and divided the world between the two countries for the purpose of conquest and evangelization. Following this papal blessing, the Treaty of Tordesillas of 1494 divided conquered lands between Spain and Portugal.[2]

Isabella of Spain (1451-1504) exemplifies a monarch driven by these spiritual and political motivations. Through her marriage to Ferdinand II of Aragon (1452-1516) in 1469, she succeeded in consolidating the kingdoms of Castile and Aragon toward establishing a unified Spain. Mentored by Franciscan monk and biblical scholar Francisco Jimenez (1436-1517), Isabella became the key figure in Spain's Catholic Reformation. Troubled by the luxurious living of some bishops, the biblical illiteracy of priests, and the moral laxity within Spain's monasteries, Isabella secured the right to appoint church leaders and to reform the monasteries. She encouraged a renewal in biblical and theological reflection by sponsoring the publication of a critical edition of Scripture, biblical commentaries, and other works of theology. Together, Isabella and Ferdinand also oversaw the Spanish Inquisition, the use of compulsion and force to convert heretics, Jews, and Muslims to the Roman Catholic Church. In 1492, as part of the Inquisition, the monarchs expelled all unconverted Jews

---

1. See Andrew F. Walls, *Crossing Cultural Frontiers: Studies in the History of World Christianity* (Maryknoll, NY: Orbis, 2017), 15-16, 49-51.

2. See Scott Sunquist and Dale T. Irvin, *History of the World Christian Movement*, vol. 2, *Modern Christianity from 1454-1800* (Maryknoll, NY: Orbis, 2012), 1-7.

and Muslims from the country. In short, Isabella's vision for reforming the Spanish church was moral, theological, and political.

Against the backdrop of this upheaval, Italian explorer Christopher Columbus (d. 1506) approached the Spanish monarchs and secured sponsorship for his intended voyage to India by sailing west in order to reach the East. Following an unexpected landing at Hispaniola (modern Dominican Republic), Columbus claimed the land for Spain, dealt violently with the indigenous inhabitants, and returned to Spain with a group of enslaved Taino people. Franciscan and Dominican missionaries followed and evangelized the local people, and a bishop was set apart by 1512. In short, Columbus's mission of discovery and conquest paired with Isabella's reforms in Spain to reveal that religious devotion, political power, and even violent compulsion were not viewed as incompatible values.

In addition to Columbus's famous voyages at the end of the fifteenth century, a number of other explorers took to the seas with mandates for conquest and evangelization. In 1487, Portuguese explorer Bartholomew Diaz (1450–1500) sailed the Atlantic along the west African coastline before discovering the Cape of Good Hope on Africa's southern tip. In 1497, another Portuguese sailor, Vasco da Gama (1469–1524), built on Diaz's work and rounded the Cape of Good Hope before reaching India. Though Columbus "discovered" the Americas for Europe, it was Italian explorer Amerigo Vespucci (1454–1512) who surveyed the South American coast in 1500 and developed the first map of the Americas, which resulted in the American continents being named after him. Also in 1500, Portuguese explorer Pedro Cabral (1467–1520) sailed too far out into the Atlantic and accidentally discovered Brazil, which he promptly claimed for Portugal. From 1519–1522, Portuguese explorer Ferdinand Magellan (1480–1521) went farther than any explorer before him and circumnavigated the globe.

ROMAN CATHOLIC MISSION STRUCTURES

During the sixteenth and seventeenth centuries, Christian mission remained wedded to imperial expansion. That is, missionary efforts largely followed on the heels of Spanish, Portuguese, and other European nations' expansions. However, other structures for missionary sending also emerged that were less tied to this Christendom paradigm.

THE JESUITS

Ignatius of Loyola (1491–1556) founded the Jesuits. Ethnically Basque, Ignatius entered the Spanish royal court at the age of fifteen. After a cannonball crushed his leg in a battle in 1521, Ignatius spent the long recovery period reading, including many Christian devotional works. Through this, Ignatius was not only converted to faith in Christ, but he also yearned to imitate the mendicant lifestyles of Francis of Assisi and Dominic. Ignatius entered the University of Paris in 1528, where he spent seven years studying theology. At Paris, six friends, including Francis of Xavier (1506–1552), joined Ignatius in a community centered on Christian living according to Ignatius's *Spiritual Exercises*. In a solemn worship service in 1534, they covenanted to live together as a society and to offer their services to the pope. In 1540, the pope issued a bull officially recognizing the Society of Jesus as a monastic order.[3]

The Jesuits continued the mendicant tradition of voluntary poverty and begging and were also characterized by the imitation of Christ, obedience, and spiritual care for believers and nonbelievers. Their allegiance to the pope further set them apart.[4] In their *Constitutions*, Ignatius wrote: "The Society also makes an explicit vow to the sovereign pontiff as the present or future vicar of Christ our Lord. This is a vow to go anywhere his Holiness will order, whether among the faithful or the infidels."[5] More than merely a monastic order, the Jesuits were a spiritual, military troop ready to go wherever the pope chose to send them—including to the ends of the earth as missionaries and to resistant peoples such as Muslims. Ignatius articulated this concise mission statement for the order: "The end of this Society is to devote itself with God's grace not only to salvation and perfection of the members' own souls, but also with that same grace to labor strenuously in giving aid toward the salvation and perfection of the souls of their neighbors."[6] By the time Ignatius died in 1556, the Jesuits included over one

---

3. See George E. Ganss, ed., *Ignatius of Loyola: Spiritual Exercises and Selected Works* (New York: Paulist, 1991), 14–26; also Christopher Hollis, *The History of the Jesuits* (London: Weidenfeld and Nicolson, 1968), 9, 14.

4. See Ganss, *Ignatius of Loyola*, 36–37, 217–18; also Hollis, *History of the Jesuits*, 14–17; Luke Clossey, *Salvation and Globalization in Early Jesuit Missions* (Cambridge: Cambridge University Press, 2008), 21–22, 29.

5. Ignatius, *Constitutions* I.1.5 (trans. Ganss, *Ignatius of Loyola*, 284).

6. Ignatius, *Constitutions* I.1.1 (trans. Ganss, *Ignatius of Loyola*, 283–84).

thousand members, with new communities springing up in Portugal, Spain, Italy, Sicily, France, and Germany as well as in Brazil and India. By 1615, the Society included over thirteen thousand members globally.[7]

For Ignatius, Jesus was the primary model for mission—"the inspiring King sent by his Father on a mission to conquer the world, in order to win all humankind to faith and salvation; and calling for cooperators who would volunteer for this enterprise."[8]

Over time, Ignatius's vision became increasingly apostolic and global. Though the words *mission* or *missions* had not been widely used in the church during the first fifteen centuries, the Jesuits were the first to adopt this vocabulary to describe their work of preaching the gospel among all nations.[9]

PROPAGANDA FIDEI

In an effort to wrest control of global mission efforts from the Spanish and Portuguese, Pope Gregory XV (1554-1623) launched the Sacred Office of the Propagation of the Gospel (*Propaganda fidei*) in 1622. Setting apart a team of thirteen cardinals—bishops just below the papal office—the pope's intent was to spread the Christian faith. This statement issued by the committee captured well the vision for the initiative:

> Do not regard it as your task, and do not bring any pressure to bear on the peoples, to change their manners, customs and uses, unless they are evidently contrary to religion and sound morals. What could be more absurd than to transport France, Spain, Italy, or some other European country to China? Do not introduce all that to them, but only the faith, which does not despise or destroy the manners and customs of any people, always supposing that they are evil, but rather wishes to see them preserved unharmed. It is the nature of men to love and treasure above everything else their own country and that which belongs to it; in consequence there is no stronger

---

7. See Ganss, *Ignatius of Loyola*, 46; also John W. O'Malley, *The Jesuits: A History from Ignatius to the Present* (Lanham, MD: Rowman & Littlefield, 2014), 33–42.

8. Ganss, *Ignatius of Loyola*, 32–33.

9. Ibid., 32–33; Clossey, *Salvation and Globalization*, 14; see also Paul Kollman, "At the Origins of Mission and Missiology: A Study in the Dynamics of Religious Language," *Journal of the American Academy of Religion* 79, no. 2 (2011): 425–58.

cause for alienation and hate than an attack on local customs, especially when these go back to a venerable antiquity. This is more especially the case, when an attempt is made to introduce the customs of another people in the place of those which have been abolished. Do not draw invidious contrasts between the customs of the peoples and those of Europe; do your utmost to adapt yourselves to them.[10]

The *Propaganda fidei* aimed to create more churches and set apart more bishops and priests. They were driven to present the gospel in its full splendor, untarnished by European—or another culture's—customs. While they valued consecrating indigenous clergy, the group required new national churches to continue to relate to Rome. One practical step for realizing these aims was creating an early mission organization, the Society for Foreign Mission, which started in Paris in 1663.[11]

ASIA

Given the political environment of the sixteenth and seventeenth centuries and the new forms and approaches to missionary sending, some of the most innovative and controversial Roman Catholic mission efforts occurred in Asia.

INDIA

Francis Xavier is arguably the most famous Roman Catholic missionary in church history. Ethnically Basque like Ignatius, Xavier was among the original group of Jesuits who gathered around Ignatius in Paris. Xavier arrived in Goa, India, in 1542 as a representative of the Portuguese king and as a papal envoy. His task was to minister to Portuguese expatriates in India but also to minister to Indian peoples.[12]

Xavier's Indian ministry began when he encountered the Paravas—a group of Tamil-speaking pearl fishers who had been baptized several years prior by some Franciscan missionaries who subsequently abandoned

---

10. *Instructions from the Propaganda fidei* (1659) (trans. Stephen Neill, *A History of Christian Missions* [London: Penguin, 1990], 153).

11. See Neill, *History of Christian Missions*, 152–56.

12. See Hollis, *History of the Jesuits*, 36–37.

the work. Apparently, the Paravas had converted to Christianity in exchange for military protection from the Portuguese against their Muslim neighbors. Xavier focused his ministry on discipling this people, who had received little teaching after their conversion. Although Xavier learned only basic Tamil, he was still able to oversee a rough translation of the liturgy in the local language. He also started a church and organized the believing Paravas into sixteen villages—strict communities centered on spiritual formation. Xavier also ministered to children, and in one month alone, he baptized some ten thousand Paravas. Given this successful ministry, the Portuguese king sent twelve more Jesuits to join Xavier. However, while the international laborers increased among the Paravas, Xavier failed to set apart any indigenous church leaders.[13]

Building on Xavier's foundational work, Italian Jesuit Roberto de Nobili (1577-1656) spent forty-two years ministering among the Tamil-speaking Madurai people. When de Nobili arrived in India in 1605, another Jesuit priest named Fernandez was already laboring there. After baptizing the Madurai, Fernandez essentially trained them to be culturally Portuguese Christians. De Nobili was convinced that to reach Indians with the gospel, missionaries must also become Indian. Eliminating everything that could possibly offend the Madurai (such as eating meat or wearing leather shoes), de Nobili dressed as an Indian holy man, mastering the classical Tamil, Telugu, and Sanskrit languages as well as the literature of the Brahmins in the process.

In an effort to distance himself from Portuguese Catholic Christianity, de Nobili deliberately cut himself off from the existing church and chose to live in a simple hut. He engaged Hindu intellectuals by holding public discussions on the nature of God and creation. Believing that only the idolatrous elements of a culture should be discarded, de Nobili labored to keep the rest of Indian culture intact. This included working within the caste system. When new believers from different castes were baptized, he chose to establish separate churches. By 1623, de Nobili reported that around one hundred Indians had been baptized.

Despite the apparent success of his methods, not everyone was pleased. Some Catholic leaders accused de Nobili of accommodating Hinduism,

---

13. See Ganss, *Ignatius of Loyola*, 47; also Neill, *History of Christian Missions*, 127-31; Hollis, *History of the Jesuits*, 35-37.

not truly preaching the gospel, and also dividing the church. Though Fernandez complained about him and other church leaders reprimanded him, de Nobili was ultimately exonerated by Pope Gregory XV in 1623. Ironically, despite distancing himself from the established Portuguese church, de Nobili was still accused of being a *Parangi* (Portuguese Catholic) by some Indians.[14] He responded to his local accusers with the following defense:

> I am not a *Parangi*. . . . I came from Rome, where my family hold the same rank as respectable Rajas (princes) hold in this country. . . . The law which I preach is the law of the true God, which from ancient times was by his command proclaimed in these countries by *sannyyasis* (holy men) and saints. Whoever says that is the law of the *Parangis*, fit only for low castes commits a very great sin, for the true God is not the God of one race but the God of all.[15]

De Nobili's response reveals his common-ground posture toward the Indians and a fascinating use of spiritual vocabulary.

JAPAN

In 1549, Francis Xavier, along with two fellow Jesuits and Yajiro—a Japanese man whom they had met in India—traveled to Japan to begin ministry there. Following in the footsteps of other missionary monks, Xavier made his first connections in Japanese society with local leaders (*daimyos*). Having gained their favor, he was provided an interpreter and given the freedom to preach the gospel throughout the country. Generally struggling with the language, Xavier encountered difficulty communicating some key biblical ideas in Japanese; therefore, he chose to transliterate them directly from Portuguese. Though connecting through language did not come naturally, Xavier greatly admired the virtues and ethics present within local Japanese culture, and he managed to discover relevant bridges on which to communicate the gospel. Stephen Neill describes this shift in Xavier's thinking, which would influence Jesuit and Roman Catholic missiology:

---

14. See Neill, *History of Christian Missions*, 156–60; also Hollis, *History of the Jesuits*, 54–58.
15. Cited in Neill, *History of Christian Missions*, 158.

In earlier years, he had been inclined to accept uncritically the doctrine of the *tabula rasa*—the view that in non-Christian life and systems there is nothing on which the missionary can build, and that everything must simply be leveled to the ground before anything Christian can be built up. . . . Now that he was confronted by a civilization with so many elements of nobility in it, he saw that while the gospel must transform and refine and recreate, it need not necessarily reject as worthless everything that has come before.[16]

After serving for two years, Xavier reported that around one hundred Japanese had been baptized. Following a struggle with poor health, Xavier died in 1552 while attempting to begin work in another mission field—China.

In the generation following Xavier's death, many Japanese responded to the gospel. Jesuits and other missionaries baptized around three hundred thousand new believers. While the initial believers came from the lower classes, later, local leaders (*daimyos*) converted with their entire communities. Building on the work of Xavier, Alessandro Valigno (1539-1606), a Jesuit superior and official papal envoy, visited Japan and encouraged missionaries to adapt to local customs, including adopting local dress and learning the language. Valigno advocated ordaining Japanese church leaders, and so he established a Japanese seminary to support this.

Despite the significant response to the gospel among the Japanese at the beginning of the seventeenth century, in the half-century that followed the government significantly persecuted the church. By 1630 almost no signs of Christianity remained in Japan.[17]

CHINA

Xavier failed to reach China; however, another Jesuit colleague, Italian Matteo Ricci (1552-1610), accessed the country and initiated some innovative ministry. Beginning in 1579, Valigno visited Macao, a Portuguese island off the mainland of China where Western missionaries could live and serve. Many church leaders at the time believed that Macao was as

---

16. Neill, *History of Christian Missions*, 133.

17. See Hollis, *History of the Jesuits*, 37-39, 42; also Neill, *History of Christian Missions*, 131-38; Liam Matthew Brockey, *Journey to the East: The Jesuit Mission to China, 1579-1724* (Cambridge, MA: Harvard University Press, 2007), 246.

close as any missionary would ever get to China; however, Valigno adamantly rejected this conclusion. Instead, he appointed Ricci and two other Jesuits to go to Macao, study Chinese, and wait for the right opportunity to enter China. The men also received training in building clocks and designing maps—professional skills that would prove to be very interesting to the Chinese. In 1583, Ricci received permission to enter the provincial capital, Zhaoqing. In 1600, he moved to Peking (Beijing), where he resided for ten years until his death.

Ricci gained favor in the Chinese capital by presenting gifts of clocks, paintings, models of Western architecture, and maps. He also adopted Chinese dress and focused his ministry on intellectuals and the upper classes. Later Jesuit missionaries, Johann Adam Schall von Bell (1592–1666) from Germany and Terrenz Screck (1576–1630) from Switzerland, both trained as astronomers. When they entered China, they brought a gift of seven thousand science books for their hosts.

Ricci was also innovative and controversial for how he contextualized the Christian message in China. For instance, he borrowed the Chinese term *Tianzhu* ("Lord of heaven") as his functional equivalent for the God of the Christian Scriptures. He used key Confucian terms and concepts, especially accepted ethical teachings, as a springboard for teaching the Christian faith and Scriptures. Ricci also considered the Chinese practice of honoring departed ancestors as acceptable and compatible with the Christian faith. At the time of Ricci's death in 1610, the Chinese church had about two thousand members, including some members of the royal family and some leading scholars. Though changing imperial favor and even persecution against the church in 1616 and 1622 presented challenges, Ricci's greatest legacy came through the indigenous Chinese clergy whom he set apart to lead the church.

Ricci's methods set the standard for Jesuit mission practices in China; however, they were also met with resistance from other missionaries, including the Dominicans and Franciscans. In 1704, nearly a century after Ricci's death, Pope Clement XI (1649–1721) denounced the Jesuit contextualization strategy in China and sent a messenger, Charles Thomas Maillard de Tournon (1668–1710), to China and other parts of Asia, ordering missionaries to cease entirely with these approaches. While many missionaries on the field labored unsuccessfully to have this decision repealed, the Chinese emperor reacted even more strongly and decreed that only those missionaries who shared Ricci's philosophy of ministry could remain in China. However, the Roman Catholic Church remained resolute in its decision, which stifled mission work in China until the twentieth century.[18]

VIETNAM

French Jesuit Alexander de Rhodes (1591-1660) arrived in Vietnam in 1623. He also employed innovative strategies in the south Asian nation. First, he excelled in language learning and developed a Latin-based alphabet for the Vietnamese language in order to translate the Scriptures. He was one of the few Catholic missionaries involved in translation during this period. Second, de Rhodes initiated communities of missionary monks—what he referred to as a company of catechists—who were trained in both Bible teaching and medicine. Similar to earlier missionary monastic communities, these communities also ministered to spiritual and physical needs. By 1627, de Rhodes had baptized nearly seven thousand believers, and by 1658, the Vietnamese church grew to some three hundred thousand believers. Despite this fruitful response, de Rhodes encountered hardships in his ministry, including being expelled from the country four times. In the end, he received a death sentence in 1645 that was later reduced to forced exile. Returning to France, he was instrumental in launching the French Society for Foreign Mission. Undeterred by his expulsion from Vietnam, de Rhodes continued his ministry in Persia, where he served for a brief stint before his death.[19]

LATIN AMERICA

Mission in Latin America—especially in the sixteenth century—generally followed this pattern: imperial conquest and expansion that set the stage for sincere missionary work by priests and monks. Columbus landed at Hispanolia in 1492, and by 1515 the Spanish had taken complete control of the island. The Spanish established a church and set apart a bishop

---

18. See Neill, *History of Christian Missions*, 139–41, 164–65; also Hollis, *History of the Jesuits*, 60–68; O'Malley, *Jesuits*, 51, 64–68.

19. See Neill, *History of Christian Missions*, 165–67.

at Santo Domingo by 1512. By 1522, churches had also been started in the neighboring Antilles.

Hernando Cortes (1485-1547) arrived in Mexico in 1519, and within two short years, he had conquered the Aztecs and taken possession of the land. By 1526, churches had been launched in Mexico City and Tlaxcala. In 1529 alone, Franciscan monks reported baptizing two hundred thousand Mexicans. Similarly, within five years of Francisco Pizarro's (1496-1541) arrival and conquest of the Incas in Peru in 1536, the Spanish gained control of the area. By 1541, a church had been started in Lima.

Following Cabral's accidental discovery of Brazil in 1500, the Portuguese established towns along the coast by the middle of the century. The Portuguese discovery of Brazilian sugar cane prompted the trafficking of African slaves across the Atlantic to South America. From 1500-1850, some ten to fifteen million Africans were enslaved and trafficked to the Americas to support European economic ventures. By 1551, the first churches were started in Brazil.

During a relatively short period of time in the sixteenth century, Catholic priests and missionaries planted new churches across the South American continent. In addition to those already mentioned in Peru and Brazil, churches were started in Caracas (1540), Asuncion (1547), and Buenos Aires (1582). Aside from regular priests and bishops leading newly established churches, Franciscan and Dominican monks carried out much of the missionary work on the continent. Later, Jesuits arrived and established *reducciones* (reductions), communities intended to train indigenous peoples in both Christianity and Western European culture.

BARTOLOMÉ DE LAS CASAS

Amid the confusion between empire and mission in Latin America in the sixteenth century, Spanish priest Bartolomé de las Casas (1484-1566) became an early advocate for justice in mission. Originally he journeyed to the New World to find wealth, but in 1510 de las Casas became the first priest ordained in the Americas. Though he continued to live the comfortable life of a Spanish colonist in his first few years of ministry, by 1514 he began to actively denounce the Spanish abuse of the American indigenous peoples and effectively began a human rights campaign.

The primary area that de las Casas confronted was the *encomienda* system. Essentially, when Spanish settlers gained control of land, they created relocation camps in which indigenous peoples lived and worked. Though viewed by some colonists as a means of evangelization, the *encomienda* system was a form of slavery. De las Casas's advocacy for the American indigenous peoples brought him before the highest levels of power in Europe. In 1542, in part through the Spanish priest's activism, the Holy Roman Emperor Charles V (Charles I of Spain) issued the New Laws, which outlawed the *encomienda*. While an edict issued in Europe was surely difficult to enforce on the other side of the Atlantic, de las Casas took it upon himself to refuse Communion to those Spanish colonists who violated the order. Eventually, de las Casas returned to Europe, where he spent his remaining days speaking, writing, and advocating for the human rights of the American indigenous peoples.

AFRICA

Roman Catholic mission work in Africa during this period was limited and largely focused on central and southern Africa. Mission success depended almost entirely on relationships with African political leaders. Following Diaz's explorations along the African coast in the late fifteenth century, initial missionary efforts began in Congo, which resulted in a church plant led by a local Congolese bishop.

Beginning in 1612, Jesuit, Dominican, and Augustinian monks labored to evangelize what is now Mozambique. In 1628, however, King Kaprazine of Mutapa (modern Zimbabwe) declared war on both the Portuguese and Christians, and war between the Africans and Europeans ensued. In 1652, the Portuguese-installed King Felipe was baptized, which resulted in a nominal acceptance of Christianity in the nation. Similarly, in 1656 Princess Jinga of Angola received baptism and then invited the pope to send more missionaries to her people.

By 1700, the baptized believers in Congo and Angola numbered around six hundred thousand. However, in the absence of deliberate mission strategies—including missionaries learning local languages and cultures, and prioritizing discipleship—the gospel advanced in central and southern Africa on the whims of kings and monarchs.

THE PROTESTANT REFORMATION

On October 31, 1517, German Augustinian monk and theologian Martin Luther (1483–1546) called for debate concerning the church's teaching on penance. He unknowingly launched a revolution that would forever change the church. Concerned with the question of salvation, he asserted that justification happened by faith alone. He argued for the priesthood of all believers, that every Christian possessed the ability to read and understand Scripture. On spiritual authority, he argued that Scripture alone represented the final authority for faith and practice. Luther demonstrated this last conviction very practically by spending the winter of 1521–1522 (while in hiding) translating the New Testament into colloquial German. Thanks to the advanced technology of the printing press, the initial run of three thousand copies sold out quickly, and the Luther Bible was on its way to being the best-selling book in sixteenth-century Germany. Luther worked continually to revise the German New Testament while also putting together a committee to complete translation of the Old Testament, which was realized in 1534. Luther's work in Bible translation set the stage for other similar projects in Europe in the sixteenth and seventeenth centuries.

Indeed, the principle of biblical authority that Luther and the other magisterial Reformers championed provided a theological foundation and fresh vision for vernacular Bible translation that invigorated future missionary work. While many reformers engaged in cross-cultural ministry encounters within Europe, and John Calvin (1509–1564) sent preachers back to his native France and even to Brazil, early Protestants did not participate in mission on a global scale.[20] The sixteenth-century Protestant Reformation did not produce a viable global missionary movement that paralleled the work of the Jesuits, who had emerged from the Catholic Reformation.

How do we explain this lack of global engagement in mission on the part of sixteenth-century Protestants? First, unlike the Catholic countries of Spain and Portugal, which possessed ships for exploration and transporting missionaries, the Protestant nations in Europe (with the exception of England) did not have these means of global transportation. Second, the wars of religion and conflicts in general across Europe in the sixteenth

---

20. See Michael A. G. Haykin and C. Jeffrey Robinson, *To the Ends of the Earth: Calvin's Missional Vision and Legacy* (Wheaton, IL: Crossway, 2014).

century severely limited land travel. While a nation such as England repeatedly shifted from Catholic to Protestant rule, this surely impacted any energy or focus Protestant Christians might have had for global mission. Third, Protestants lacked missionary sending structures. As our study has shown, monastic orders (Celts, Franciscans, Dominicans) functioned as the key means of sending in the medieval church. The Reformers were so focused on eliminating the works righteousness they associated with the monasteries that they opted to shut them down altogether. While they did not value monastic orders as a means for mission, it appears that no other alternative structures for sending missionaries to the world were considered. To be sure, many Reformers, such as Calvin, sent preachers across Europe; however, these structures paled in comparison to what future Protestant groups would develop for global sending.[21]

Ultimately, the general Protestant focus on Europe seems best explained by how the magisterial Reformers understood the meaning of mission. When Luther read Matthew 28:18–20, he interpreted Jesus's Great Commission as making disciples through baptism and catechesis. The magisterial reformers strived to renew the church through the pure preaching and teaching of the Scriptures. This ministry extended to evangelizing families and bringing the Reformation to bear in society. Reformation mission could best be described as a mission to evangelize and teach the established church. While the arena of God's mission is the whole earth and we are to "declare his glory among the nations" (Ps 96:3), the early Protestant Reformers remind us that mission to our Jerusalems will always be needed.

EARLY PROTESTANT GLOBAL MISSION

NORTH AMERICA

Despite the sixteenth-century emphasis on Europe, a flicker of Protestant global focus can be observed in the seventeenth and eighteenth centuries. Similar to the mandates given by European Catholic monarchs in

---

21. See Scott Sunquist, *The Unexpected Christian Century: The Reversal and Transformation of Global Christianity, 1900–2000* (Grand Rapids: Baker Academic, 2015), 11–13; and Glenn Sunshine, "Protestant Missions in the Sixteenth Century," in *The Great Commission: Evangelicals and the History of World Missions*, ed. Martin I. Klauber and Scott M. Manetsch (Nashville: B&H Academic, 2008), 14–15.

the sixteenth century, part of the English (Protestant) charters to settle Virginia, Connecticut, Pennsylvania, and Massachusetts included a call to evangelize Native Americans. John Donne's (1572–1631) sermon on Acts 1:8 delivered to the Virginia Company in 1622 illustrates some of this vision:

> The Acts of the Apostles were to convey that name of Christ Jesus, and to propagate his gospel throughout the whole world. Beloved, you too are actors on this same stage. The end of the earth is your scene. Act out the acts of the apostles. Be a light to Gentiles who sit in darkness. Be content to carry him over these seas, who dried up one red sea for his first people, and who has poured out another red sea—his own blood—for them and for us.[22]

Although conflict existed between English settlers and indigenous Americans, the Anglican Church formed one of the earliest Protestant mission societies in 1701, the Society for the Propagation of the Gospel in Foreign Parts, in order to evangelize both Native Americans and African slaves in the American colonies.

On top of his duties as a full-time Puritan minister, John Eliot (1604–1690) began to minister to the Algonkian people in the mid-seventeenth century. He learned Algonkian so well that he translated the Bible into the Native American dialect by 1663—one of the earliest efforts in missionary Bible translation following the Reformation. By 1671, some thirty-six hundred Algonkian had embraced the gospel. Convinced that these new converts could not grow spiritually in their native context, Eliot extracted them from their tribal contexts and established praying towns—new Christian communities designed for the purpose of teaching, fellowship, and accountability.

David Brainerd (1718–1747) was arguably the most famous American missionary to Native Americans in the eighteenth century. Influenced by the revival preaching of George Whitefield (1714–1770), Brainerd left Yale College and became an itinerant preacher among indigenous peoples in Massachusetts, Pennsylvania, New York, and New Jersey. His most fruitful work, accomplished through preaching to small groups, occurred among

---

22. Cited in Esther Chung-Kim and Todd R. Hains, eds., *Acts*, Reformation Commentary on Scripture, New Testament 6 (Downers Grove, IL: IVP Academic, 2014), xliii.

the Delaware Indians in New Jersey. Despite his passion for the ministry, Brainerd contracted tuberculosis and died at the age of twenty-nine. Brainerd may have been forgotten in mission history if it had not been for his friend and father-in-law to be, Jonathan Edwards (1703-1758), who published *An Account of the Life of the Late Reverend Mr. David Brainerd* in 1749.

While Edwards is largely remembered in American Christian history for being a philosophical theologian and a preacher during the First Great Awakening (1730s and 1740s)—particularly his famous sermon "Sinners in the Hands of an Angry God"—he also influenced the church toward mission. Edwards not only supported and encouraged Brainerd's work but, following Edwards's dismissal as a minister of the Northampton church in 1750, he spent the better part of a decade ministering to Native Americans in Massachusetts. Edwards's greatest contribution to global mission happened when he published Brainerd's journals. When they were read by Christians in the English-speaking world—such as William Carey (1761-1834) and Henry Martyn (1781-1812)—they inspired and mobilized a new generation to mission service.[23]

INDONESIA

Protestant missionary work also followed on the heels of commercial and political expansion, particularly through the Dutch East India Company, into South and Southeast Asia in the seventeenth century. In 1627, Dutch statesman and Christian scholar Hugo Grotius (1583-1645) sought to bolster mission work by authoring the book *On the Truth of the Christian Religion*, which was to be distributed by Dutch sailors in Sri Lanka and Indonesia. Later, the Dutch founded a seminary in Indonesia and initially sent out twelve ministers for the island nation. A number of Dutch ministers became proficient in local Indonesian languages, and the New Testament was translated into Malay in 1668. By 1800, the Dutch claimed to have baptized one hundred thousand believers on the island of Java and another forty thousand on Ambon.[24]

---

23. See Timothy George, "Evangelical Revival and the Missionary Awakening," in Klauber and Manetsch, *Great Commission*, 46-50.

24. See Neill, *History of Christian Missions*, 190-91.

Figure 6. Map of Confessional Divisions in Europe during the Reformation

Sweden

Russia

Poland

ALTIC SEA

BLACK SEA

Ottoman Empire

Venice

Naples

INDIA

In 1705, King Frederick IV of Denmark (r. 1699-1730) commissioned Protestant mission work in Tranquebar, the Danish-controlled areas of South India. The king and missionaries adhered to a movement known as Pietism—a group within the Lutheran church that desired to experience heartfelt religion as much as they wanted to articulate sound doctrine. Led by famous theologians such as Philip Jakob Spener (1635-1705) and August Herman Franke (1663-1727), the Pietists valued practicing spiritual disciplines, including prayer, and Bible study groups. This environment of spiritual renewal acted as a catalyst for global mission participation.

Unable to find any willing Danish volunteers, Frederick IV sent two German Pietists, Bartholomäus Ziengenbalg (1682-1719) and Heinrich Plütschau (1677-1752), to Tranquebar. Although they faced opposition from Danish merchants and even Danish clergy in established churches, Ziengenbalg and Plütschau labored to master the Tamil language, and Ziegenbalg completed the translation of the Tamil New Testament in 1714 and also began work on the Old Testament. Along with language learning, the Germans focused on understanding local culture and thought in order to contextualize their Lutheran Christianity into Indian forms. Although they ministered in a communal society, they emphasized preaching the gospel and calling for individual conversions. They established schools in order to provide general education for their host people and theological seminaries to train and set apart national church leaders.[25]

By 1750, the Church of England began a second early Protestant mission society, the Society for the Propagation of Christian Knowledge, which specialized in providing printed materials for mission. Focusing their work on southern India, the Anglican group collaborated well with German Lutheran missionaries sent from Denmark. One of their earliest projects was translating the Anglican Book of Common Prayer into Tamil.

Finally, another German Lutheran missionary, Christian Friedrich Schwartz (1726-1798), labored for nearly a half century in India. Trained in theology at the Pietist University of Halle in Germany, Schwartz was also

---

25. See Hans-Werner Gensichen, "Ziegenbalg, Bartholomäus," in *Biographical Dictionary of Christian Missions*, ed. Gerald H. Anderson (New York: Macmillan Reference USA, 1998), 761; and Gensichen, "Plütschau, Heinrich," in Anderson, *Biographical Dictionary of Christian Missions*, 540-41.

sent to India by the Danish crown. Continuing the legacy of Ziengenbalg and Plütschau, Schwartz mastered multiple Indian languages—Tamil, Urdu, and Persian—and finished Ziengenbalg's translation of the Old Testament. He also strived to contextualize the gospel in the Indian context. Remembered for pursuing simplicity, Schwartz planted a church in Tanjore that grew to some two thousand believers before his death. In many ways, his ministry set the stage for William Carey's nineteenth-century work.[26]

THE MORAVIANS

While Protestants were beginning to engage in global mission during the eighteenth century, the first signs of a missionary movement—a precursor to the mission societies of the nineteenth century—came with the emergence of the Moravians (*Unitas Fratrum*). The group was founded by Count Nicolaus Ludwig von Zinzendorf (1700-1760). This German nobleman abandoned a career in public service for ministry after being influenced by the Pietists and studying under August Hermann Franke at Halle. While at the university, Zinzendorf participated in a student group called the "Order of the Grain of the Mustard Seed," which celebrated taking the gospel to the nations.

In 1722, Zinzendorf opened up his estate at Berthelsdorf, which was later renamed Hernhutt ("the Lord's watch"), to Protestant refugees. The diverse community constructed dwellings and shops while striving to live in Christian community. Five years into the experiment, the Moravians experienced an apparent spiritual revival, which prompted them to begin an around-the-clock prayer meeting that lasted for one hundred years.[27] In this environment of renewal, the community began to set their eyes on the spiritual needs of the world. In 1732, the Moravian Church began sending its first missionaries around the world. As they were building from their Pietist roots, proclaiming a gospel of love was central to their mission focus. Also, since many Moravians already worked as carpenters and artisans, they continued to use these skills to support themselves on the

---

26. See Hans-Werner Gensichen, "Schwartz, Christian Friedrich," in Anderson, *Biographical Dictionary of Christian Missions*, 606-7; also Neill, *History of Christian Missions*, 198-200.

27. See J. E. Hutton, *History of the Moravian Church* (London: Moravian Publication Office, 1909), 217-20.

field. During this period, a high percentage of Moravian believers—about one in sixty—served as cross-cultural missionaries.

In the eighteenth century, Moravian missionaries ventured to the East and West Indies, Greenland, North America, Suriname, and South Africa. A number of them ministered amid significant hardships. In order to get close to African slaves on the sugarcane plantations in St. Thomas (Virgin Islands), John Dober (1706–1766) and David Nitschmann (c. 1695–1772) sold themselves as indentured servants. Christian David (1690–1751) endured the difficult conditions of Greenland to preach the gospel to the Greenlandic Eskimo people. He also clashed with another Lutheran missionary, who accused the Moravians of preaching a sentimental gospel that did not require moral change. While serving among Native Americans in the Hudson River Valley and establishing a discipleship community in Pennsylvania, David Zeisberger (1721–1808) saw many of his disciples massacred by Patriot troops during the American Revolution.[28]

SUMMARY

Due to imperial expansion during the sixteenth and seventeenth centuries, Christian mission became inextricably linked with imperial motivations. While the Catholic countries of Spain and Portugal seemed to unapologetically fuse empire with mission, many Protestant nations (also England, Holland, Denmark) followed suit. The same vessels carrying explorers and colonizers carried Franciscan and Dominican monks. The British and Dutch East India companies hired chaplains to minister to European sailors and also to Asian peoples.

What impact did this reality have on Christian mission? First, because church and mission efforts were so closely linked with political power during the period of exploration and discovery, this seems to be the period when Christianity became officially branded as a Western religion. Many Western missionaries believed political power was compatible with mission efforts. Many also operated under the assumption that Western culture was superior. Therefore, part of evangelizing a people meant civilizing

---

28. See Ruth A. Tucker, *From Jerusalem to Irian Jaya: A Biographical History of Christian Mission* (Grand Rapids: Zondervan, 2004), 100–113.

(or Westernizing) them. Second, some pushed back against these imperial tendencies and formed new missionary sending structures such as
the *Propaganda fidei* in which mission emphases could be controlled by
the church and not the state. Third, many sincere Roman Catholic and
Protestant missionaries during this period experienced conflict across
the world with their own countrymen who were there to make money and
exploit the local peoples. Preaching the gospel meant affirming the image
of God in the host peoples encountered and showing them dignity, which
was counter to many imperial agendas such as the *encomienda* system in
Latin America. Finally, mission work for some—most notably Bartolomé
de las Casas—included standing up for indigenous peoples and advocating
for their human rights against the exploitation from European imperialists.

WHO WERE THE EARLY MODERN MISSIONARIES?

While regular priests such as de las Casas began churches and engaged in
mission, monks continued to lead the way in Roman Catholic mission efforts.
Franciscan, Dominican, and later Augustinian monks actively evangelized.
The Jesuits accomplished the most significant work. However, because
of the controversies they created and due to their perceived arrogance, the
pope dissolved the Jesuit order in 1773. Though this action was overturned
in 1814, the Jesuit global mission enterprise never fully recovered.

Many of the earliest Protestant missionaries participated in cross-
cultural mission on top of other ministry duties as pastors and chaplains.
Ziengenbalg and Plütschau were set apart as official missionaries to India
by the Pietist king of Denmark. Finally, the Moravians followed in the way
of Paul, supporting themselves as carpenters and artisans while engaging
in gospel ministry.

WHAT DID THE EARLY MODERN MISSIONARIES DO?

Connected with Leaders

Continuing the approach of missionaries from the early church and medieval period, many Christian evangelists during this period began their work
by making contact with political leaders. In Japan, Xavier sought the favor
of local leaders (*daimyos*), which opened doors to reaching the general
populace. In China, Matteo Ricci also made favorable inroads with political leaders through his gifts of technology. Finally, the sixteenth-century

Catholic missionary approach in southern Africa depended entirely on monarchs accepting baptism and leading their people to do the same. Although large segments of the population responded to the new faith, Christian adherence in the region seemed largely nominal.

Learned Culture and Contextualized the Gospel

Beginning with Francis Xavier's shift in thinking about the Japanese, the Jesuits believed that their host peoples still bore the image of God and that their cultures contained noble starting points for communicating the gospel. Although Xavier struggled to learn languages in India and Japan, later Jesuits such as Ricci and Nobili mastered Asian languages, which gave them insight into grasping their audience's worldview. This cultural insight led to contextual mission strategies—Ricci's choices about naming God in the Chinese language and allowing Confucian thought to shape Chinese Christianity, and de Nobili's posture as an Indian holy man engaging in spiritual dialogue. Early Protestant missionaries in India, Ziengenbalg, Plütschau, and Schwartz, also excelled at language learning, understanding culture, and striving to contextualize Lutheran churches in southern Indian forms.

Evangelized and Discipled

Sixteenth- and seventeenth-century missionaries emphasized evangelism and discipleship. Some did a rather poor job of it, while others excelled in this aspect of mission. Because the Spanish and Portuguese prioritized the economic and political aspects of imperialism over the spiritual concerns of mission, missionaries to the Americas conducted mass baptisms with little or no Christian teaching that followed. Similarly, because of politically motivated conversions in southern Africa, little attention was given to discipleship, and the new converts possessed only a superficial understanding of the gospel.

Beginning with Xavier in southern India, the Jesuits did a better job teaching the Christian faith and starting churches through their discipleship villages. In Latin America, the Jesuit *reducciones* offered an environment for spiritual growth, community, meaningful work, and protection from imperial powers despite the fact that they were largely training their disciples in Western Christianity. Similarly, John Eliot's praying-town strategy for the Algonkian believers provided a similar context for discipleship, although the approach meant extracting these new believers from their native contexts.

The Protestant Reformation value of salvation by grace alone influenced how Protestant missionaries articulated the gospel and called nonbelievers to faith and repentance. The magisterial Reformers demonstrated this value through evangelism and catechesis in the towns that they were striving to reform. For Calvin, this included establishing programs in Geneva to instruct children in the gospel.[29] This was also evident in the public preaching ministries of George Whitefield in North America and John Wesley (1703-1791) in the British Isles, and also through the small group evangelistic preaching of David Brainerd among Native Americans. The Pietist movement, which celebrated understanding doctrine but also experiencing God in a heartfelt, personal manner, influenced Protestant missionaries to share a gospel of God's love and to insist on individual, personal conversions. Ziengenbalg and Plütschau emphasized personal conversions in their ministry in India even though they ministered in a communal culture in which important decisions such as religious faith are made collectively.

Set Apart Indigenous Leaders

Despite the strong colonial flavor of global mission during this period, a number of mission groups valued training and setting apart national Christian leaders. Alessandro Valigno launched a seminary in Japan to train leaders. Matteo Ricci discipled a few Chinese men who became leaders in the Chinese church. Similarly, in its quest to plant churches that were not European in character, the *Propaganda fidei* celebrated ordaining national church leaders who would, of course, possess a strong connection to Rome. Finally, in their efforts to contextualize Lutheran Christianity into Indian forms, Ziengenbalg and Plütschau also labored to set apart Indian clergy.

---

29. See Dolf Britz, "Politics and Social Life," in *The Calvin Handbook*, ed. Herman J. Selderhuis (Grand Rapids: Eerdmans, 2009), 437.

Translated Scripture

Although Bible translation had been central to early Christian mission, very little translation work occurred during the medieval period. Western Roman Catholics venerated the Latin Vulgate Scriptures to such a point that translating the Bible into local languages was not considered necessary. In light of this trend, Alexander de Rhodes's translation of the Vietnamese Scriptures made him a trailblazer among seventeenth-century Catholic missionaries.

A direct application of the Reformation value of biblical authority, a renewed vision for Bible translation is probably the greatest legacy of the Protestant Reformation toward global mission. Luther's work to translate the New Testament into colloquial German inspired many Protestants to translate Scripture into local languages. In the sixteenth century alone, translations appeared in Italian, French, Dutch, Czech, Danish, Swedish, Icelandic, and English.[30] In the preface to the 1515 Danish Scriptures, Christiern Pederson writes: "Nobody ought to think that the Gospels are more sacred in one tongue than in another: they are as good in Danish or in German as they are in Latin."[31] Due to government and church opposition, the French, Spanish, and English translations were developed elsewhere in Europe, and the first French translations were published anonymously. Because of his work on the English Bible, William Tyndale (1494-1536) was captured by Henry VIII's soldiers and executed in 1536.[32]

Beginning with John Eliot's Algonkian translation in 1663, Bible translation became a common feature among Protestant mission work from the seventeenth century onward. Dutch missionaries made the Scriptures available in Formosan (Taiwan) Chinese (1661) and Malay (1668); Ziengenbalg, Plütschau, and Schwartz worked on the Tamil Scriptures; and the Danish Lutheran missionary Paul Egede (1708-1789) published the Greenlandic Eskimo New Testament (1766).

---

30. See S. L. Greenslade, ed., *Cambridge History of the Bible*, vol. 3, *The West from the Fathers to the Reformation* (Cambridge: Cambridge University Press, 1963), 94-174.

31. Bent Noak, "Scandinavian Versions," in Greenslade, *Cambridge History of the Bible*, 3:137.

32. See Matthew Barrett, *God's Word Alone—The Authority of the Bible* (Grand Rapids: Zondervan, 2016), 58-61; also S. L. Greenslade, "English Versions of the Bible," in Greenslade, *Cambridge History of the Bible*, 3:141-47.

Emerged from Spiritual Awakening

One of the enduring trends in evangelical global mission that began in this period is that revival and spiritual awakening often precedes significant missionary movements. Perhaps the greatest observation about Moravian mission was their commitment to prayer. After experiencing a spiritual revival at Hernhutt, the group launched an around-the-clock prayer vigil, which certainly contributed to more missionaries being sent to the world. This Moravian spirituality also influenced John Wesley in his conversion and his eventual call to ministry.

Although the North American church did not immediately become a global mission sender following the First Great Awakening, the preaching of George Whitefield inspired David Brainerd to mission among Native Americans. In addition to his preaching and mission work in Massachusetts, Jonathan Edwards organized prayer meetings for the purpose of spiritual revival. New works of Christian literature often accompany spiritual revivals. Edwards's publication of Brainerd's journals seems to represent this reality, and the work served to inspire others to volunteer for missionary service.

FURTHER READING

Britz, Dolf. "Politics and Social Life." In *The Calvin Handbook*, edited by Herman J. Selderhuis, 437-48. Grand Rapids: Eerdmans, 2009.

Brockey, Liam Matthew. *Journey to the East: The Jesuit Mission to China, 1579-1724.* Cambridge, MA: Harvard University Press, 2007.

Chung-Kim, Esther, and Todd R. Hains, eds. *Acts.* Reformation Commentary on Scripture, New Testament 6. Downers Grove, IL: IVP Academic, 2014.

Clossey, Luke. *Salvation and Globalization in Early Jesuit Missions.* Cambridge: Cambridge University Press, 2008.

Ganss, George E., ed. *Ignatius of Loyola: Spiritual Exercises and Selected Works.* New York: Paulist, 1991.

Gensichen, Hans-Werner. "Plütschau, Heinrich." In *Biographical Dictionary of Christian Missions*, edited by Gerald H. Anderson, 540-41. New York: Macmillan Reference USA, 1998.

———. "Schwartz, Christian Friedrich." In *Biographical Dictionary of Christian Missions*, edited by Gerald H. Anderson, 606-7. New York: Macmillan Reference USA, 1998.

———. "Ziegenbalg, Bartholomäus." In *Biographical Dictionary of Christian Missions*, edited by Gerald H. Anderson, 761. New York: Macmillan Reference USA, 1998.

George, Timothy. "Evangelical Revival and the Missionary Awakening." In *The Great Commission: Evangelicals and the History of World Missions,* edited by Martin I. Klauber and Scott M. Manetsch, 45–63. Nashville: B&H Academic, 2008.

Greenslade, S. L., ed. *Cambridge History of the Bible, vol. 3, The West from the Fathers to the Reformation.* Cambridge: Cambridge University Press, 1963.

Haykin, Michael A. G., and C. Jeffrey Robinson. *To the Ends of the Earth: Calvin's Missional Vision and Legacy.* Wheaton, IL: Crossway, 2014.

Hollis, Christopher. *The History of the Jesuits.* London: Weidenfeld and Nicolson, 1968.

Hutton, J. E. *History of the Moravian Church.* London: Moravian Publication Office, 1909.

Kollman, Paul. "At the Origins of Mission and Missiology: A Study in the Dynamics of Religious Language." *Journal of the American Academy of Religion* 79, no. 2 (2011): 425–58.

Neill, Stephen. *A History of Christian Missions.* London: Penguin, 1990.

Noak, Bent. "Scandinavian Versions." In Greenslade, *Cambridge History of the Bible,* 3:135–40.

O'Malley, John W. *The Jesuits: A History from Ignatius to the Present.* Lanham, MD: Rowman & Littlefield, 2014.

Sunquist, Scott. *The Unexpected Christian Century: The Reversal and Transformation of Global Christianity, 1900–2000.* Grand Rapids: Baker Academic, 2015.

Sunquist, Scott, and Dale T. Irvin. *History of the World Christian Movement, vol. 2, Modern Christianity from 1454–1800.* Maryknoll, NY: Orbis, 2012.

Sunshine, Glenn. "Protestant Missions in the Sixteenth Century." In *The Great Commission: Evangelicals and the History of World Missions,* edited by Martin I. Klauber and Scott M. Manetsch, 12–22. Nashville: B&H Academic, 2008.

Tucker, Ruth A. *From Jerusalem to Irian Jaya: A Biographical History of Christian Mission.* Grand Rapids: Zondervan, 2004.

Walls, Andrew F. *Crossing Cultural Frontiers: Studies in the History of World Christianity.* Maryknoll, NY: Orbis, 2017.

4
The Great Century of Christian Mission (1800–1900)

Amid Western colonial expansion and evangelical renewal movements, Protestant mission came into its own and became a significant global movement in the nineteenth century. Historian Kenneth Scott Latourette refers to this time as the "great century" for Christian mission. Building on the thought and initiative of English missionary pioneer William Carey (1761-1834), Christians in the West began to see mission as a central purpose of the church. While Carey and others caught a vision for world evangelization, they went further and developed mission societies—volunteer sending structures—in order to send and support missionary laborers going to Asia, Africa, and the Americas. In this chapter, we will first describe the context of the nineteenth-century world before exploring the work and innovation of missionaries and mission societies in this period. Finally, we will conclude by summarizing some key approaches, principles, and values for nineteenth-century mission. Because the mission story in this period is so vast, I will necessarily limit the discussion to Protestant mission, which is not intended diminish the work of Roman Catholic, Orthodox, or other missionary movements.[1]

---

1. For Roman Catholic and Orthodox mission work in this period, see Stephen Neill, *A History of Christian Missions* (London: Penguin, 1990), 335–79; also Robert L. Gallagher and John Mark Terry, *Encountering the History of Missions: From the Early Church to Today* (Grand Rapids: Baker Academic, 2017), 74–88.

THE NINETEENTH-CENTURY WORLD

COLONIALISM

On a global political scale, the Great European Migration continued. In the late eighteenth and nineteenth centuries, such movement led to the founding of new nations, including the United States (1776), New Zealand (1840), Canada (1867), and Australia (1901). Of course, the nations of Europe continued to colonize other parts of the world, particularly within Africa and Asia. The British Empire took control of India, Burma, Sri Lanka, Egypt, and east Africa. The French colonized north and west Africa (today known as Francophone Africa), parts of Southeast Asia, and some Pacific Islands. Germany and Belgium developed their colonial interests in southern Africa, while Holland expanded into southern Africa and Indonesia. Since Protestant mission efforts followed on the heels of European colonial and commercial expansion, mission and empire continued to be viewed as synonymous in the eyes of many colonized peoples.

INDUSTRIALIZATION

While individual European nations were exploiting colonized lands for raw materials and other commercial interests, Europe itself underwent its own Industrial Revolution in the early part of the nineteenth century. Industrialization, in turn, gave rise to factories supported by machines. Not only did this change the location and rhythm of work, but it also reshaped family and social structures. As village dwellers migrated to the cities in hopes of better wages and a better life, industrialization spawned urbanization. Industrialized economies further provided a foundation for Karl Marx (1818–1883) and Friedrich Engels's (1820–1895) *Communist Manifesto* (1848), a sociopolitical philosophy that gained increasing influence in the nineteenth and twentieth centuries.

CURRENTS OF THOUGHT

The nineteenth century continued to experience the latter developments of the Enlightenment (c. 1685–1815), an intellectual movement that questioned tradition, exalted reason and science as the key means of knowledge, and promoted individualism. The Enlightenment worldview challenged biblical ideas such as miracles, the supernatural and demonic world, and also the presence of God in human affairs. Applying Enlightenment principles, German biblical scholars from the Tübingen school, including New Testament scholar Friedrich Schleiermacher (1768–1834), raised critical questions about the historicity and authorship of Scripture. This skepticism toward biblical ideas, particularly the traditional account of creation (Gen 1–2), received a further boost when Charles Darwin (1809–1882) published his *Origin of Species* in 1858. While it's no surprise that many secular scientists embraced Darwin's theory of evolution, some biblical scholars and theologians were likewise won over.

GLOBAL RELIGIONS

In addition to these shifts in thought, attitudes toward religion were changing as well. During this period, the great world religions—Islam, Hinduism, and Buddhism—experienced decline. The Roman Catholic Church was no exception, losing power and influence. In 1870, when Italy became a sovereign nation, the Papal States were abolished, and the Roman Catholic Church's territory became limited to the Vatican. Following the French Revolution in 1789, France embarked on journey of *laïcité* (secularization), which included legislation in 1905 that made the nation a secular republic free of the influence of the Catholic Church. Across the sea, the American colonies demonstrated different ideas about the place of an official state church; the United States adopted separation of church and state, with the first amendment to the US Constitution advocating for freedom of religion. These developments in Europe and the United States heralded the end of the idea of Christendom.

EVANGELICAL REVIVALS

Despite these changing attitudes toward religions, the century underwent numerous evangelical revivals. From 1800 to 1830, North America experienced what was called the Second Great Awakening. Camp meetings in Kentucky, Ohio, West Virginia, and North Carolina, along with the renewed evangelistic preaching in New England, fueled the revivals. New church plants sprang up, particularly among the free-church minded Presbyterians, Methodists, and Baptists. In fact, during this period in American history, regular church attendance grew from 10 percent to 40 percent of the population. Outside North America, other evangelical renewal movements developed in Norway, Germany, Switzerland, France,

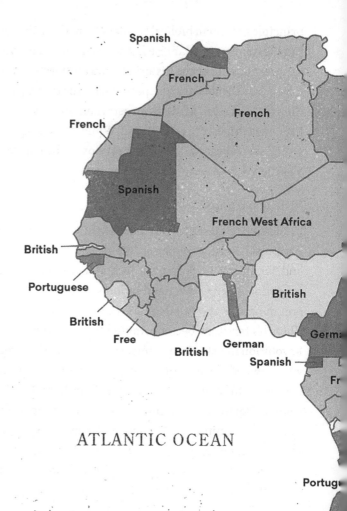

African Colonies after the Berlin Conference of 1884

Figure 7. Map of the European Colonization of Africa

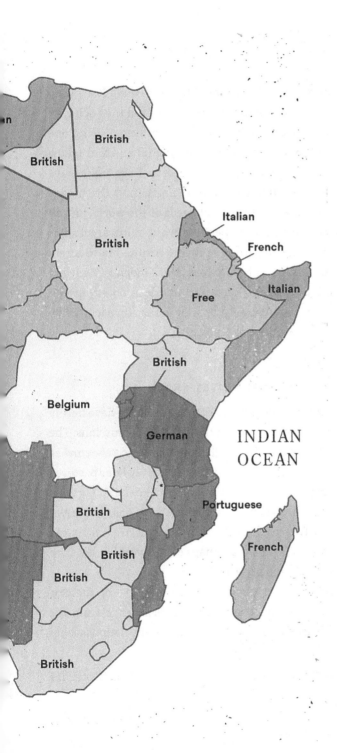

and Britain in the nineteenth century. In many of these cases, evangelical revivals translated into new vision and commitment to global mission sending.[2]

The haystack prayer meeting offers an enlightening case study. A group of students at Williams College (Massachusetts) organized the Society of the Brethren, which met once or twice a week for prayer. During one meeting in the summer of 1806, Samuel Mills (1783–1818) and four fellow students found themselves in a massive thunderstorm. They took refuge inside a nearby haystack, where they continued their meeting. On this day, the focus of prayer became the great spiritual needs of the world, and all but one student pledged themselves to become cross-cultural missionaries. Beyond mere sentiment, the group's prayers resulted in concrete missionary engagement. Mills went on to form the American Board of Commissioners for Foreign Missions (hereafter American Board) in 1810, the first North American mission society, as well as the American Bible Society and the United Foreign Mission Society.[3]

WILLIAM CAREY (1761–1834)

Growing up in Northampton, England, William Carey could have hardly imagined being referred to one day as the father of modern missions. The son of a weaver, Carey first apprenticed and later labored as a shoemaker until the age of twenty-eight. Initially a lay preacher, Carey later pastored two small Baptist congregations while continuing to make shoes. Through reading the *Voyages* of the English explorer Captain James Cook (1728–1779), Carey's vision for the spiritual needs of the world caught fire. Enamored with data, stories, and maps, Carey placed maps of the world in his shop, which guided him into prayer and deeper study.

Carey became convinced that global mission ought to be the central focus of the church. He encountered some resistance from his Particular Baptist church leadership, who believed that the nations would

---

2. See Edward L. Smither, "The Impact of Evangelical Revivals on Global Mission: The Case of North American Evangelicals in Brazil in the Nineteenth and Twentieth Centuries." *Verbum et Ecclesia* 31, no. 1 (2010).

3. See Alan Neely, "Mills, Samuel John, Jr.," in *Biographical Dictionary of Christian Missions*, ed. Gerald H. Anderson (New York: Macmillan Reference USA, 1998), 460.

be brought into the kingdom by another move of the Spirit in the last days.[4] Carey remained unmoved and adopted as his foundational missional text Matthew's Great Commission—"make disciples of all nations" (Matt 28:18-20). In 1792, he published *An Enquiry into the Obligations of Christians to Use Means for the Conversion of the Heathens*, a short treatise that surveyed mission history as well as some global religious and cultural demographics. As the title suggests, Carey argued that the church ought to function as God's means for mission in every generation.

A committed Calvinist who believed in God's sovereignty in salvation, Carey also advocated the active participation of the church in mission. At a gathering of Baptist ministers in Nottingham in 1792, Carey famously challenged his colleagues, "Expect great things from God; attempt great things for God." In the same year, he helped form the Baptist Missionary Society (BMS). Well-known Baptist theologian Andrew Fuller (1754-1815) became the society's first secretary, while John Thomas (1757-1801), a physician, was appointed as the first missionary candidate. Carey also volunteered himself for missionary service.

William and Dorothy Carey did not share the same call for mission work. Uneducated and illiterate, Dorothy had hardly ventured outside her home village; India did not figure into her life's calling. Initially refusing to join her husband, she changed her mind and accompanied him to India, arriving in 1793. At the time, the British East India Company controlled India—a precursor to British colonial rule that began in 1858—and the company generally opposed the work of missionaries. Because of this pressure, the Careys moved to the interior of the country and later to West Bengal, where William worked in an indigo factory. These experiences helped him learn the local language and adapt to the culture. Unfortunately, Dorothy lived a different story. Isolated from the local culture, her primary occupation was caring for her children. Tragedy struck the Carey home when their five-year-old son Peter died, precipitating Dorothy's struggles with mental illness. Though William clearly loved his wife and family, he coped with this tragedy and the hardship of

---

4. See Thomas J. Nettles, "Baptists and the Great Commission," in *The Great Commission: Evangelicals and the History of World Missions*, ed. Martin I. Klauber and Scott M. Manetsch (Nashville: B&H Academic, 2008), 89–92.

cross-cultural living by withdrawing to spend hours a day in language study and Bible translation work.[5]

In 1800, the Carey family moved to the Dutch-controlled colony of Serampore near Calcutta. Joining colleagues Joshua Marshman, William Ward, and their families, they formed the Serampore mission. Since the families lived together in one large household, the Careys received much-needed support, especially since Dorothy was unable to care for her children. The Serampore team also proved to be an early example of a missionary team, collaborating on mission strategy.

The Serampore mission team championed five key values:

- evangelism through preaching throughout all of India;
- Bible distribution in all national languages;
- quick establishment of local churches;
- training and setting apart indigenous church leaders;
- and conducting a thorough contextual study of Indian peoples.

Laboring to understand their context, they strived to keep Indian cultures intact while also denouncing practices that contradicted Scripture. For instance, the Serampore mission opposed infanticide and also the *sati* practice—the Hindu tradition of widows casting themselves on the funeral pyre of their deceased husbands.

To support these values, the Serampore team employed a number of strategies. First, they started schools and launched Serampore College (1818). They trained Christians in theology and non-Christians in a variety of subjects while integrating a Christian worldview in their teaching. Second, they started a printing press and publisher, in order to distribute Scripture and other literature. Third, they planted a church at Serampore, which grew to some six hundred baptized believers by 1818. Finally, despite the fact that Carey was an untrained linguist whose initial translations were incomprehensible, he contributed to Bible translation work in thirty-six Indian languages. His work included complete Bibles in Bengali,

---

5. See Andrew D. McFarland, "William Carey's Vision for Missionary Families," in *The Missionary Family: Witness, Concerns, Care*, ed. Dwight P. Baker and Robert J. Priest (Pasadena, CA: William Carey Library, 2014), 98–115.

Sanskrit, and Marathi; New Testaments in twenty-three other languages; and portions of Scripture in another ten.

Apart from Carey's work as a church planter and Bible translator, perhaps his greatest legacy to the modern Protestant missionary movement was modeling his value of expecting great things from God and attempting great things for God. Through the pain and hardship endured in the context of family life, he also demonstrated perseverance amid suffering in mission. Though Carey was not the first Protestant missionary in history or even the first Protestant missionary to India, he is remembered as the father of modern missions because of these innovations and because he was on the forefront of a missionary movement from the English-speaking world. Indeed, from 1792 and the founding of the Baptist Missionary Society until 1960, 80 percent of the Protestant missionaries in the world came from English-speaking nations.[6]

MISSION SOCIETIES

Protestant mission efforts took off in the nineteenth century in part because of the creation of many new mission societies. While Roman Catholics had monastic orders and a network like the *Propaganda fidei*, in previous centuries Protestants lacked a means for sending gospel laborers to the world. The Moravians were the main exception. But in the eighteenth century, sending organizations were created.

Following on the heels of the Baptist Missionary Society, founded by Carey and colleagues in 1792, the London Missionary Society (LMS) launched in 1795. Though theologically Reformed, the mission was interdenominational in focus, attracting laborers from Presbyterian, Methodist, Baptist, and other backgrounds. The LMS initially sent missionaries to Oceania (Pacific Islands) and Africa.

Early in the eighteenth century, the Anglican Church had already formed the Society for the Propagation of the Gospel in Foreign Parts for mission to Native Americans and African slaves in the American colonies, and the Society for the Propagation of Christian Knowledge to provide printed materials for mission. In 1799 the Anglican Church Missionary

---

6. See Neill, *History of Christian Missions*, 222–26.

Society (CMS) was birthed through the vision of two members of the British East India Company and the Clapham group, an evangelical activist group that included British politician and abolitionist William Wilberforce (1759-1833). Originally called the Society for Missions to Africa and the East, the group's fields of ministry included Africa, India, China, and the Middle East.

Continental Europeans also started mission organizations at this time. In 1815, German Pietists formed the Berlin Missionary Society with a vision for evangelizing southern Africa. Later in the nineteenth century, they sent laborers to China and east Africa. In the same year, the Swiss interdenominational Basel Mission started. Initially sending missionaries to the Gold Coast of Africa (Ghana), the mission was innovative for two reasons: setting up a training school for missionary candidates and emphasizing community development in mission by teaching skills such as printing, tile manufacturing, and weaving on their ministry fields. Other European Protestant mission societies were formed in France, Denmark, Sweden, and Norway during this period.

Following evangelical revivals in North America, US Americans started mission societies, too. In 1810, just four years after the haystack prayer meeting, Samuel Mills launched the American Board. Composed of members from Congregational churches, the American Board was the first official mission group from the United States. In 1814, the American Baptist Missionary Board launched with an initial focus on China. Later, Methodists and Presbyterians formed mission arms within their denominational structures. In 1845, following a split with Baptists from the northern states over the question of slavery, the Southern Baptist Convention was founded, and it included a Foreign Mission Board.

Driven by what some have called the voluntary principle, missionary candidates put aside career ambitions in public service, business, or established ministry and committed their lives to proclaiming the gospel among the nations.[7] Though missionaries had always volunteered and sacrificed, it was during the nineteenth century that *missionary* became an accepted vocation for European and North American Protestants. Before

---

7. See David J. Bosch, *Transforming Mission: Paradigm Shifts in Theology of Mission* (Maryknoll, NY: Orbis, 1991), 253.

the end of the nineteenth century, one famous missionary, David Livingstone (1813-1873) would be honored with a state funeral in Westminster Abbey. In the twentieth and twenty-first centuries, Livingstone and Mary Slessor (1848-1915) would be commemorated on Scottish pound notes.

ASIA

INDIA

Aside from William Carey and the Serampore team, many other missionaries and organizations began serving in India in the first half of the nineteenth century prior to British colonial rule. For years the Church of England had been supplying chaplains to the British East India Company. While caring for the souls of British expatriates, many Anglican ministers caught a vision for ministering to Indian peoples as well. In 1820, Thomas Middleton (1769-1822), the bishop of Calcutta, founded Bishop's College, which not only educated Indian peoples in the liberal arts but also trained national priests and religious education teachers. In 1823, Reginald Heber (1783-1826) became the bishop of Calcutta and reached out to William Carey to collaborate in mission across denominational lines. Prior to his death, Heber composed the famous hymn "Holy, Holy, Holy" (1826) in an effort to convey the holiness of the triune God in contrast to the Hindu perspectives of deity that he encountered. In 1832, Daniel Wilson (1778-1858), a member of the evangelical activist group the Clapham sect, was appointed bishop of Calcutta. One of the earliest ministers or missionaries to openly denounce India's caste system, Wilson referred to it as a cancer to the church. He wanted to see it dismantled in order to grow the church in India.

Just as the Portuguese Roman Catholics had done in the sixteenth century, the Anglicans also engaged the historic Thomas church in South India. In 1815, Colonel John Munroe founded a seminary in Kottayam to train Thomas Christian priests. He invited Anglican teachers from the Church Missionary Society to serve as professors. While some Thomas Christians became Anglicans, overall the Indian Christians resisted the Anglican influence, and by 1836 all official ties between the CMS and the Thomas church had been severed. Despite this, CMS missionary Benjamin Bailey (1791-1871) labored to translate the Scriptures into Malayalam, completing the New Testament in 1829 and the Old Testament

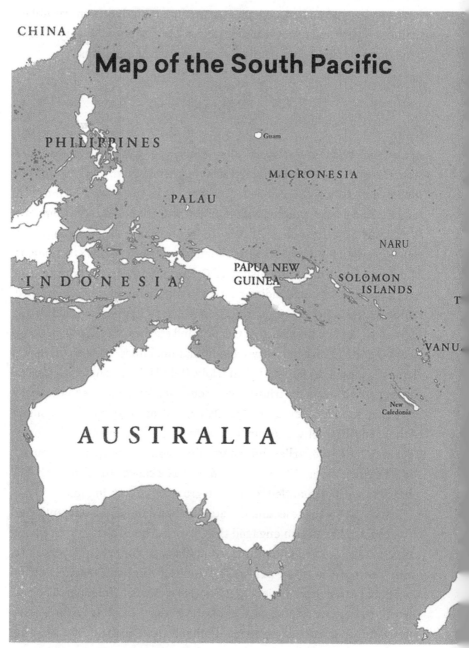

Figure 8. Map of the South Pacific

Hawaii

K
I
R
I
B
A
T
I

U

Tokelau

Wallis and Futuna   SAMOA   Cook
                                   Islands

                          Niue
FIJI   TONGA

SOUTH PACIFIC
OCEAN

NEW
ALAND

in 1841. Abraham Malpan (1796–1845), an Indian professor of Syriac at the Kottayam seminary, led a biblical reform movement within the Thomas church beginning in 1836. Sometimes referred to as the Martin Luther of India, he emphasized Bible study, moral reform among priests, and eradication of unbiblical practices such as prayers for the dead and venerating saints. Malpan also labored in Bible translation, making Scripture available in the vernacular of south India.

Henry Martyn (1781–1812) played an important role in early Anglican mission to India as well as Persia and the Arab world. Since he served as a chaplain for the East India Company, he never officially held the title missionary. However, after reading Jonathan Edwards's *Life of David Brainerd* in his youth, Martyn became impassioned for global mission. While his ministry included itinerant preaching and engaging Muslims in a rather polemical manner, Martyn's greatest contribution was translating Scripture. Unlike William Carey, Martyn received training in linguistics at Cambridge and succeeded in translating the New Testament into Hindi, Persian, and Arabic before his untimely death at the age of thirty-one. In this respect, Martyn's life mission statement, "Now let me burn out for God," became a reality.

Aside from the Anglicans, many other missionaries and mission groups labored in India in the precolonial period. In 1830, Church of Scotland missionary Alexander Duff (1806–1878) arrived in Calcutta. Duff believed that the key means to reaching India was education, particularly by educating the upper classes in various subjects in English. Although Duff failed to appreciate Indian models of education and believed that Western culture was superior, by 1848 over thirty upper-caste Bengalis had accepted baptism. Duff was also instrumental in launching the University of Calcutta in 1857. Other missionaries emulated his educational approach to mission during the nineteenth century.

American John Scudder (1793–1855) holds the distinction of being the first medical missionary. Originally sent out with the American Board, Scudder established a hospital in Sri Lanka, especially for combatting cholera and yellow fever. Later, he moved to Madras (India), where he continued his medical work. Scudder's approach to mission included establishing schools and churches as well as printing and distributing evangelistic literature. Scudder's legacy is remarkable: all six of his children followed his calling as missionary doctors in South India, while another three generations of Scudders—forty-two people in all—continued in some form of missionary service.

Although India officially came under British rule in 1858, missionary activity from Britain and other Western nations continued. In fact, many sincere, believing Christians served in the British colonial government, laboring for the welfare of Indian peoples. Many were favorable to Christian missionary work, including starting schools, colleges, and hospitals. Despite this, an anti-Western Hindu revival and nationalist movement arising in 1875 challenged Western missionaries to rethink their mission approaches. William Miller (1838-1923), a missionary from the Free Church of Scotland, departed from the view held by Duff and others—that education was a means to teach Western Christian values. Having served as principal of Madras Christian College and later vice-chancellor of Madras University, he saw the Christian university as an environment for sincere and meaningful worldview dialogue between Hindu students and Christian professors.

In addition to engaging Hindus with Christian ideas, others such as Henry Martyn and William Muir (1819-1905) focused on India's Muslims. A layman living in India, Muir published a tract in 1887 titled "The Rise and Decline of Islam." Largely reviving some ideas from Thomas Aquinas (1225-1274), Muir emphasized the prophet Muhammad's immoral character, Islam's false teachings, its spread through violence, and its tendency toward sexual indulgence. His approach was largely an attack on the faith without a sincere attempt to understand it; Muir was one of the few to focus on Muslims in this period.

The peoples of northeast India proved to be the most receptive to the gospel in the latter half of the nineteenth century. In 1845, German Lutheran missionaries began work among the Kolarian people (Bihar). By 1857, they had baptized around nine hundred believers, and by the mid-twentieth century, the church included some two hundred thousand Kolarian believers. In 1841, Welsh Methodists started working with the Khasi people (Assam). Within fifty years, they had translated the Scriptures into the vernacular, and the church included ten thousand new believers. In 1863, Norwegian missionary Lars Skrefrud began ministry among the Santals: and by 1910, the church had grown to fifteen thousand believers.

Finally, Methodist missionaries from Wales and Baptist workers from Britain and the United States successfully evangelized the Garo, Abor, Mini, and Naga peoples by the end of the nineteenth century.

Following the ministry of Carey and the Serampore team, India remained a constant focus for Protestant mission work throughout the nineteenth century. Despite the challenges of communicating the gospel to Hindus, Muslims, and others as well as the difficulties of being on mission in a colonial context, Protestant missionaries saw the church in India grow to around one million believers by 1900.[8]

CHINA

The Jesuits largely drove mission work in China in the seventeenth and early eighteenth century. But that changed with the dissolution of the order in 1773. Though China remained largely closed to foreigners in the first half of the nineteenth century, the London Missionary Society still appointed Robert Morrison (1782–1834) to serve there. Following studies in medicine, astronomy, and Chinese, Morrison sailed for China in 1807. In 1809, he joined the British East India Company as a translator. In addition to these duties, Morrison spent a great deal of his time in translation and published a Chinese New Testament in 1813. Sadly, the Chinese authorities and the East India Company resisted his translation work. Undeterred, Morrison completed a translation of the Old Testament in 1819 and a Chinese-English dictionary in 1823. The latter resource served missionaries to China for many years to come. Because of the challenges in China, Morrison relocated to Malacca (Malaysia) in 1818 and established the Anglo-Chinese College, a school for Malay and Chinese children. The aim of the school was to cultivate dialogue between Eastern and Western ideas and to be a gentle witness to Chinese students living outside their homeland. Though Morrison baptized only ten Chinese believers during his missionary career, he pioneered the study of Chinese language and culture in Britain, which mobilized many more missionaries to the Far East.

Karl Gutzlaff's (1803–1851) story in mission demonstrates both innovation and controversy. The German Lutheran served in Thailand, Korea, and Singapore before moving to Macau in 1831. A gifted linguist and Bible

---

8. See Neill, *History of Christian Missions*, 226–37.

translator, Gutzlaff worked on translations in Thai, Cambodian, and Lao before joining a team to revise the Chinese Scriptures in 1840. Due to the Chinese government's restriction on missionary activity, Gutzlaff started a school in 1844 to train Chinese evangelists and then sent them throughout the country to preach and distribute Scripture. The initial reports were very encouraging—many Chinese people were accepting Bibles and believing the gospel. Gutzlaff organized a speaking tour of Europe to report on these good results and to raise more funds for the mission. The only problem was that his Chinese disciples—many of them opium addicts—had fabricated the reports and sold the Bibles to support their drug habits. When Gutzlaff learned the truth he was heartbroken; however, he went forward with his speaking tour as if the reports were actually true. Eventually the truth came to light, and Gutzlaff died a broken man in 1851. Although Gutzlaff's missionary career ended in scandal, the Chinese Evangelization Society—the mission he founded—managed to survive and continue its work. In 1854, the mission recruited a young Englishman named James Hudson Taylor (1832–1905) to the work in China.

Shortly after his conversion at the age of seventeen, Hudson Taylor reported a calling to be a missionary to China. As part of his preparation for cross-cultural service, Taylor studied theology and completed an apprenticeship in medicine. He also ended an engagement with a woman who did not share his missionary vision. Arriving in China in 1854, Taylor spent the first seven years studying Chinese.

The treaty of Nanking of 1842 opened China to international commerce and Christian mission. Foreigners were allowed to live in several port cities along the coast. As a result, most Western missionaries lived on mission compounds separate from the Chinese population. Taylor became discouraged by and critical of what he perceived as the missionaries' laziness and luxurious living. He refused to live in the mission compound and joined Scottish Presbyterian missionary William Burns (1815–1868), who was already making trips into the Chinese interior. Taylor began wearing Chinese clothing and even dyed his hair black in order to blend in among his host people in the Chinese interior. Though Taylor was merely continuing the strategies of the seventeenth-century Jesuits, his methods were considered controversial among other Protestant missionaries. Because of his attitude and approaches, some members of the missionary community even attempted to oppose his courtship of and eventual marriage to Mary Dyer.

In 1860, Hudson and Mary (Dyer) Taylor returned to England due to Hudson's poor health. Though he made the most of this home assignment by doing further medical studies, Taylor's greatest work—and his greatest legacy in mission—was founding the China Inland Mission (CIM) in 1865. The vision for CIM was based on six guiding values. First, the group was to be interdenominational but also hold to historic Christian teachings. Certainly, the controversies of the day (the influence of Darwin's *Origin of Species*, developing schools of higher criticism, and developing liberal theology) motivated the CIM to cling to historic Christian teaching. Second, though its founders embraced conservative theology, CIM required little formal theological education. Since formal theological studies could take many years, CIM missionaries would study more informally, as Taylor had, and therefore be available for mission service much sooner. Third, China Inland Mission would be field led. Critical decisions for mission strategy needed to be made in the context of the work, not from a home office in Europe or the United States. Fourth, CIM would be a faith mission. Funding for mission would not come through a centralized source such as a denomination. Instead, missionaries would strive to develop partners who would personally support mission through prayer and financial giving. Fifth, following Taylor's example, CIM workers would adopt Chinese clothing and strive to identify with their host culture. Sixth, CIM's mission priority was to evangelize all of China. By 1882, CIM workers had visited every province within the country, and other groups such as the YMCA adopted this approach.

By 1895, China Inland Mission had grown to 641 missionaries. By 1934, that number had doubled to 1,368 workers, making it the largest mission organization in the world. Overall, CIM was a rather blue-collar mission organization, drawing most of its members from more modest backgrounds. There were, however, notable exceptions. In 1885, after reading Taylor's book *China's Spiritual Need and Claims*, seven well-educated students (six from Cambridge) laid aside their career ambitions and joined CIM.

Despite attempts to contextualize mission efforts, missionaries in China still faced opposition. After more than a half century of tolerating the presence of foreigners and international business, the Chinese people launched a popular uprising against foreign interests known as the Boxer Uprising (1899–1901). During this period of unrest, many foreigners fell victim to violent attacks, including 188 Protestant missionaries and some children who lost their lives. Once the uprising subsided, many families of the victims filed suit against the Chinese government and were awarded reparations. Though many CIM members died during the uprising, Taylor and the mission refused to seek reparations and openly forgave the attackers. This peaceful and nonretaliating response seemed to impress the Chinese people and gave the CIM and their message more credibility.[9]

Charlotte ("Lottie") Moon (1840–1912), the most famous figure in Southern Baptist mission history, also brought innovation to mission in China in the latter part of the nineteenth century. Raised in Virginia, Moon grew up in a family of women who defied traditional gender roles. Her older sister Oriana earned a medical degree, served as a doctor for the Confederate Army during the Civil War, and also served for a brief period in mission in Palestine. In 1872, Lottie's younger sister Edmonia became the first single female missionary to be appointed by the Southern Baptists. She served in northern China. The following year, Lottie—who had received a master of arts degree and was working as a teacher—joined her sister in China with the Foreign Mission Board. After a decade of teaching school in the port city of Dengzhou, Moon moved into the interior of the country and focused on evangelism and church planting.

Around 1885, Moon began writing letters to South Baptist women's groups, sharing the great need for laborers and financial resources. In 1887, she proposed that a special missions offering be collected at Christmas time. Over time, this collection—now known as the Lottie Moon Christmas offering—became the key means for funding Southern Baptist mission work around the world.

Moon persevered through turbulent times in China, including the first Sino-Japanese War in 1894, the Boxer Uprising, and the nationalist uprising and overthrow of the Qing Dynasty in 1911. Finally, she was an early

---

9. Neill, *History of Christian Missions*, 238–45; also Daniel H. Bays, *A New History of Christianity in China* (Chichester, UK: Wiley-Blackwell, 2012), 84–87.

advocate of missionary care, urging missionaries to take a furlough every ten years.[10]

Christian mission continued in China through the beginning of the twentieth century despite the clear challenges encountered by Taylor, CIM, Moon, and others. By 1914 some fifty-four hundred missionaries were serving in the country, and the church had grown to five hundred thousand baptized believers.

JAPAN

American missionaries—Presbyterian, Baptist, and Episcopalian among others—entered the country around 1859 and focused on translating Scripture and starting schools. When the last shogun (military dictators who had ruled the country since the twelfth century) resigned in 1867, the country increasingly opened to outside influences, including Christian missionaries. Around 1866, Protestants baptized their first Japanese believer, and they planted their first church in 1872. By 1888, as many as twenty-five thousand Japanese believers worshiped in Protestant churches. Most of these had come to faith through schools run by Protestant missionaries.

While international missionaries initiated ministries in the latter half of the century, Japanese national church leaders also quickly emerged. Shimeta Niishima (1843-1890) traveled to the United States as one of the earliest international students. After studying science, Christianity, and theology—completing a seminary degree—he returned to his home country ten years later as a missionary with the American Board. Niishima's vision was to reach Japan through education, and to that end, he founded Doshisha University in 1875. Kanzo Uchimura (1861-1931) became a great Bible teacher who attracted thousands to his lectures. Opposed to organized religion generally and Western-style churches in Japan specifically, he founded the non-church movement. Uchimura was not really opposed to the idea of the church; rather, he opposed Western forms being imposed on Japanese believers. Finally, Masahisa Uemura (1858-1925) was ordained as a Presbyterian minister in 1879. Convinced that only the Japanese could effectively evangelize Japan, he argued that Western

---

10. See Ruth A. Tucker, *From Jerusalem to Irian Jaya: A Biographical History of Christian Mission* (Grand Rapids: Zondervan, 2004), 294-98.

missionaries should leave the country. A gifted theologian and teacher, he founded Tokyo School of Theology in 1904.

KOREA

Following a treaty with the United States in 1882, Korea opened to business and relations with the rest of the world. Although King Gojong (r. 1863–1897) allowed Christian doctors and educators to enter the country, he opposed open evangelism. In 1885, Presbyterians and Methodists arrived in the country and opened schools, orphanages, and collaborated to translate the Bible. By 1886, they had baptized the first Korean believers. In 1906, the country experienced a spiritual revival. By 1910, the same year that Japan annexed Korea, over thirty thousand believers were worshiping in Presbyterian and Methodist churches.

Church growth in Korea can be attributed in part to the vision of John Nevius (1829–1893)—a Presbyterian missionary serving in China—who visited Korea in 1890. First, Nevius urged that all Christians should see themselves as ministers and serve wherever they lived. Second, the Korean church should set apart its own leaders and financially support them. Third, ministry methods and infrastructure should not be developed beyond what the Koreans could sustain. Finally, church buildings should be constructed in local styles and with local resources. Nevius's thought paralleled the three-self method—that churches should be self-led, self-supporting, self-propagating. Rufus Anderson (1796–1880) of the American Board and Henry Venn (1796–1873) of the Anglican Church Missionary Society had independently proposed this philosophy. Increasingly, nineteenth-century mission leaders were concerned with fostering indigenous churches free of dependency on Western mission societies and denominations.[11]

BURMA

Adoniram Judson (1788–1850) and Ann Judson (1789–1826) are often remembered as the first traditional American missionaries sent from North America—those sent as official missionaries through an established mission board. Appointed by the Congregationalist American Board, the Judsons were originally assigned to India, where they were to collaborate

---

11. See Neill, *History of Christian Missions*, 276–82.

with Baptist missionaries. During their four-month journey by ship from Boston to India, the Judsons studied Baptist theology to better understand their coworkers' doctrine. They arrived in India as convinced Baptists and were baptized by William Carey. They parted company with the American Board and joined the newly formed American Baptist Mission. Forced out of India in 1813 by the British East India Company, they relocated and began work in Burma.

The Judsons primarily focused on evangelism and Bible translation. Adoniram built a traditional Burmese *zayat* (used for religious purpose and village assemblies), where he preached regularly. After six years, they had baptized ten new believers. By 1824, Adoniram had completed a Burmese dictionary, and by 1834, he finished the entire Burmese Bible translation. Ann had translated Daniel and Jonah, developed a Burmese catechism, translated Matthew's Gospel into Thai, and also wrote an early history of mission to Burma.

The couple also encountered much hardship. In 1824, during the Anglo-Burmese war, Adoniram was accused of being a spy and was imprisoned for nearly two years. Ann regularly visited her husband and brought him food while tirelessly lobbying the Burmese government for his release. Though she eventually succeeded, she died shortly after Adonoriam's release because of the ongoing stress and exhaustion. Losing Ann plunged Adoniram into an extended period of grief and depression. Through hardship and collaboration in ministry, the Judsons demonstrated an early example of a married couple partnering in the work of mission.[12]

Another American Baptist missionary, George Boardman (1801–1831), labored in Burma among the Karen people. The Karen, who already believed in a creator God and had their own account of the fall of humanity, were receptive to Boardman's preaching. By 1851, the Karen church included some thirty thousand believers. Boardman's preaching activity took a toll on his health, and he died prematurely in 1831. His widow, Sarah, married Adoniram Judson in 1834.[13]

---

12. See Dana Robert, "Judson, Ann ('Nancy') (Hasseltine)," in Anderson, *Biographical Dictionary of Christian Missions*, 346; also William H. Brackney, "Judson, Adoniram," in Anderson, *Biographical Dictionary of Christian Missions*, 345–46.

13. See Neill, *History of Christian Missions*, 248–49.

INDONESIA

Missionaries continued ministry in Indonesia, in part because the Dutch held strong economic and political interests there. The Netherlands Missionary Society reported that most of the inhabitants on the island of Celebes had embraced the gospel by 1900. On Sumatra, German missionary Ludwig Ingwere Nommensen (1834–1918) labored among the Batak people. By 1911, the Scriptures had been translated into Batak, and the church numbered over one hundred thousand believers. Though the church struggled to become independent from foreign leadership and support, Indonesia remained the most receptive part of the Muslim world to the gospel during this period.[14]

SOUTH PACIFIC

Missionaries came, missionaries were killed and cannibalized, more missionaries caught a vision for the work and came, kings believed, and the gospel spread. This condensed—if dramatic—history accurately describes nineteenth-century mission history in the South Pacific Islands. Although many missionaries lost their lives in the process, the South Pacific Islands proved to be the most fertile soil for Christian mission during the nineteenth century.

Founded in part to reach the South Pacific, the London Missionary Society sent laborers to Tahiti in 1796. Missionaries made favorable contact with King Pomare II (r. 1782–1821), who believed the gospel and was publicly baptized in 1819. By 1838, the whole Bible was translated into Tahitian.

Three of the first missionaries to Tonga were murdered in the late eighteenth century. In 1826, English Methodist missionary John Thomas (1796–1881) arrived on the island and began preaching with the aid of the Tahitian Scriptures. The pinnacle of his thirty years in ministry was baptizing King Tupou in 1831. The king began to rewrite the laws of Tonga based on the principles of his newfound faith.

In 1817, the London Missionary Society (LMS) sent John Williams (1796–1839) to begin work in the Society Islands. Williams put into practice a number of innovations during his two decades of mission. In addition to translating the Bible into the Rarotongan language in 1834, he believed that

---

14. Neill, *History of Christian Missions*, 294–97.

national evangelists were best suited to evangelize Oceania. Since transportation to the islands was a constant challenge, Williams convinced the LMS to purchase a ship to facilitate itinerant preaching and discipleship. By 1834, national teachers had visited all of the Tahitian islands. Around 1830, Williams initiated work in Samoa by leaving eight Tahitian evangelists to minister there. Later, when European missionaries returned to the island, they discovered two thousand new Samoan believers. In 1839, Williams placed three Samoan teachers in New Hebrides. However, when he traveled back to visit the work, Williams himself was attacked and cannibalized.

Tongan evangelists first brought the gospel to Fiji in 1823. Later, European Methodists also began to minister on the island. Around 1845, the island experienced a spiritual revival, which included King Thakombau (1815-1883) embracing the gospel and receiving baptism.

The American Board initiated mission work on Hawaii in 1820. Since the local chiefs favored the missionaries, they had freedom to preach. More than twenty thousand Hawaiians, about one-fifth of the population, were baptized in just two decades.

Finally, in 1858, Scottish Presbyterian missionary John Paton (1824-1907) began serving in Tanna in New Hebrides. Aside from dealing with regular threats on his life from cannibals, Paton lost his wife and four of his children to sickness or disease. Paton persevered and later moved to the island of Aniwa, where he translated the Scriptures and saw much of the island's population embrace the gospel.[15]

MIDDLE EAST

Samuel Zwemer (1867-1952), nicknamed the apostle to Islam, pioneered ministry in the Arab-Muslim world. After completing university and seminary studies in his home state of Michigan, Zwemer pledged to serve in the Muslim world after attending a Student Volunteer Movement meeting. Finding no mission organization that would send him to the Arab world, Zwemer and two friends, James Cantine (1861-1940) and John Lansing (d. 1906), founded the American Arabian Mission in 1889. In a unique approach to faith missions, Zwemer traveled and spoke, raising Cantine's financial support, while Cantine did the same for Zwemer. Five years later,

---

15. Neill, *History of Christian Missions*, 251-56, 298-300.

Zwemer's denominational mission (Reformed Church) became a supporting partner with the American Arabian mission.

In 1890, Zwemer joined Cantine in Lebanon, where they studied Arabic under renowned Arabic scholar Cornelius Van Dyke (1818–1895). In 1865, Van Dyke had completed a revised translation of the entire Arabic Bible. After spending some time in Egypt with Cantine and Lansing, Zwemer eventually settled on the island of Bahrain, where he opened a Bible bookshop. Bible and literature distribution became a central part of Zwemer's ministry. Zwemer also met his wife, Amy, a Church Missionary Society worker from Australia. The Zwemers had four children, two of whom died of dysentery and were buried in Bahrain.

In addition to evangelism and literature ministry, Zwemer began a ministry of writing around 1900. In all, he authored over sixty books in English intended to educate the church in the West on Muslim beliefs and to mobilize more laborers for mission among Muslims. After 1905, Zwemer's ministry became increasingly focused on mobilization. Based in the United States from 1905 to 1910, he traveled and spoke for the Student Volunteer Movement. In 1906, he organized a global consultation in Cairo for reaching the Muslim world, and in 1910, he spoke at the Student Volunteer convention in New York City. In 1912, he relocated to Cairo, where he engaged in personal evangelism. While based in Cairo, Zwemer also traveled around the Muslim world—to North Africa, India, Iran, China, Indonesia, and South Africa—encouraging and training missionaries to Muslims and holding dialogues with Muslim leaders. In 1925, he preached at an evangelistic crusade in South Africa. On different nights, he preached in English, Dutch, and Arabic.

In 1929, Zwemer accepted an appointment as professor of Christian mission at Princeton Theological Seminary, one of the earliest professorships in mission studies in the United States. During this time, he became the founding editor of the academic journal *The Muslim World*. Zwemer spent the last decade of his life based in New York City focused on preaching, teaching, and writing.

Though Zwemer personally saw very few Muslims embrace Christ, his approach proved groundbreaking. Initially believing that Islam was a false religion, Zwemer's earlier evangelistic work was more polemical in nature. Later, he shared the gospel more through dialogue. Having become an expert on Muslim teachings, he skillfully engaged Muslim theologians and leaders. Convinced that the printed page was a ubiquitous missionary, Zwemer also valued distributing Christian literature, including Arabic Bibles and tracts he had developed. Since the vast majority of nineteenth-century Arabs were not literate, his literature ministry primarily reached the educated elite. Zwemer probably contributed most significantly to Muslim missions by exposing the Western church to the world of Islam and through mobilizing many laborers to minister among Muslims. His books conveyed vision, understanding, and skill for ministering to Muslims.[16]

AFRICA

WEST AFRICA

In 1804, German missionaries working with the Anglican Church Missionary Society began ministry in Sierra Leone. Later, British Methodists joined in the work. During the first twenty years of ministry, fifty missionaries died of sickness or disease, which earned West Africa the title "the white man's graveyard." In 1827, the Anglicans founded Fourah Bay College, a Western-style university that trained ministers and teachers. In 1851, missionaries of African descent from the West Indies began serving in Sierra Leone; however, many of them struggled as much as their European counterparts with sickness and adapting to the living conditions.

In 1828, the Basel Mission began work in Ghana. While committed to mastering African languages, the Basel team started schools and incorporated agricultural and economic development into their mission work. In Ghana, they helped local people to harvest and sell cocoa. In 1838, Methodist missionary Thomas Birch Freeman (1809–1890) joined the ministry in Ghana. Half British and half African, Freeman adapted well to the local culture and focused his ministry on training laypeople in evangelism.

Colonized by Britain in 1851, Nigeria would become Africa's largest country. While Anglicans and Methodists initially engaged in significant

---

16. See Alan Neely, "Zwemer, Samuel Marinus (1867–1952)," in Anderson, *Biographical Dictionary of Christian Missions*, 763; J. Christy Wilson, "The Legacy of Samuel Zwemer," *International Bulletin of Mission Research* 10 (July 1986): 117–21.

evangelism, the church spread most through Nigerians who had embraced the gospel in Sierra Leone and returned home proclaiming their newfound faith.

In 1864, the Church of England ordained its first African bishop, Samuel Ajayi Crowther (1809-1891). Trained for ministry at Fourah Bay College, Crowther had previously labored on the Yoruba Bible translation. Desiring to apply his three-self church model, Church Missionary Society leader Henry Venn advocated appointing Crowther as a national church leader and missionary. Tasked with evangelizing Nigeria and Niger, Crowther struggled learning the languages and cultures of these regions. Unfortunately, the CMS did not appoint another African leader following Crowther's passing.[17]

Mary Slessor (1848-1915) was a pioneer for single women participating in mission. Born into poverty in Scotland, Slessor drew inspiration from another Scot of modest standing who became a missionary in Africa—David Livingstone. Arriving in Nigeria in 1876 with the Presbyterian mission, Slessor served as an itinerant evangelist, pushing into areas where the gospel had not been preached, particularly among the Okoyong and Efik peoples. She mastered local languages and culture. She also challenged the tribal practice of killing newborn twins, which was based on the belief that twins resulted from demonic activity. Her conviction also led her to rescue many twins and abandoned children, even adopting some as her own children. When southern Nigeria came under British control, Slessor went to work as a diplomat for the British government in Okoyong.[18]

Protestant work began in neighboring Cameroon in 1843. Joseph Merrick (1808-1849), a missionary from Jamaica, learned both the Isubu and Douala languages and translated the Gospel of Matthew into Isubu. British Baptist missionary Alfred Saker (1814-1880) labored translating the Doula Scriptures, completing the project in 1872.

---

17. See Andrew F. Walls, "Crowther, Samuel (or Ajayi)," in Anderson, *Biographical Dictionary of Christian Missions*, 160-61.

18. See Tucker, *From Jerusalem to Irian Jaya*, 170-75.

EAST AFRICA

Protestants began to evangelize Uganda in the last quarter of the nineteenth century. Anglican missionaries started their work in the country in 1876 and were received favorably by King Muteesa I (r. 1856–1884). By 1882, the first Ugandans were being baptized. In 1885, CMS missionary Alexander Mackay (1849–1890) completed translation of the Gospel of Matthew into the Luganda language.

Toward the end of the century, Alfred Tucker (1849–1914) served as the Anglican bishop for East Africa, overseeing the church in the modern nations of Uganda, Tanzania, and Kenya. Influenced by Venn's three-self model, Tucker strived to set apart national church leaders and to promote equal partnership between national and international missionaries. Though some European missionaries opposed Tucker's vision and resisted his efforts, the Ugandan church grew to some sixty-five thousand believers under his leadership. National Christians translated Mark's Gospel and labored to evangelize their own people.[19]

SOUTHERN AFRICA

Nineteenth-century Protestant missionary activity to southern Africa might be the most familiar part of mission history to Western Christians today. But few Christians today would recognize the name Robert Moffat (1795–1883). Originally rejected for missionary service by the London Missionary Society, the Scottish Congregational missionary joined the LMS work in southern Africa in 1816. This initial rejection did not seem to have an effect on him, as he spent nearly a half-century ministering among the Bechuana people. After ministering in Cape Dutch, Moffat mastered the Tswana language; he had translated the entire Bible into it by 1857. Like others, Moffat began a school and also planted a church. Because of an apparent spiritual awakening that began in 1829, the church grew to over two hundred believers within a decade. Even the feared African King Mzilikazi (r. 1823–1868) sent a delegation to Moffat to inquire about Christianity. One of Moffat's sons later served as a missionary to Mzilkazi's Matabele kingdom. Though Moffat mastered Tswana, he devoted little time to studying African culture and religions. Also, his parental approach—his

---

19. See Neill, *History of Christian Missions*, 221.

posture of superiority toward local peoples—suppressed indigenous Christian initiative and leadership. Perhaps more than others, Moffat exemplified the civilizing tendency (conveying the superiority of Western culture) of some Western missionaries during this period.

David Livingstone, Moffat's son-in-law, is arguably the most famous Western missionary and explorer in church history. Born into poverty in Scotland, Livingstone began working in a cotton mill at the age of ten. After pursuing medical studies at a London hospital and studying theology informally, Livingstone joined the LMS work in southern Africa in 1841. During his first decade of service, Livingstone engaged in traditional missionary work, including setting up three new mission stations in the region. During this period he also married Moffat's daughter Mary.

In 1852, Livingstone started his exploration work. Setting out first for Angola, he later traveled through the heart of Africa to Mozambique on the east coast. Maintaining scientific and geographic records, Livingstone began to make Africa known to the outside world. He is credited with discovering Victoria Falls between modern Zambia and Zimbabwe. In 1857, Livingstone published his *Missionary Travels and Research in South Africa* and returned to Britain as a national hero. At this point, he left the LMS and took a position with the British government. In 1858, he returned to Africa to navigate the Zambezi River; and in 1865, he embarked on an unsuccessful expedition to find the source of the Nile River. When Livingstone died in 1873, his African coworkers buried his heart in Africa and sent his body and personal papers to England. Livingstone was honored with a state funeral in Westminster Abbey.

Though he parted ways with the LMS in 1852, he remained committed to evangelism. A passion to get to new villages and communities that had not been exposed to the gospel actually drove his exploration. Relatedly, Livingstone labored to bring about transformation in Africa specifically through ending the slave trade. Striving to open Africa to Christianity and commerce, he was convinced that if Europe and the West did business with Africa, then Africans would cease trafficking other Africans in the global slave trade. Finally, due to his fame as an explorer and his speaking tours in Britain, he mobilized many more missionaries for Africa. The Anglican Universities' Mission to Central Africa was founded in 1857 as a direct result of Livingstone's pleas for more laborers for the harvest in Africa.

Despite Livingstone's innovation in mission, he too encountered failure. First, he struggled to lead and organize mission efforts, although he was a great visionary and mobilizer. Second, despite his vision for transformation in Africa, his exploration work actually facilitated slave traders opening new markets for human trafficking. Finally, Livingstone failed to prioritize the health and well-being of his family. During his early years of exploration, he left his wife and children in rather unsafe areas while he carried on his journeys. Later, he sent them back to Britain where they subsisted in near poverty. During his national speaking tour in 1857, Livingstone only managed to spend three days with his family. While the world got to know the famous Dr. Livingstone through his books and speeches, his own children never really knew their father personally.[20]

In 1820, Welsh LMS missionary David Jones (1796–1841) began serving on the southern African island of Madagascar. Jones made favorable contact with King Radama I (r. 1810–1828). Though he was not personally interested in spiritual matters, because Radama believed that Christian ethics would benefit his people, he gave missionaries much freedom to preach and establish schools. Jones and David Griffiths (1792–1863) worked together to translate the New Testament, a catechism, a hymnbook, and some schoolbooks into Malagassy. By 1831, they had baptized their first believers. Following King Ramada's death, the Malagassy church suffered much persecution, forcing international missionaries to leave. However, when European missionaries returned to the island around 1850, they found that the national church had quadrupled in size amid the period of hardship.[21]

NORTH AFRICA

Despite North Africa's rich early Christian history, the region was almost entirely Muslim in the nineteenth century and largely ignored by Protestants. In 1876, English missionaries George and Jane Pearse arrived in Algeria to minister to French troops stationed there. When they discovered the significant unreached Muslim majority, they sought to reach more than just the French. In 1882, a number of mission groups merged

---

20. See Neill, *A History of Christian Missions*, 264–67.

21. See Neill, *A History of Christian Missions*, 269–70.

to form the North African Mission, the earliest mission society focused on the Muslim world.

The North African Mission did not allow Lilias Trotter (1853–1928) to join their work on account of her health. However, she affiliated with them in Algeria, where she brought fresh ideas as a single woman in a Muslim context. She challenged European forms of mission such as evangelistic meetings. Instead she proposed a contextualized café-style approach to ministry, including North African–style poetic readings of Scripture. Ministering through arts, crafts, and literature, Trotter strived to connect with children and their mothers. Despite the growing number of laborers for North Africa at the turn of the century, few North African Muslims embraced the gospel.

LATIN AMERICA

Protestant mission societies slowly began to work in Latin America toward the end of the nineteenth century. However, most Protestants regarded Latin America as already evangelized because of the long-standing presence of the Roman Catholic Church. Even the majority of the delegates at the 1910 Edinburgh World Missionary Conference did not view the region as a legitimate mission field.

As North America and Europe experienced evangelical revivals during the nineteenth century, these perspectives on Roman Catholic countries began to change. Argentine theologian José Míguez Bonino (1924–2012) describes the missionaries as surprisingly unified: "Despite their confessional diversity (mostly Methodists, Presbyterians, and Baptists) and origin (North American and British), all shared the same theological horizon, which can be characterized as evangelical."[22] One of the earliest mission societies that grew out of the Second Great Awakening in North America was the American Bible Society (1816). Formed with the evangelical conviction that Scripture was authoritative, the ABS quickly began working in Brazil, printing Portuguese Scriptures and deploying missionaries to sell and distribute Bibles throughout the country. Between 1855 and 1914, Baptist, Methodist, Presbyterians, Episcopalian, and British Bible Society

---

22. José Miguez Bonino, *Faces of Latin American Protestantism* (Grand Rapids: Eerdmans, 1995), 27.

missionaries also began ministries in Brazil, Colombia, Chile, and Paraguay. By 1914, over five hundred thousand Latin American Christians were worshiping in Protestant churches.

Scottish Presbyterian Robert Reid Kalley (1809–1888) offers a helpful representative example of evangelical Protestant mission work in Latin America at this time. Upon learning of Brazilian Emperor Pedro II's (r. 1831–1889) concessions toward Protestants, he settled near Rio de Janeiro in 1855. Kalley distributed Scripture and witnessed door-to-door; he was the first Protestant minister to preach in Portuguese. In 1858, he planted the first known Protestant church in the country. Kalley recruited Portuguese-speaking believers from his previous ministry in Madeira (an island southwest of Portugal) to serve in the Brazilian work. In addition to preaching in the local language, Kalley wrote hymns in Portuguese. Opposed to foreign denominations controlling the Brazilian church, Kalley deliberately set apart Brazilian church leadership. Finally, Kalley did not ignore social issues but remained a vocal opponent of the slave trade, which continued in Brazil until 1888.[23]

NORTH AMERICA

Although the United States began sending missionaries around the globe in the nineteenth century, evangelists continued to cross boundaries for the gospel within North America as well.

During the Second Great Awakening, Presbyterian evangelist James McGready (1763–1817) began preaching in camp meetings in North Carolina. He described the response to William McGee's (1768–1817) sermon at Gasper River, Tennessee, in 1800 this way:

> The power of God seemed to shake the whole assembly. Towards the close of the sermon, the cries of the distressed arose almost as loud as his voice. After the congregation was dismissed the solemnity increased, till the greater part of the multitude seemed engaged in the most solemn manner. No person seemed to wish to go

---

23. See Edward L. Smither, *Brazilian Evangelical Missions in the Arab World: History, Culture, Practice, and Theology* (Eugene, OR: Pickwick, 2012), 25–26; also Smither, "Impact of Evangelical Revivals on Global Mission."

home—hunger and sleep seemed to affect nobody—eternal things were the vast concern. Here awakening and converting work was to be found in every part of the multitude; and even some things strangely and wonderfully new to me.[24]

The most famous camp meetings took place in Cane Ridge, Kentucky, where crowds of ten thousand to twenty-five thousand gathered to hear the gospel preached by the likes of Presbyterian evangelist Barton Stone (1772-1844). Given that the largest town in Kentucky in this period had only eighteen hundred residents, the camp meetings were significant gatherings. In addition to significant numbers of conversions, many new Methodist, Baptist, and Presbyterian churches were planted as a result of these revivals.

Though much less emotional in nature, revivals were also taking place in New England. Timothy Dwight (1752-1817), the grandson of Jonathan Edwards, actively preached in this part of America overtaken by deism and Unitarian theology. The renewal movement in New England also touched the university, as revival occurred among students at Yale.

In addition to this mission activity during the Second Great Awakening, others focused on reaching Native American peoples in the northwest territories of the United States. Moved by the visionary messages of American Board mobilizer Samuel Parker, Marcus Whitman (1802-1847) and Narcissa Whitman (1808-1847) joined the work and headed west to the Oregon territories only a day after they were married in 1836. They formed a team with Henry Spalding (1803-1874) and Eliza Spalding (1807-1851), although the couples experienced a great deal of conflict during the journey west.

Once in Oregon, the couples focused on different Indian tribes. The Whitmans settled in Waiilatpu and ministered to the Cayuse, a tribe that had been hostile toward outsiders. A trained doctor, Marcus offered medical care to the Cayuse, while Narcissa started a school for children. Several other families joined them, and they built a mission compound with an expanding farm that became a comfortable and prosperous dwelling. The Spaldings settled in Lapwai and ministered to the Nez Perce people,

---

24. Cited in Charles L. Thompson, *Times of Refreshing: A History of American Revivals from 1740-1877, with Their Philosophy and Methods* (Amazon Digital Services, 2013), 83-84.

engaging in evangelistic preaching, church planting, and translating hymns into the local language. They also started a school.

Resenting the Whitmans for their affluence and blaming the missionaries for a measles outbreak that killed half of the tribe, the Cayuse attacked the Whitman mission compound in 1847, killing Marcus, Narcissa, and a dozen others. They held fifty-three other women and children captive for one month, escalating tensions between Native Americans and white settlers.

Though forced to leave the area because of the massacre in 1847, Henry Spalding returned to minister to the Nez Perce and Spokane Indians. Both groups responded to the gospel, and Spalding reportedly baptized one thousand new believers. The Whitmans and Spaldings' story illustrates mission in a different colonial context in North America with an outcome of violent resistance to the more powerful whites as well as spiritual harvest.[25]

SUMMARY

Not unlike that of previous centuries, nineteenth-century global mission was carried out in a context of Western imperialism and commercial expansion. Though William Carey and Adoniram Judson clashed with the British East India Company, others such as Marcus Whitman seemed to pursue mission on the coattails of the colonial enterprise. Though Christendom (an official union of church and state) was being dismantled, many Protestant missionaries approached their ministry from a place of economic and even political power. This certainly had an effect on how cultural groups around the world perceived the gospel, the church, and forms of Christianity.

On the other hand, evangelical revivals and awakenings fueled Protestant mission work. Nineteenth-century revivals, such as the Second Great Awakening in North America, translated directly into global missionary movements. A student such as Samuel Mills could participate in a life-changing prayer group in 1806 and then be at work launching mission societies just a few years later.

---

25. See Tucker, *From Jerusalem to Irian Jaya*, 88–96.

Finally, the nineteenth-century Protestant church seemed to grasp its obligation and responsibility for engaging the world with the gospel. Beginning with Carey's assertion that the church was the *means* for God's mission in fulfilling the Great Commission, Protestants became activists for world evangelization.

WHO WERE THE NINETEENTH-CENTURY MISSIONARIES?

With the emergence of mission societies, which included at times support and recognition from governments, the missionary vocation found official recognition among Protestants during the nineteenth century. Though Western business and military interests abroad did not always appreciate the presence of missionaries, other influential leaders such as William Wilberforce celebrated and supported mission work.

Men

For much of the nineteenth century, men were regarded as the missionaries, and, if married, their spouses were simply missionary wives. Although William Carey deeply cared for his wife, Dorothy, when she followed him to India, she did so not in pursuit of her own calling but in obedience to her husband's vision. Others such as Alexander Duff and David Livingstone chose to leave their families in Britain for many years while they served in mission.

Married Couples

Despite this tendency, we do observe some healthy examples of couples partnering together in ministry in this period. While Adoniram and Ann Judson worked together in Bible translation in Burma, Ann also pursued her own projects, such as writing an early history of mission. Of course, during Adoniram's imprisonment, Ann played a key role lobbying the Burmese government for her husband's release. Toward the latter part of the century, Canadian Presbyterian missionaries Jonathan (1859-1936) and Rosalind (1864-1942) Goforth served together in small group evangelism in China. Samuel Zwemer first recruited his future wife, Amy, to the Arabian mission team because of her valuable skills as a nurse. Before the Zwemers became a married couple, they were single teammates focused on a common vision.

Single Women

Though some groups such as the American Board did not accept single women in their mission, the nineteenth century also saw single women participate in mission as they never had before. Mary Slessor labored as a pioneer evangelist in Nigeria, an advocate for abandoned children, and as a British diplomat to Nigeria. Lottie Moon was one of the earliest single women appointed by the Southern Baptists. Like Slessor, she not only opened up new mission fields in China, but she also helped Baptists rethink the roles and responsibilities of women in ministry. Of course, her letter-writing campaign to Baptist women in North America forever revolutionized how Southern Baptists raised money for mission work.[26]

National Missionaries

Despite the prevailing parental and colonial attitudes of some missionaries, we do observe the good early work of some national evangelists, church leaders, and missionaries during this period. Samuel Crowther's ministry in Nigeria and Niger, and Shimeta Niishima, Kanzo Uchimura, and Masahisa Uemura's work in Japan, show evidence for this encouraging trend. Of course, many other national missionaries—Pacific Island evangelists, and Nigerians reached in neighboring Sierra Leone who returned home with the gospel—remain nameless in mission history.

Non-Western Missionaries

Finally, though the narratives of white males dominate nineteenth-century missionary history, some non–North Americans and non-Europeans began to serve. Jamaican missionary Joseph Merrick acquired the Isubu and Douala languages of Cameroun and translated Matthew's Gospel into Isubu. Despite facing great challenges, African-background believers from the West Indies labored in Sierra Leone. Finally, George Leile, a former slave and pastor from Savannah, Georgia, pioneered Baptist mission work on the island of Jamaica in the late eighteenth and early nineteenth centuries.

---

26. See Tucker, *From Jerusalem to Irian Jaya*, 287–98.

WHAT DID THE NINETEENTH-CENTURY MISSIONARIES DO?

Started Mission Societies

If Protestants lacked the means for sending laborers to the world in the sixteenth, seventeenth, and eighteenth centuries, they more than made up for it through the creation of mission societies in the nineteenth century. Both denominational and interdenominational societies offered partnership and accountability for local churches to engage in mission. They developed infrastructures to direct financial and human resources for global mission work.

The societies offered missionaries the opportunity to labor as teams, thereby guarding against isolation, burnout, and moral failure. Of course, as we have seen, missionaries did not always get along and function as healthy teams.

Hudson Taylor and the China Inland Mission influenced mission societies toward being more culturally intelligent and entrepreneurial. By empowering leadership at the field level, CIM could make decisions that made sense in their contexts of ministry. This faith mission approach inspired entrepreneurial types such as Samuel Zwemer to raise up a team of prayer and financial partners. It also allowed more churches and Christians to play a more direct role in global mission.

Formed Mission Stations

Carey, Livingstone, the Whitmans, and many others settled onto their fields of ministry and constructed houses and other facilities, which created self-contained and safe communities. Though the mission station functioned as a base for preaching, church planting, translation, and other ministries, it also allowed the missionaries to maintain traditions and habits from their home cultures. In some cases, it stifled adaptation and connection to their host cultures. Because mission stations were comfortable and even affluent environments, local people regarded them as colonial establishments.

Evangelized the Interior

Hudson Taylor seethed at the mission-station approach, which, in his mind, kept his fellow missionaries in China isolated, comfortable, and lazy. Earlier in the century, the Serampore team began talking about evangelizing the whole of India and making Scripture available in as many languages as possible. Karl Gutzlaff and Robert Burns inspired Taylor to move out of the places where foreigners could easily live and where the church was established and to push into the interior toward reaching an entire nation. Mary Slessor, Lottie Moon, and others also championed these values. They took risks to open new places of ministry, and they made other missionaries uncomfortable in the process.

Planted Churches

Many missionaries engaged in church planting in the nineteenth century. Sometimes this meant starting expatriate churches in colonial lands, such as new Anglican congregations in India and Africa. In other cases, they planted new national churches that worshiped in the vernacular. Though Robert Reid Kalley was Scottish and Presbyterian, he cultivated local churches that were Brazilian in style and culture.

In Japan, Kanzo Uchimura founded the non-church movement, an idea that caught on in India in particular during the twentieth century. Uchimura was truly opposed to the idea of Western church forms being imposed on the Japanese. For this reason, Anderson, Venn, and Nevius's argument for self-sustaining churches—churches built with the physical and cultural building materials of the host people—became more important.

Though church planting was a large focus of nineteenth-century mission, this was actually a shortcoming in Hudson Taylor's initial work in China. Greatly emphasizing language learning, contextualization, and evangelism, the early China Inland Mission work did not prioritize gathering communities of new believers into local churches.

Translated Scripture

Protestants continued to cherish the Reformation value of biblical authority, and they made Bible translation a regular feature of mission practice. Evangelical renewal movements also seemed to fuel a desire to translate Scripture. Commenting on this connection Eric Fenn notes: "New spirituality . . . so closely connected with the recovery of biblical truth meant that the Bible moved into the center of faith and practice again."[27]

---

27. Eric Fenn, "The Bible and the Missionary," in *Cambridge History of the Bible*, vol. 3, *The West from the Fathers to the Reformation*, ed. S. L. Greenslade (Cambridge: Cambridge University Press, 1963), 387.

Bible translation benefited global mission during this period in at least two ways. First, at times, the Bible was able to reach places that missionaries could not physically access. For example, two of the four Gospels in Korean were translated outside the country and then smuggled in. When the first Protestant missionaries arrived in the late nineteenth century, they encountered Korean believers ready for baptism who had already believed the gospel through reading these Scriptures. Similarly, in the Middle East, Samuel Zwemer valued the printed page, both Scripture and Christian literature, as the missionary that could go anywhere, especially where missionaries could not go.

Second, Scriptures in the vernacular served to correct cultural mistakes made by missionaries and paved the way toward indigenous, local forms of Christianity. As southern African believers imbibed Scripture in their heart languages, the civilizing messages of well-meaning European missionaries could be drowned out. Vernacular Scripture has also critiqued syncretistic patterns and rooted out the influences of non-Christian primal religions.

Zwemer, Ann Judson, David Jones and David Griffiths, and others translated additional works into the vernacular. These included catechisms, evangelistic tracts, hymns, and other books. While these books certainly aided the development of local Christianity in these areas, their impact was limited to those who were literate or became literate through the aid of missionaries.

Learned Culture and Contextualized the Gospel

Though some nineteenth-century missionaries preferred to communicate in English or a trade language and introduced Western forms of education and church, many others mastered local languages and sought to make Christianity at home within the host culture. The Serampore team valued understanding the cultures of India and allowing only the gospel to dictate areas of culture that ought to change. Carey, the shoemaker from England who lacked formal academic credentials, became an expert on Indian culture and was eventually appointed professor of Oriental studies at a university in Calcutta.

Hudson Taylor and the CIM made understanding and identifying with local culture a central part of their work. In North Africa, Lilias Trotter questioned the use of Western-style evangelistic meetings and adopted a café-style gathering that made sense in her context. Adoniram Judson borrowed the meeting house (*zayat*) idea from Burmese culture in order to organize evangelistic meetings.

Started Hospitals and Schools

Many nineteenth-century mission societies constructed hospitals and schools, an approach later referred to as institutional missions. In some contexts, such as Korea, the government did not allow open evangelism or church planting, but they did permit Christian doctors and educators to enter the country. In other open areas, missionaries still chose to minister to human needs through relieving suffering, encouraging wellness, and promoting development through education. John Scudder seemed to balance word and deed ministry by serving as a caring physician and a committed evangelist. Although most mission schools promoted the superiority of Western education, culture, and even the English language—whether consciously or unconsciously—the institutional approach nevertheless demonstrated Christian compassion and holistic witness in mission.

Emphasized Community Development and Business

Related to the institutional approach, the nineteenth century also saw mission societies such as the Basel mission encourage community and economic development in addition to evangelistic proclamation. Through his desire to open Africa for Christianity and commerce, David Livingstone also believed that business and trade would contribute to Africa's economic transformation and serve to end the global slave trade.

Set Apart Indigenous Leaders

Venn, Anderson, and Nevius's value for self-led churches began to catch on during the nineteenth century. While the Serampore team made this one of their core values, missionary church planters in Japan, Uganda, and Brazil embraced this as well. The commitment to setting apart leaders included launching theological colleges such as Fourah Bay College (Sierra Leone) and Bishop's College (India). Though these colleges based their curriculum on Western theology and Western modes of education, we recognize the effort to equip national leaders for ministry.

Suffered and Persevered in Mission

Despite obvious shortcomings on the part of nineteenth-century missionaries, they nevertheless persevered in the work of mission amid suffering and hardship. Some risked their lives to bring the gospel to the peoples of the South Pacific, including cannibals. Others died from disease in the white man's graveyard of west Africa, while others buried their spouses and children on the mission field and remained faithful to their work. William Carey battled the emotional pain of watching his wife slip away into mental illness. Ann Judson advocated tirelessly for her husband, who was unjustly imprisoned in a Burmese jail. When Ann died shortly after his release, Adoniram Judson fell into a deep, extended depression.

An early advocate for missionary care, Lottie Moon suggested that missionaries should return to their home country every so often for renewal and encouragement. She suggested a furlough every ten years. Even that proposal showed the resilience and commitment that many nineteenth-century, cross-cultural missionaries had toward their ministries.

FURTHER READING

Bays, Daniel H. *A New History of Christianity in China*. Chichester, UK: Wiley-Blackwell, 2012.

Bonino, José Míguez. *Faces of Latin American Protestantism*. Grand Rapids: Eerdmans, 1995.

Bosch, David J. *Transforming Mission: Paradigm Shifts in Theology of Mission*. Maryknoll, NY: Orbis, 1991.

Brackney, William H. "Judson, Adoniram." In *Biographical Dictionary of Christian Missions*, edited by Gerald H. Anderson, 345–46. New York: Macmillan Reference USA, 1998.

Fenn, Eric. "The Bible and the Missionary." In *Cambridge History of the Bible*, vol. 3, *The West from the Fathers to the Reformation*, edited by S. L. Greenslade, 383–407. Cambridge: Cambridge University Press, 1963.

McFarland, Andrew D. "William Carey's Vision for Missionary Families." In *The Missionary Family: Witness, Concerns, Care*, edited by Dwight P. Baker and Robert J. Priest, 98–115. Pasadena, CA: William Carey Library, 2014.

Neely, Alan. "Mills, Samuel John, Jr." In *Biographical Dictionary of Christian Missions*, edited by Gerald H. Anderson, 460. New York: Macmillan Reference USA, 1998.

———. "Zwemer, Samuel Marinus (1867-1952)." In *Biographical Dictionary of Christian Missions*, edited by Gerald H. Anderson, 763. New York: Macmillan Reference USA, 1998.

Neill, Stephen. *A History of Christian Missions*. London: Penguin, 1990.

Nettles, Thomas J. "Baptists and the Great Commission." In *The Great Commission: Evangelicals and the History of World Missions*, edited by Martin I. Klauber and Scott M. Manetsch, 89-107. Nashville: B&H Academic, 2008.

Robert, Dana. "Judson, Ann ('Nancy') (Hasseltine)." In *Biographical Dictionary of Christian Missions*, edited by Gerald H. Anderson, 346. New York: Macmillan Reference USA, 1998.

Smither, Edward L. *Brazilian Evangelical Missions in the Arab World: History, Culture, Practice, and Theology*. Eugene, OR: Pickwick, 2012.

———. "The Impact of Evangelical Revivals on Global Mission: The Case of North American Evangelicals in Brazil in the Nineteenth and Twentieth Centuries." *Verbum et Ecclesia* 31, no. 1 (2010).

Thompson, Charles L. *Times of Refreshing: A History of American Revivals from 1740-1877, with Their Philosophy and Methods*. Amazon Digital Services, 2013.

Tucker, Ruth A. *From Jerusalem to Irian Jaya: A Biographical History of Christian Mission*. Grand Rapids: Zondervan, 2004.

Walls, Andrew F. "Crowther, Samuel Adjai (or Ajayi)." In *Biographical Dictionary of Christian Missions*, edited by Gerald H. Anderson, 160-61. New York: Macmillan Reference USA, 1998.

Wilson, J. Christy. "The Legacy of Samuel Zwemer." *International Bulletin of Mission Research* 10 (July 1986): 117-21.

5
The Global Century of Christian Mission (1900–2000)

At the beginning of the twentieth century, around 95 percent of the world's Christians lived in Europe and North America. By the end of the century it was a very different story. The majority of the world's Christians now resided in the Global South—Asia, Africa, and Latin America. If the nineteenth century was the "great century" for Christian mission, the twentieth was the "global century." Despite significant violence and global conflicts, as well as the bitterness and uncertainty of a postcolonial world, the gospel continued to make great advances around the world. In this chapter, we first explore the political, social, and religious backgrounds as well as the tendencies and trends in mission practice. Next, we briefly observe how the gospel planted itself in the fields of Asia, Africa, and Latin America, meeting the key missionary players along the way. Finally, in this chapter we give more focus to new trends and strategies that defined twentieth-century evangelical mission.

THE TWENTIETH-CENTURY WORLD

WARS AND CONFLICTS

The assassination of Austro-Hungarian Archduke Franz Ferdinand (1863–1914) in Sarajevo plunged many nations into World War I (1914–1918). Entering the war rather late, in 1917, the United States and its president Woodrow Wilson (1856–1924) aimed to win the war to end all wars. In reality, World War I became just the first chapter in a series of twentieth-century wars. Defeated in the first war, Germany emerged again as a global power under Adolf Hitler (1889–1945) and launched World War II (1939–1945).

These world wars were followed by other regional conflicts. The Korean War (1950–1953) divided Korea between a communist, dictator-led North and a democratically focused South at the forty-eighth parallel. The Vietnam conflict clawed on for twenty years through the mid-1970s, establishing communist-controlled North Vietnam. Tension continued to rise in the Middle East between Israel and its neighbors. Iran and Iraq—two Muslim countries—engaged in an eight-year war through most of the 1980s. Following Iraqi leader Saddam Hussein's (1937–2006) invasion of Kuwait in 1990, the United States and other allies rolled into the region to liberate Kuwait and restore stability to the oil-rich region in what Arabs called the Second Gulf War.

The twentieth century also witnessed horrific periods of genocide. In 1915, the Ottoman Turks slaughtered 1.5 million of their Armenian neighbors. From 1941 to 1945, Hitler's Nazi regime killed as many as six million European Jews during the Holocaust. In 1994, in the predominantly Christian nation of Rwanda, the dominant Hutu tribe commenced a campaign of ethnic cleansing, killing as many as one million of their Tutsi neighbors in just one hundred days. Ethnic cleansing also arose during the Balkan War (1992–1995), when the Orthodox Christian Serbs brutally slaughtered twenty-five hundred Bosnian Muslims on the Mehmet Pacha Bridge, dumping their bodies into the Drina River.

Islamic fundamentalist movements flourished throughout the twentieth century. A number of factors contributed to this phenomenon. In 1923, while constructing the modern Turkish state, Mustapha Kamal Attaturk (1881–1938) dismantled the Ottoman Empire—the last remaining Muslim caliphate (dynasty). This left the world of Islam, which had existed since the seventh century as *din wa dawla* ("religion and state"), floundering in an identity crisis. In addition to this vacuum of power, Western foreign policy decisions in the Middle East, as well as the creation of the state of Israel in 1948, fueled a number of fundamentalist movements.

For example, Hasan al-Bana (1906–1979) launched the Muslim Brotherhood in 1928, responding to Egypt's economic decline. Bana strived to institute sharia law in Egypt. He was inspired by reformer Muhammad ibn Abd-al Wahab (1703–1792), who interpreted Islam only from the Qur'an and hadiths in order to root out syncretism in Islam. Though unsuccessful in Bana's day, the Muslim Brotherhood briefly came to power in Egypt in 2011 and 2012.

Responding to Western influences, including the Western-backed leadership of Shah Mohamed Reza Pahlavi (1919-1980), Ayatollah Khomeini (1900-1989) successfully led an Islamic revolution in Iran in 1979. Khomeini established a cleric-led government and instituted Islamic law in the Shi'a country. In 1992, the Iranian revolution was exported to Algeria, which plunged the country into a ten-year civil war that claimed the lives of one to two hundred thousand Algerians.

Toward the end of the twentieth century, other fundamentalist groups attempted to gain power through violence and terror. In the 1970s, Hezbollah attempted to control Lebanon, while Hamas defended the Palestinian cause against Israel. Emerging from an Islamic school in Pakistan, the Taliban seized Afghanistan toward the end of the twentieth century. Finally, led by Osama bin Laden (1957-2011), al-Qaeda managed to recruit thousands of young men to perpetrate acts of terror on soft targets around the world, including the West. The most infamous act came on September 11, 2001, when hijackers slammed planes into the World Trade Center buildings in New York City.

SHIFTS IN THE POLITICAL LANDSCAPE

The twentieth century also witnessed many changes in global politics. In 1917, Vladimir Lenin (1870-1924) and other Russian communists launched the Bolshevik Revolution, overthrowing the tsar and instituting a communist experiment that would persist through most of the century. In 1922, the Union of Soviet Socialist Republics (USSR) was formed, comprising Russia and fourteen other countries. As the USSR and the United States both increased in political and military power, they engaged in an arms race and Cold War that lasted most of the twentieth century. In 1992, under the leadership of Mikhail Gorbachev (b. 1931), the Soviet Union was officially dismantled.

During this period, China likewise proved a testing ground for the political theory of Karl Marx and Friedrich Engels. In 1949, a communist revolution birthed the People's Republic of China. Later, in 1967, the government carried out the Cultural Revolution, in which they purged the country of intellectuals and other thought leaders who might pose a threat to the communist movement. As a result, the official state religion became atheism. The government suppressed the church and expelled international Christian missionaries from the country.

In 1948, the United Nations recognized the new modern state of Israel. Beginning with the British Balfour Declaration of 1917, Britain and other nations began to look favorably on the idea of a Jewish state. Rejecting proposals for creating the state in present Uganda, the Jews insisted on occupying the land promised to Abraham. While some evangelical Christians, especially in North America, viewed this as a fulfillment of biblical prophecy, most of Israel's Arab neighbors felt very differently and refused Israel's right to exist. Further, creating the Jewish state meant expelling and displacing the Palestinians from their land, inciting further conflict.

POSTCOLONIALISM AND NATIONALISM

For the first half of the twentieth century, European imperialism continued as it had in the nineteenth century. However, in 1947, India gained its independence from Great Britain, leading to the formation of Pakistan and Bangladesh. During the 1950s and 1960s, African and Asian nations began claiming their independence. In some cases, this was a peaceful process. In others, such as Algeria's fight for independence from France, it was a violent and bloody conflict.

Many of these new nations struggled to flourish, experiencing great instability during the latter half of the century. Plagued by tribalism, Africa saw numerous civil wars and coups d'état. Southeast Asian nations such as Korea and Vietnam endured civil war, while Cambodia's leader Pol Pot (1925–1998) slew over two million of his people during the 1970s. The postcolonial era also spawned a great number of dictators who allowed their citizens little social or political freedom. Finally, this period witnessed the rise of nationalist movements, often accompanied by anti-Western sentiments, resulting in negative and resistant attitudes toward Christian missionaries.

Nationalist ideologies also developed in Europe and North America. Hitler's Nazi regime was founded on a fundamental faith in white supremacy, the ideological basis for extinguishing Jews and other non-Aryan peoples. Inspired by these views, groups such as the Ku Klux Klan in the United States fought for white supremacy and actively suppressed blacks, people of color, and other minorities. Institutional racism was advanced in America through segregation, black codes, and Jim Crow laws, and in South Africa through apartheid.

REVERSE GLOBAL MIGRATION

From the sixteenth to nineteenth centuries, Europeans migrated to the rest of the world; however, in the twentieth century, a reverse migration back to Europe and North America began to take place. Before ceding independence to the north African nations between 1956 and 1962, France encouraged migration from north Africa to support its developing economy. Over time, millions of north African Muslims came to live in France, some as guest workers and others who became French citizens. Similarly, to rebuild its economy following World War II, Germany recruited international workers from Korea, such as miners and medical personnel. International students from Africa, Asia, and Latin America also began studying in the West. Immigrant entrepreneurs launched businesses in the West, particularly in the United States.

Others immigrated to the West to flee political tyranny, civil war and unrest, and poverty. Rejecting the lack of freedom in Iran in 1979, Iranians began to seek asylum and immigrate to Britain, the Scandinavian countries, Canada, and the United States. Thousands fled the communist regime in Vietnam, and many came to America as refugees. At the same time, countless Cubans fleeing the Castro regime risked their lives and boarded small vessels for Florida. Refugees from many African nations contributed to a developing "refugee highway" across the continent in hopes of making it to Europe. In the latter half of the twentieth century, millions of Filipinos left the poverty of their home country for better work opportunities in Saudi Arabia and the Gulf States, Europe, and Canada.

SHIFTS IN THEOLOGY

Nineteenth-century shifts in thought, including Darwinism and biblical higher criticism, caused many Western Christians to embrace liberal theology. They rejected the historic teachings of Scripture (e.g., the virgin birth; the death, burial, and resurrection of Christ; a literal hell) and the exclusive claims of Christianity (Christ is the only way to God). As a result, many began to redefine Christian mission as focusing entirely on human social needs. Emphasizing humankind's goodness, some missionaries no longer challenged nonbelievers to repent and believe the gospel but instead to pursue a full humanity.

Theologically conservative Christians responded with a movement of Christian fundamentalism. Beginning with the publication of *The Fundamentals of the Christian Faith* (1909–1915), fundamentalists sought to maintain the historic tenets of the Christian faith. They began forming Bible colleges as conservative centers for theological education, including Moody Bible Institute (1886), the Bible Institute of Los Angeles (1908), Philadelphia College of the Bible (1913), Columbia Bible College (1923), and other schools during this period.

While these schools produced many pastors and missionaries, the fundamentalist movement tended to isolate the church from the broader culture. This continued in the United States until the 1950s, when theologian Carl F. H. Henry (1913–2003) advocated a new fundamentalism, which gave rise to modern evangelicalism.[1]

MODERN PENTECOSTALISM

Amid global revivals in the early twentieth century, including ones in Wales and Korea, the Asuza Street revival in 1906 gave birth to the modern Pentecostal movement. Growing out of the African Methodist Episcopal Church in Los Angeles and the preaching of Charles Parham (1873–1929), the movement spread quickly across the United States. In 1915, the spark fanned to a global flame. Emphasizing speaking in tongues, healing, and miracles, Pentecostal churches broke down barriers of race, culture, and socioeconomics, drawing together diverse peoples for worship. During the second half of the twentieth century, the most rapid global church growth has taken place within Pentecostal churches. The movement has also permeated Protestant, Anglican, and even Roman Catholic churches, blurring the lines between church traditions within global Christianity.

MISSION SOCIETIES

While Britain had been the primary sending country for global mission in the nineteenth century, the United States held that distinction in the twentieth century. Building on the values of the nineteenth-century voluntary principle, the American entrepreneurial spirit manifested itself in

---

1. See Brian Stanley, *The Global Diffusion of Evangelicalism: The Age of Billy Graham and John Stott* (Downers Grove, IL: InterVarsity, 2013).

the creation of new mission societies. In the final decade of the nineteenth century, American evangelical groups including the Evangelical Alliance Mission (1890), Central America Mission (1890), the Gospel Missionary Union (1894), African Inland Mission (1895), and Sudan Interior Mission (1898) formed. As their names indicate, some groups launched in order to minister in particular regions of the world.

In 1913, C. T. Studd (1860-1931) founded the quintessential faith mission, Worldwide Evangelization Crusade. While praying for and receiving financial gifts for mission, WEC members chose not to ask churches or individuals for money. During this period, Latin American Mission (1921) and Unevangelized Fields Mission (1931) also started.

Since twentieth-century mission was marked by a great deal of innovation and new strategies, a number of the new organizations reflected that. In 1942, Cameron Townsend (1896-1982) founded Wycliffe Bible Translators with the task of making Scripture available in all of the world's languages. Focused on disaster relief and community development, World Vision began its work in 1950. Convinced that reaching the university campus today would result in reaching the world tomorrow, Bill Bright (1921-2003) and Vonette Bright (1926-2015) pioneered Campus Crusade for Christ (Cru) in 1951. Focused on mobilizing young people for short-term mission, George Verwer (b. 1938) founded Operation Mobilization in 1957, while Loren Cunningham (b. 1936) created Youth with a Mission in 1960. Believing that mobilizing laborers for mission should be the first priority of the church, Fuller Theological Seminary professor Ralph Winter (1924-2009) founded the U.S. Center for World Mission in 1976. Finally, Pioneers (1976) and Frontiers (1982) were initiated with a vision to reach unreached peoples with the gospel. While Pioneers sent laborers to all parts of the world, Frontiers focused uniquely on the Muslim world.

STUDENT VOLUNTEER MOVEMENT

The Student Volunteer Movement was birthed in 1886 in Mt. Herman, Massachusetts, following a four-week YMCA collegiate camp led by American evangelist Dwight L. Moody (1837-1899). Though Moody's focus was North America and the camp did not have a deliberate global focus, the revivalist atmosphere nevertheless sparked a vision for global missions. During the camp, Princeton Theological Seminary professor Robert Wilder

(1863–1938) challenged the students with what became known as the Princeton Pledge: "I purpose, God willing, to become a foreign missionary." Around one hundred students responded to this call in 1886. In 1888, the Student Volunteer Movement was officially constituted, adopting this watchword: the "evangelization of the world in this generation." Between 1886 and 1920, over eighty-seven hundred individuals—university educated and sometimes affluent—followed through on their pledge and went into overseas missionary service.[2]

One charismatic figure who led SVM was C. T. Studd. Previously a record-setting cricket player at Cambridge University, Studd gave away his inheritance to become a faith missionary. After ten years of ministry in China, he returned to England due to poor health. From 1894 to 1900, Studd traveled for the SVM in Britain and the United States, laboring to mobilize other students toward global mission service. Later, Studd continued his missionary service in India (1900–1906) and Congo (1913–1931).

In addition to serving as director of the YMCA, a mission society in nineteenth and early twentieth centuries, John R. Mott (1865–1955) led the SVM for thirty years. Because of his tireless travel and efforts to motivate young people to Christian service, Mott received the Nobel Peace Prize in 1946. Robert Speer (1867–1947), the global mission coordinator for the Presbyterian church in North America, also served as traveling secretary and a mobilizer for the SVM.

Despite the significant number of volunteers sent to the world, the SVM began to succumb to liberal theology in the 1920s. The 1928 World Missionary Conference in Jerusalem emphasized social and humanitarian work over gospel proclamation and conversion. Similarly, in the 1932 work *Re-thinking Missions*, Harvard professor William Ernest Hocking and a group of Protestant laymen sought to redefine evangelism as "ministry to the secular needs of men." They asserted, "The time has come to set the educational and other philanthropic aspects of mission work free from organized responsibility to the work of conscious and direct evangelism."[3]

---

2. See Michael Parker, *The Kingdom of Character: The Student Volunteer Movement for Foreign Missions (1886–1926)* (Lanham, MD: University Press of America, 1998), 2–21; also Dana L. Robert, "The Origin of the Student Volunteer Watchword: 'The Evangelization of the World in this Generation,'" *International Bulletin of Missionary Research* 10, no. 4 (October 1986): 146.

3. William Ernest Hocking, *Re-thinking Missions: A Laymen's Inquiry after 100 Years* (New York: Harper and Brothers, 1932), 326.

Responding to this dichotomy between the human and spiritual aspects of Christian ministry, Mott argued: "There are not two gospels, one social and one individual. There is but one Christ who lived, died, and rose again, and relates himself to the lives of men. He is the Savior of the individual and the one sufficient Power to transform his environment and relationships."[4] Despite appeals from Mott and Speer, the SVM continued on this trajectory, and the movement ultimately morphed into the World Council of Churches.[5]

EDINBURGH WORLD MISSIONARY CONFERENCE

In June 1910, over twelve hundred Protestant delegates met in Edinburgh, Scotland, for a historic global mission consultation. John R. Mott moderated, and many from the SVM led the gathering. The SVM watchword "the evangelization of the world in this generation" framed the conference. Prior to the meeting, eight study groups explored topics such as carrying the gospel to the non-Christian world, missionary preparation, and mission and governments.[6]

While the conference contributed to the birth of the World Council of Churches and the twentieth-century ecumenical movement, only Protestant mission leaders attended. The conference also excluded predominantly Roman Catholic countries because these were already considered Christian contexts. Finally, the gathering remained a predominantly Western affair: the vast majority of the twelve hundred delegates came from Europe and North America. Arguably the most prophetic word announced to the attendees came from Samuel Azariah (1874–1945), the future Anglican bishop of South India and one of the few non-Western church leaders present. Reflecting back on the work of nineteenth-century Protestant mission efforts with an eye toward the future of mission, Azariah declared: "Through all the ages to come the Indian church will rise up in gratitude to attest the heroism and self-denying labors of the missionary body. You have given your goods to feed the poor. You have given

---

4. Cited in Ruth A. Tucker, *From Jerusalem to Irian Jaya: A Biographical History of Christian Mission* (Grand Rapids: Zondervan, 2004), 324.

5. See Tucker, *From Jerusalem to Irian Jaya*, 312–34.

6. See "Edinburgh 1910 Conference," Centenary of the 1910 World Missionary Conference, http://www.edinburgh2010.org/en/resources/1910-conference.html (accessed June 25, 2018).

your bodies to be burned. We also ask for love. Give us friends."[7] Azariah appealed to equal partnership between Western Christians and indigenous Christians. Indeed, as the twentieth century progressed, national Christians would lead the way in world evangelization.

ASIA

CHINA

Societies such as China Inland Mission continued their work during the first half of the twentieth century amid great turmoil. The country suffered continual upheaval between 1911 and 1927 under the leadership of various warlords. By 1927, the majority of international missionaries departed the country. Under the leadership of Chiang Kai Chek (1887-1975), a professing Christian, the church enjoyed a measure of freedom during the entirety of the 1930s. Throughout the Sino-Japanese War (1937-1945), the Japanese persecuted many Chinese Christians and international missionaries. During this time, Scottish missionary and 1924 Olympic Gold medalist Eric Liddell (1902-1945) was interned in a Japanese prison camp, where he eventually died.

At the start of the 1949 Communist Revolution, about four thousand Protestant missionaries were laboring in the country, and the church had grown to about one million Chinese believers. Within a few short years, the government expelled nearly all of the missionaries and seized the mission hospitals and schools. Through virulent propaganda campaigns, the Chinese government declared Christianity a Western evil. During the 1967 Cultural Revolution, in addition to eliminating intellectuals, the government also destroyed churches and persecuted Christians. Despite great oppression, the Chinese church began to experience significant growth after 1980, particularly within the house church movement. By the end of the twentieth century, the church in China had grown to an estimated one hundred million Christians. The bulk of this expansion occurred through the ministry of national believers.

---

7. Cited in Brian Stanley, *The World Missionary Conference: Edinburgh 1910* (Grand Rapids: Eerdmans, 2009), 119.

INDIA

Christian missionaries engaged a twentieth-century India that was religiously and culturally diverse. Having spent the first half of the century under British control, India spent the latter half of the century navigating its postcolonial identity. For this reason, the ministry of American Methodist E. Stanley Jones (1884–1973) proved significant. A product of the Student Volunteer Movement, Jones began his work in India in 1907. Jones's guiding principle was to focus on the person of Christ more than Christianity as a religion, particularly its Western forms. Jones's key strategy became known as the Ashram movement—a community in which members of various castes and religions lived together. In this environment, Hindus, Muslims, Jains, and Christians gathered at table and participated in interfaith dialogue. By 1940, Jones had initiated forty Ashram communities in India. In addition to his field work, Jones authored thirty books on evangelism and ministry in the Indian context.[8]

KOREA

The twentieth-century Korean church story was marked by revival, spiritual expansion, and also suffering. Shortly after a revival that broke out in Pyongyang in 1906, Japan annexed the country in 1910.[9] Until World War II ended in 1945, Japan dominated Korea, both politically and culturally. By 1939, all international missionaries had been expelled from the country. In 1945, the thirty-eighth parallel was established officially separating North and South Korea. In 1950, North Korea invaded it southern neighbors, leading to three years of war.

Despite these difficulties, in the second half of the twentieth century South Korea experienced some of the most rapid Christian growth of anywhere in the world. By the year 2000, over 40 percent of the country professed Christianity in some form, while 16 percent of the population identified as evangelical Christians. In 1958, Korean pastor David Yonggi Cho (b. 1936) founded Yoido Full Gospel Church. With nearly one million

---

8. See "E. Stanley Jones," Asbury University, http://www.asbury.edu/offices/library/archives/biographies/e-stanley-jones (accessed June 25, 2018).

9. See Mark Shaw, *Global Awakening: How Twentieth-Century Revivals Triggered a Christian Revolution* (Downers Grove, IL: IVP Academic, 2010), 33–54.

members organized into cell groups, Yoido became the largest single congregation of Christians in the world by the late twentieth century.

JAPAN

The bombing of Hiroshima in 1945 and Japan's subsequent defeat in World War II decimated Japanese society, leaving it in need of rebuilding. American General Douglas McArthur (1880–1964) proposed that one thousand Christian missionaries volunteer for service in Japan. By 1963 over four thousand missionaries, primarily North Americans, were serving among the Japanese. While some may have responded to McArthur's appeal, many others were motivated by their own calling to evangelize the nation.

Individual relationships proved the most effective means of reaching the Japanese with the gospel. Despite this, by the end of the century, Japanese congregations remained small, while the number of evangelical Christians remained less than 0.5 percent of the Japanese population.[10]

MIDDLE EAST

Throughout the 1950s, many predominantly Muslim countries in the Middle East, Asia, and Africa gained their independence from Europe—countries that were at least nominally Christian. Over time, most international missionaries, particularly those from the West, were expelled, and visas for Christian mission work were revoked.

In this context of hostility toward the Western Christian world, Kenneth Cragg (1913–2012) offered a winsome model for Christian witness among Muslims. An Anglican bishop, Cragg served Anglican congregations in Jerusalem, Cairo, Beirut, and Nigeria, as well as in his native Great Britain. In addition to his Christian theological training, Cragg mastered the Arabic language and became a world-renowned scholar of the Qur'an. In fact, Muslim scholars often sought out Bishop Cragg for his perspectives on the Qur'an and Islamic theology. Cragg authored over fifty books that compared and contrasted Christian and Muslim thought. Cragg urged Christians to learn what Muslims believe, cultivate a sincere appreciation for Muslim beliefs and traditions, and strive to build honest friendships with Muslims. Building on this basis of friendship and understanding, a Christian could sustain meaningful

---

10. See Stephen Neill, *A History of Christian Missions* (London: Penguin, 1990), 424–27.

dialogues with Muslims and even invite them to follow Christ. Continuing the work of Samuel Zwemer, Cragg served as the editor of the *Muslim World* journal and taught Arabic and Islamic Studies at Hartford Seminary.

During the postcolonial era, Christian mission work was greatly restricted in the Muslim world. Many missionaries began to access closed contexts as professionals—teachers, entrepreneurs, and nonprofit workers. Based on the apostle Paul's ministry model in Acts 18, this approach became known as tentmaking.[11] Tentmaking missionaries ministered in word and deed through their tangible service in the marketplace and by sharing a verbal witness. Missionaries have engaged in respectful dialogue with Muslims and strived to plant contextualized churches. During the latter part of the century, new mission societies launched with growing emphases on the Muslim world. In 1982, Greg Livingstone (b. 1940) launched Frontiers with the specific focus of planting churches among Muslims.[12]

AFRICA

In the twentieth century, the peoples of Africa endured significant hardship and pain. During the twentieth century, every country in Africa was a European colony except Ethiopia. The postcolonial period was turbulent and marked by tribalism, numerous coups d'état, and the emergence of military governments and dictatorships. In countries such as Congo, Benin, Angola, and Mozambique, Marxist regimes assumed power. In addition to this political upheaval, over twenty million sub-Saharan Africans have contracted HIV/AIDS since 1980. Finally, much of the continent has battled extreme poverty, droughts, and famine.

Despite these challenges, the church in Africa grew from ten million believers in 1910 to nearly four hundred million in 2010. According to Philip Jenkins, this marks the most significant growth in any religion in any region in world history.[13] By 1980, approximately one in six Africans

---

11. See J. Christy Wilson, *Today's Tentmakers: Self-Support: An Alternative Model for Worldwide Witness* (Eugene, OR: Wipf & Stock, 2002).

12. See Greg Livingstone, *Planting Churches in Muslim Cities: A Team Approach* (Grand Rapids: Baker Academic, 1993); also Frontiers, http://frontiers.org (accessed June 25, 2018).

13. See Phillip Jenkins, "Now That Faith Has Come," plenary address, Evangelical Theological Society National Meeting, San Diego, 2007; Jenkins, *The Next Christendom: The Coming of Global Christianity* (Oxford: Oxford University Press, 2011).

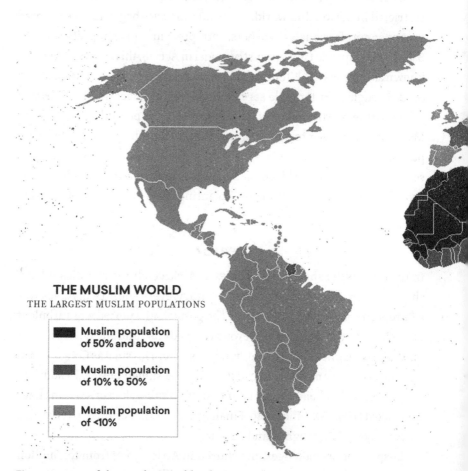

THE MUSLIM WORLD
THE LARGEST MUSLIM POPULATIONS

Muslim population
of 50% and above

Muslim population
of 10% to 50%

Muslim population
of <10%

Figure 9. Map of the Muslim World today

identified as Christians. Several sub-Saharan countries reported significant evangelical populations, including Uganda (46 percent), Kenya (35 percent), Central African Republic (35 percent), and Nigeria (23 percent). A few evangelical Christians also became heads of state in Africa in the latter part of the twentieth century.

LIBERIA AND IVORY COAST

Similar to what happened in China, most of the church growth in Africa during this period was accomplished by national Christians. These included professional ministers and missionaries as well as lay Christians. Originally a member of the Methodist and Episcopal churches in Liberia, William Wadé Harris (c. 1860-1929) pursued his calling as a wandering prophet-evangelist in west Africa. Beginning around 1914, Harris spent the next fifteen years—the final ones of his life—traveling between Liberia and Ivory Coast, reportedly baptizing some one hundred thousand West Africans. His message included calling his fellow Africans to abandon fetishes and idols, and to repent and be baptized. Harris valued the visible work of the Holy Spirit. Observers reported that his message was accompanied by miracles, healing, and speaking in tongues. Harris's ministry also set the stage for the development of African independent churches. These were church movements not necessarily connected to a historic Western denomination. Often Pentecostal in doctrine, they were culturally African in worship forms.[14]

SUDAN

While Africans such as Harris led the way in twentieth-century mission in Africa, international missionaries also contributed. In 1901, Rowland Bingham (1872-1942) braved Sudanese living conditions, launching Sudan Interior Mission. Through prayer, faith, and quinine—a key means to combat malaria, allowing missionaries to remain in the country—SIM began numerous mission stations across Sudan. Their ministry included evangelism, church planting, and medical mission. Following its independence from Britain in 1955, Sudan expelled all Christian missionaries in 1964. Despite this, over twenty-five hundred churches had been planted by 1970.

---

14. See David Shenk, "The Legacy of William Wadé Harris," *International Bulletin of Missionary Research* 10, no. 4 (October 1986): 170-76.

ETHIOPIA

In 1928, SIM expanded its work into neighboring Ethiopia. During the Italian occupation of the country (1935–1939), all international missionaries were expelled. Beginning in 1935, when there were only fifty evangelical Christians in the country, missionaries invested time translating Mark's Gospel and other Christian literature into Amharic. Because of these resources and the witness of the national church, the Ethiopian evangelical church grew to about ten thousand believers by 1941.

LATIN AMERICA

Today, the majority of the world's Roman Catholics live in Latin America. By the end of the twentieth century, about 80 percent of Latin American peoples were baptized Catholics. Yet, by 1980, only a small minority of the population were attending Sunday Mass. Brazilians often say that Catholics only go to church three times in their lives: for their baptism, their wedding, and their funeral.

At the beginning of the twentieth century, relatively few evangelical Christians were worshiping in Latin America. Some Protestant missionaries, such as those attending the 1910 Edinburgh World Missionary Conference, avoided ministry in Latin America because they viewed it as an evangelized region. Other Protestants such as Robert Speer and A. T. Pierson challenged this assumption. In 1913, they helped organize a conference in New York to consider evangelical mission work in Latin America. In 1916, another gathering met in Panama to discuss further strategies for Latin America, while subsequent conferences with similar goals were held in Montevideo (Uruguay) in 1925 and Havana (Cuba) in 1929. Speer and others formed the Committee of Cooperation for Latin America, while a similar group was started to focus specifically on Brazil. Finally, in 1930, a federation of evangelical churches for Latin America was founded.[15] As a result, some Protestant mission groups began evangelizing nominal Catholics, while others ministered among indigenous tribal peoples. During this time, a number of mission societies were founded for

---

15. See Kenneth S. Latourette, *A History of the Expansion of Christianity* (New York: Harper & Brothers, 1937–1945), 7:172–73.

tribal work, including South American Indian Mission, Andes Evangelical Mission, Wycliffe Bible Translators, and New Tribes Mission.

Following the 1906 Asuza Street Revival, Pentecostal Christianity spread quickly to South America. For example, in 1910, two Swedish Baptist immigrants residing in the Chicago area—Gunnar Vingren (1879-1933) and Daniel Berg (1884-1963)—reported being led to ministry in Brazil because of a miraculous vision. Justo González writes:

> In the summer of 1910, in his kitchen in South Bend, one of the members of Vingren's church who has the gift of prophecy declares that God was calling Vingren to a great mission elsewhere. A few days later, the prophet told Berg essentially the same. The prophet did not know where their mission was, but he knew that the place was called Pará, and that the two were to sail from New York on November 5. Since no one knew where Pará was, Vingren and Berg went to the library and there discovered that there was a state by that name in northern Brazil. They then traveled to New York, where they learned that there was a ship, the *Clement*, leaving New York for Pará on November 5! Without further arrangements, they bought two passages in steerage and arrived in Belem do Pará two weeks later, with ninety dollars between the two of them and without knowing one word of Portuguese.[16]

Vingren, who had previously served as a pastor, focused on evangelism, while Berg supported them both through his work as a metalworker. Though initially worshiping with Baptists in Belem do Pará, as their language abilities increased and their Pentecostal leanings became apparent, they were forced to leave the church. Later, they started the Missão da Fé Apostolíca (Mission of the Apostolic Faith). In 1918, they affiliated with the Assemblies of God denomination in North America. They established Assemblies of God churches in every state in northern and northeast Brazil by 1920, and in every region of the country by 1944. Since 1950, the Brazilian denomination has grown from one hundred thousand members to 14.4 million, making it the largest Assemblies of God communion in the

---

16. Justo L. González and Ondina E. González, *Christianity in Latin America: A History* (Cambridge: Cambridge University Press, 2007), 282.

world.[17] By the end of the twentieth century, Pentecostals made up nearly 70 percent of evangelicals in Latin America.

Some international missionaries laboring among Latin American tribal peoples encountered suffering and even martyrdom. In 1944, while trying to make contact with the Ayoré people of Bolivia, Bob and Cecil Dye of New Tribes Mission were murdered by the Ayoré. In 1956, Jim Eliot, Nate Saint, Ed McCully, Peter Fleming, and Roger Youderian lost their lives while attempting to make peaceful contact with the Waodoni people of Ecuador. Though the Waodoni had a history of violence with outsiders, Nate Saint's sister Rachel and Jim Eliot's widow, Elisabeth, went to live among the Waodoni and started a church among them.[18]

After a half-century of missionary efforts in Latin America, some leaders introduced fresh ideas and approaches to mission. Having grown up in Costa Rica to missionary parents, Kenneth Strachan (1910–1965) assumed leadership of Latin American Mission in 1950. Frustrated that evangelistic efforts had not led to lasting spiritual fruit, Strachan introduced a new strategy called Evangelism-in-Depth, a local church–initiated evangelism campaign emphasizing follow-up and discipleship. Strachan implemented his strategy in Nicaragua, Costa Rica, and Guatemala. In addition, Strachan hired more national Christians to work with Latin American Mission, striving to make the group more relevant to Latin American culture.

Other Latin American mission leaders introduced new ideas about theology of mission. In 1970, a diverse group of theologians, pastors, and church leaders formed the Latin American Theological Fraternity (FTL). Rejecting liberation theology (which greatly emphasizes economic justice for the poor) and criticizing North American fundamentalism, which seemed to ignore the social needs of Latin America, the FTL proposed "a fresh exploration . . . into the depths of the biblical text, with the questions raised by the Latin American context."[19] They read Scripture in light of Latin America's very real social problems, including poverty, injustice, and oppression—issues that are addressed in Scripture and in the earthly

---

17. See Edward L. Smither, *Brazilian Evangelical Missions in the Arab World: History, Culture, Practice, and Theology* (Eugene, OR: Pickwick, 2012), 29–34.

18. See Tucker, *From Jerusalem to Irian Jaya*, 352–63.

19. See Samuel Escobar, *Changing Tides: Latin America and World Mission Today* (Maryknoll, NY: Orbis, 2002), 114.

ministry of Jesus. Celebrating mission in word and deed, theologians such as René Padilla (b. 1932) and Samuel Escobar (b. 1934) introduced the notion of *mission integrale* (holistic mission) to the global church.

Over the course of the twentieth century, more and more Latin Americans became evangelicals. In Brazil, only 143,000 Christians identified as evangelicals in 1890. By the year 2000, Brazilian evangelicals numbered as high as twenty-five million. Today, every country in Latin America is at least 4 percent evangelical, while countries such as Guatemala (26 percent), El Salvador (22 percent), and Panama (18 percent) boast an even larger evangelical presence. The Latin American church began to actively send missionaries to the world in the latter part of the twentieth century.

SUMMARY

Political change and upheaval, wars, violence, and suffering shaped much of twentieth-century global history. These realities doused much of the optimism for human progress present in the West at the turn of the century. Liberal theology, which had been founded on such optimism and that had emphasized mission as humanization, also began to be questioned over the course of the twentieth century.

Many cultural groups across the world also began to negotiate new cultural identities during the latter half of the century. Stemming from postcolonial developments, global migration, and the beginnings of globalization, the world was changing, and people were changing with it. The Filipino teenager born and raised in Toronto would see and experience the world very differently from her parents who had migrated to Canada for a better life. The Algerian engineer may have become more devoted to Islam after his time studying in North America, or he may have seriously considered the gospel after being shown hospitality by followers of Christ.

This period, marked with upheaval and change, has been referred to as the "unexpected Christian century" for global mission.[20] In 1910, the "average" Christian family in the world was an English family attending a Sunday service at an Anglican church in London. By 2000, this family

---

20. See Scott W. Sunquist, *The Unexpected Christian Century: The Reversal and Transformation of Global Christianity, 1900–2000* (Grand Rapids: Baker, 2015).

would still be Anglican, but they were now African Christians attending an Anglican service in Nigeria or Rwanda. In 1910, about 95 percent of the world's Christians lived in North America or Europe. By the end of the twentieth century only 40 percent of the world's Christians lived in the West.

Scholars of world Christianity have referred to this phenomenon as the rise of the Global South. By the end of the twentieth century, the center of global Christianity had shifted from Europe and North America to Latin America, Africa, and Asia. Sometimes referred to as "non-Western," "third world," "two-thirds world," or "developing world," majority world Christianity simply means that the largest group of global Christians now live in Latin America, Africa, and Asia.[21] While the leadership of the 1910 Edinburgh conference was largely Western, the "look" of the global church and its leadership became primarily non-Western by the end of the twentieth century.

WHO WERE THE TWENTIETH-CENTURY MISSIONARIES?

Entrepreneurs and Visionaries

With the American church becoming the number-one sender of global missionaries in the twentieth century, many entrepreneur types and visionaries became missionaries and catalysts for mission efforts. John R. Mott ably led the Student Volunteer Movement, and visionaries such as Cameron Townsend, George Verwer, Greg Livingstone, and Ralph Winter considered new approaches to mission in the twentieth century.

Women

Building on the pioneering work of Mary Slessor and Lottie Moon in the nineteenth century, both single and married women enjoyed an increased role in global mission during the twentieth century. Over time, mission groups found that single women were often the best missionaries to pioneer work in a hostile area. Following the slaughter of Jim Eliot, Nate Saint, and the Waodoni mission team in Ecuador in 1956, Eliot's widow Elisabeth (1926–2015) and Saint's sister Rachel (1914–1994) went back to the tribe,

---

21. A. Scott Moreau, Gary R. Corwin, and Gary B. McGee, *Introducing World Missions: A Biblical, Historical, and Practical Survey* (Grand Rapids: Baker Academic, 2004), 12–13.

made peaceful contact, and evangelized them. Rachel continued to minister among the Waodoni until her death in 1994.

National Global South Believers

The spread of the gospel in the twentieth century was largely accomplished by national believers. While this fact does not discount the courageous and faithful service of Western missionaries, it was the likes of William Wadé Harris and countless unnamed national Christians who evangelized their own people. This is only natural. First, national missionaries could proclaim the gospel in a culturally meaningful way. Second, whereas Western missionaries were expelled or restricted from some contexts (e.g., China, Korea, and Ethiopia), national believers were present to do the work of ministry. The presence and effective work of national Christians and church leaders naturally raised the very healthy question—what role should Western or international missionaries play moving forward?—a question that must be continually pondered in mission during the present day.

WHAT DID THE TWENTIETH-CENTURY MISSIONARIES DO?

Translated Scripture

Given the challenges and complexities facing mission in the twentieth century, many mission leaders responded with innovation, strategic thinking, and resilience. While selling Spanish Bibles in Guatemala in 1917, Cameron Townsend met a man from the indigenous Kaqchikel people who posed the haunting question: If your God is so smart, why doesn't he speak my language? Townsend spent the remainder of his life striving to resolve this issue for cultural groups without Scripture in their languages.

While Bible translation efforts had been reignited following the Protestant Reformation, Townsend took it to a new level when he founded first the Summer Institute of Linguistics in 1934 and later Wycliffe Bible Translators in 1942. Originally focused on translating Scripture for indigenous peoples in the Americas, SIL and Wycliffe's work quickly became more global in scope. Kenneth Pike (1912–2000), a linguist from the University of Michigan, led SIL and Wycliffe to apply the twentieth-century advancements in linguistics for Bible translation. Part of their work included publishing the *Ethnologue*, which provides up-to-date research on the world's more than seven thousand languages and dialects. In the twenty-first century, Wycliffe aims to begin translation work in all of the remaining global languages without Scripture.[22]

Planted Churches

Building on the nineteenth-century three-self philosophy—that churches should be self-led, self-supporting, and self-propagating—a number of twentieth-century missionaries focused their work on effective church planting. Roland Allen (1868–1947), an Anglican missionary who served first in China and later Kenya, published two key works on church planting: *Missionary Methods: St. Paul's or Ours?* (1912) and *The Spontaneous Expansion of the Church and the Causes that Hinder It* (1927). Rejecting the mission-compound approach and the planting of Western-style churches, Allen argued that the apostle Paul's emphasis on evangelism and church planting should be normative for the missionary and that Spirit-led church movements with lay ministers should replace Western, paternal models. Though Allen's ideas were not greatly appreciated in his own day, missionary church planters began to rediscover and apply his principles during the 1960s.[23]

Continuing Allen's focus on spontaneous expansion, other twentieth-century church planters emphasized church planting movements. Describing this phenomenon as "a rapid multiplication of indigenous churches planting churches," David Garrison observes that these movements have been characterized by prayer, abundant evangelism, the authority of Scripture, local and lay leadership, house churches, and intentional planting of rapidly reproducing churches.[24] Such movements have been particularly fruitful in restricted areas such as China and the Muslim world.

Donald McGavran (1887–1990) pioneered the church growth movement. He was troubled by the mission-station approach and concerned about meaningful church planting within India's caste system. Instead

---

22. See "Vision 2025," Wycliffe Global Alliance, http://www.wycliffe.net/vision2025 (accessed June 25, 2018); also "About," *Ethnologue: Languages of the World*, https://www.ethnologue.com/about (accessed June 25, 2018).

23. Charles Henry Long, "Allen, Roland," in *Biographical Dictionary of Christian Missions*, ed. Gerald H. Anderson (New York: Macmillan Reference USA, 1998), 12–13.

24. David Garrison, *Church Planting Movements: How God Is Redeeming a Lost World* (Monument, CO: WIGTake, 2004), 21; see also Garrison, *A Wind in the House of Islam* (Monument, CO: WIGTake, 2014).

he advocated "the homogeneous unit principle," because he believed
that it was best to plant churches in existing social networks. He wrote:
"[Human beings] like to become Christians without crossing racial, linguistic, or class barriers."[25] Though not opposed to multicultural congregations,
McGavran saw the homogenous unit as a strategic starting point in church
planting. In addition, McGavran celebrated people movements in church
planting. That is, more than just individuals coming to faith, McGavran
suggested that groups of people—extended families, villages, and others
in communal societies—ought to embrace the gospel together and launch
new churches. Finally, he placed a high value on what he called the recep-
tivity principle—prioritizing ministry where the spiritual harvest was ripe.

Emphasized People Groups

At the Lausanne Congress on World Evangelization in 1974, Ralph Winter
gave a short but powerful paper arguing that the key to completing the
Great Commission was not through focusing on countries but rather
through engaging people groups. Winter argued that when Scripture spoke
of the "families of the earth" (Gen 12:1-2) or the "nations" (Matt 28:18-20),
it was referring to ethno-linguistic peoples. He defined a people group
as "a significantly large grouping of individuals who perceive themselves
to have a common affinity with one another. For evangelistic purposes,
it is the largest group within which the gospel can spread as a church
planting movement without encountering barriers of understanding or
acceptance."[26] The Joshua Project, a global database on the status of world
evangelization and church planting, lists around twenty-four thousand
people groups in the world today.

Winter argued that the priority in mission ought to be reaching
unreached peoples. The Joshua Project defines an unreached people group
as having "no indigenous community of believing Christians able to evangelize [their own] people group."[27] Some missiologists have suggested that

---

25. Donald A. McGavran, *Understanding Church Growth* (Grand Rapids: Eerdmans, 1980),
223.

26. "People Groups," Joshua Project, https://joshuaproject.net/help/definitions (accessed
June 25, 2018).

27. "Unreached People Groups," Joshua Project, https://joshuaproject.net/help/definitions
(accessed June 25, 2018).

if a people group have less than 5 percent Christian adherents or are less than 2 percent evangelical, then they remain incapable of evangelizing themselves. Winter's vision became the gospel for every person and a church for every people group.

Since 1974, Winter's thinking has challenged mission organizations to refocus their strategic priorities and resource allocations. Groups such as Pioneers were founded to focus on least-reached peoples, while the Southern Baptist International Mission Board completely restructured their organization at the end of the twentieth century in light of unreached peoples. Through founding the U.S. Center for World Mission and launching the Perspectives study program, Winter helped the church in North America and beyond to gain a vision for the least reached.

Evangelized through Preaching

Another key approach to twentieth-century global mission was proclamation, particularly through organized evangelistic meetings, often referred to as crusades, and open-air campaigns. Billy Graham (1918–2018) was the most famous and prolific evangelist during the latter half of the century. After graduating from Wheaton College, Graham initially pastored local churches before joining Youth for Christ as a traveling evangelist. Though Graham's first organized crusade took place in Grand Rapids, Michigan, in 1947, his eight-week crusade in Los Angeles in 1949 truly launched his global ministry. Beginning with the London crusade in 1954, Graham began to hold evangelistic meetings outside the United States, in Europe, Africa, Asia, and Latin America.

While most of his outreaches took place in countries open to Christian proclamation, Graham also preached in some otherwise restricted areas. At the height of the Cold War in 1982, Graham preached for five nights in Moscow, and he later returned to the Soviet Union in 1984 and 1988. In 1988, he also held a series of meetings in China.

Between 1947 and his last crusade in New York City in 2005, Graham preached over four hundred evangelistic crusades in 185 countries. An estimated eighty-four million people attended these meetings. Another 130 million heard Graham proclaim the gospel on radio and television as the Billy Graham Evangelistic Association began to leverage these media forms for ministry. Graham's legacy included preaching a simple gospel and inviting hearers to respond by making a personal decision for Christ.[28] While Billy Graham was the most famous twentieth-century crusade-style evangelist, others such as Argentinian evangelist Luis Palau (b. 1934) and German Pentecostal preacher Reinhard Bonke (b. 1940) have also adopted this approach.

Emphasized Humanitarian Work

Amid the twentieth century's challenges, including global poverty and disasters both natural and manmade, many Christian organizations began to focus on humanitarian work. Following an initial period of service in Korea, Bob Pierce (1914–1978) started World Vision in 1950 with a focus on children at risk, particularly those orphaned during the Korean War. After expanding its work to Latin America, Africa, the Middle East, and Eastern Europe, World Vision broadened its focus to community development projects (e.g., clean water, education, health, microfinance) in the 1970s. By the end of the century, the group engaged in justice mission, particularly on behalf of women and children.[29]

In 1970, Pierce founded Samaritan's Purse with a vision "to meet emergency needs in crisis areas through existing evangelical mission agencies and national churches."[30] The group has focused on relieving suffering caused by earthquakes, hurricanes, wars, and famine. In the mid-1970s, Franklin Graham (b. 1952), son of Billy Graham, began working alongside Pierce. When Pierce died of leukemia in 1978, Graham became the organization's leader.

In addition to World Vision and Samaritan's Purse, other groups such as Compassion International (1952) and Food for the Hungry (1971) got their start in the latter half of the twentieth century. While these groups focus purely on relief and development, many evangelical mission organizations and denominations also initiated compassion ministry arms during this period.

---

28. "Profile: William (Billy) F. Graham, Jr.," Billy Graham Evangelistic Association, https://billygraham.org/about/biographies/billy-graham/ (accessed June 25, 2018).

29. See "Our History," World Vision International, https://www.wvi.org/our-history (accessed June 25, 2018).

30. "History," Samaritan's Purse, https://www.samaritanspurse.org/our-ministry/history/ (accessed June 25, 2018).

Twentieth-century evangelical mission leaders wrestled with the tension between proclamation and caring for human needs in mission. The 1974 Lausanne gathering, initiated and funded by Billy Graham's ministry, opened with a great focus on proclamation. However, through their presentations, Latin American Theological Fraternity leaders Samuel Escobar and Rene Padilla challenged the delegates to think more deeply about the place of social action in mission. Both Billy Graham and John Stott (1921–2011), an Anglican priest and leading theologian of Lausanne, humbly listened to these voices from the majority world. Following Lausanne, Stott spent time with these leaders in Latin America learning more about mission in their context. As a result, the following article on "Christian Social Responsibility" was included in the Lausanne Covenant:

> Although reconciliation with other people is not reconciliation with God, nor is social action evangelism, nor is political liberation salvation, nevertheless we affirm that evangelism and socio-political involvement are both part of our Christian duty. For both are necessary expressions of our doctrines of God and man, our love for our neighbor and our obedience to Jesus Christ. The message of salvation implies also a message of judgment upon every form of alienation, oppression and discrimination, and we should not be afraid to denounce evil and injustice wherever they exist. When people receive Christ they are born again into his kingdom and must seek not only to exhibit but also to spread its righteousness in the midst of an unrighteous world. The salvation we claim should be transforming us in the totality of our personal and social responsibilities. Faith without works is dead.[31]

Engaged in Short-Term Missions

During the twentieth century, many evangelical Christians, especially North Americans, began participating in short-term mission (STM) work. Short-term missions range from one week to two years. While some mission organizations initially resisted the idea of short-term missions, by

---

31. Lausanne Covenant, article 5, https://www.lausanne.org/content/covenant/lausanne -covenant (accessed June 25, 2018).

the latter part of the century, most groups embraced STM as a viable strategy, particularly for mobilizing future long-term workers. In 1957, George Verwer founded Operation Mobilization with a great emphasis on mobilizing young people to one- and two-year mission opportunities. In 1960, Loren Cunningham started Youth with a Mission with a similar focus.

By 2005, over 1.6 million North American Christians were participating in short-term mission trips, with the average trip lasting about eight days. Many local churches, including youth groups, have added local and international mission trips to their outreach strategy. Christian high schools and universities have also promoted STM among their students.

On one hand, the STM trend has helped church members gain exposure to the needs of the world and become globally focused Christians—those who pray, give financially, and advocate for the needs of the unreached. Short-term teams often include medical professionals, construction workers, and athletic trainers and coaches. These Christians put their valuable skills to work in ministry in areas of great needs. On the other hand, short-term work has raised a number of problems and challenges. Some teams have invested little time in cultural training, while others have promoted STM trips with their churches or youth groups as exotic adventures. In the case of North Americans, this posture has only perpetuated the "ugly American" stereotype among many global peoples. The STM phenomenon has also raised questions regarding the use of money in mission. For example, should a short-term team of ten Americans raise $20,000 to work at an orphanage in Haiti for a week, or would it be better for the group to send that money to the orphanage's long-term staff so they can enhance the work?[32]

Leveraged Technology in Mission

A large number of twentieth-century missionaries proved to be innovative with the developing technology available. In the earlier part of the century, around 160 Protestant printing presses were in operation producing and distributing Christian literature. Toward the middle of the century, a number of new evangelistic publishing houses, including Christian

---

32. See Robert J. Priest, *Effective Engagement in Short-Term Missions: Doing It Right!* (Pasadena, CA: William Carey Library), 2008; also David A. Livermore, *Serving with Eyes Wide Open: Doing Short-Term Mission with Cultural Intelligence* (Grand Rapids: Baker, 2006).

Literature Crusade (1941) and Operation Mobilization Publishing (1968), were founded. Following World War II and the emergence of the iron curtain in the Soviet bloc regions, many mission organizations prioritized distributing evangelistic literature in restricted areas.

Beginning with Betty Greene's (1920–1997) work with Mission Aviation Fellowship in 1946 in the jungles of South America, evangelical mission groups also valued aviation as a means to resource missionaries in remote areas.[33] Trained pilots and mechanics could fly medical supplies and personnel into needed areas. To facilitate Bible translation, Wycliffe added its Jungle Aviation and Radio Service (JAARS) division in 1948. Later, other groups such as New Tribes Mission, SIM, and African Inland Mission developed mission-aviation teams. While some pilots received their training in the military, others trained at Christian colleges, which had begun adding mission aviation to their curricula.

In addition to Billy Graham's crusades being broadcast on radio and satellite television, other ministries also invested in media. Moved by a conviction to proclaim the gospel in restricted access and resistant areas, Clarence Jones (1900–1986) started Heralding Christ Jesus' Blessings (HCJB) radio in Ecuador in 1931. By 1981, HCJB was broadcasting Christian programming in fifteen languages around the world. In 1948, Far East Broadcasting Company (FEBC) began a similar work with a focus on Asia. By 1970, FEBC included a network of twenty-one radio stations broadcasting in forty different Asian languages. Finally, in 1954, Paul Freed, a missionary in the Middle East, founded Transworld Radio (TWR). Broadcasting from Africa, the Americas, Asia, the Middle East, Europe, and central Asia, TWR became the largest gospel radio network in the world.

Under the leadership of Paul Eschelman, Campus Crusade for Christ released the "Jesus Film" in 1979, a movie depicting the life of Christ based on Luke's Gospel. After 250 showings in North American theatres, the film began to be dubbed into other languages, which launched the Jesus Film Project. By the year 1999, the "Jesus" had been translated into over five hundred languages. It has been shown outdoors, on national television broadcasts, and satellite TV, and distributed through audiocassettes,

---

33. See "Betty Greene," Mission Aviation Fellowship, https://www.maf.org/about/history/betty-greene (accessed June 25, 2018).

videocassettes, and DVDs. The most translated movie in the history of the industry, in some instances the "Jesus" was the first movie dubbed into some of the world's languages. Toward the end of the century, the Jesus Film Project and Wycliffe began partnering to translate and distribute the movie and the Gospel of Luke together.[34]

Valued Partnership

Beginning with the 1910 World Missionary Conference in Edinburgh, Protestants demonstrated the value of partnership and collaboration in global mission. During the same decade, global mission consultations took place in New York City (1913) and Panama (1916).

In 1966, the Billy Graham ministry initiated the World Congress on Evangelism, which convened in Berlin. With the aim to "define and clarify biblical evangelism for our day,"[35] over seven hundred evangelical delegates wrestled with obstacles and new approaches to global evangelism in the twentieth century.

The Berlin conference paved the way for the 1974 Lausanne Congress on World Evangelization, also initiated by Billy Graham. While the Berlin meeting was dominated by American issues and personalities, the Lausanne gathering gave a platform to global church leaders to address their contextual challenges in mission. From July 16–25, 1974, twenty-four hundred delegates from 150 nations gathered to discuss mission within the twentieth-century global political, economic, and religious landscape. Probably the two most significant developments from Lausanne 1974 were Winter's assertion that unreached people groups should be the priority in mission, and Padilla and Escobar's call for a more holistic approach to mission. Through the resulting Lausanne Covenant, a more global evangelical theology of mission also emerged.[36]

Lausanne II met in Manila in 1989. Building on Winter's people group focus, Luis Bush challenged the delegates to focus their work on the

---

34. See "The History of Jesus Film Project," Jesus Film Project, https://www.jesusfilm .org/about/history.html (accessed June 25, 2018).

35. See Billy Graham Center at Wheaton College, https://www.wheaton.edu/academics/ academic-centers/billy-graham-center/ (accessed June 25, 2018).

36. See "The Legacy of the Lausanne Movement," Lausanne Movement, https://www .lausanne.org/our-legacy (accessed June 25, 2018).

10/40 window—the region between 10 and 40 degrees latitude between North Africa and Asia where the majority of unreached peoples live. From Manila, hundreds of mission partnerships and networks emerged to face the issues of mission at the end of the twentieth century.

Out of Lausanne 1974, an authentic global network developed. While additional congresses were held in Manila and Cape Town (2010), the Lausanne Movement has largely been fueled by working groups.[37] The first Lausanne gathering also inspired other mission congresses such as the Curitiba, Brazil, conference in 1976 and the first COMIBAM (Ibero-America Mission Conference) in São Paulo in 1987. These meetings helped to forge strategic mission networks from Latin America.

Mobilized Laborers

Student Volunteer Movement leaders such as John R. Mott, Robert Speer, C. T. Studd, and Samuel Zwemer invested a great deal of energy mobilizing new laborers for global mission in the earlier part of the twentieth century. As new mission societies emerged, organizations also emphasized mobilizing new personnel.

Though the SVM declined during the 1930s, the Urbana Missions Conference, organized by InterVarsity Christian Fellowship, met for the first time in 1946. From that first gathering of 575 students, the conference met every three years through the rest of the century at the University of Illinois-Champagne Urbana. While as many as twenty thousand students have attended individual conferences, InterVarsity reports that around three hundred thousand students have participated in Urbana through the years, with many attendees going on to serve in global mission as a result.[38]

Studied Missiology

Often regarded as the pioneer of missiology, the academic study of mission, Gustav Warneck (1834–1910) taught at the University of Halle (Germany) from 1897 to 1908.[39] In addition to Warneck, Samuel Zwemer, Roland Allen,

---

37. See "All Issue Networks," Lausanne Movement, https://www.lausanne.org/all-issue-networks (accessed June 25, 2018).

38. See "About Urbana," Urbana, https://urbana.org/about-urbana (accessed June 25, 2018).

39. See Hans-Werner, Gensiche, "Warneck, Gustav," in Anderson, *Biographical Dictionary of Christian Missions*, 718.

and Herman Bavinck (1895–1964) contributed to missiology as professors and writers during the first half of the twentieth century. In 1973, Ralph Winter and Gerald Anderson founded the American Society of Missiology,[40] while in 1990, David Hesselgrave and Donald McGavran initiated the Evangelical Missiological Society.[41] Along with others, these networks have encouraged missiological reflection through conferences and academic publications. Since Christian universities and theological seminaries were adding professors of mission to their faculties, they also developed undergraduate and graduate degrees programs in mission, missiology, and intercultural studies.

FURTHER READING

"About." Ethnologue: Languages of the World. https://www.ethnologue.com/about. Accessed June 25, 2018.

"About Urbana." Urbana. https://urbana.org/about-urbana. Accessed June 25, 2018.

"All Issue Networks." Lausanne Movement. https://www.lausanne.org/all-issue -networks. Accessed June 25, 2018.

"Betty Greene." Mission Aviation Fellowship. https://www.maf.org/about/history/ betty-greene. Accessed June 25, 2018.

Billy Graham Center at Wheaton College. https://www.wheaton.edu/academics/ academic-centers/billy-graham-center/. Accessed June 25, 2018.

"Edinburgh 1910 Conference." Centenary of the 1910 World Missionary Conference. http://www.edinburgh2010.org/en/resources/1910-conference.html. Accessed June 25, 2018.

"E. Stanley Jones." Asbury University. http://www.asbury.edu/offices/library/ archives/biographies/e-stanley-jones. Accessed June 25, 2018.

Escobar, Samuel. *Changing Tides: Latin America and World Mission Today*. Maryknoll, NY: Orbis, 2002.

Frontiers. http://frontiers.org. Accessed June 25, 2018.

Garrison, David. *Church Planting Movements: How God Is Redeeming a Lost World*. Monument, CO: WIGTake, 2004.

———. *A Wind in the House of Islam*. Monument, CO: WIGTake, 2014.

Gensiche, Hans-Werner. "Warneck, Gustav." In *Biographical Dictionary of Christian Missions*, edited by Gerald H. Anderson, 718. New York: Macmillan Reference USA, 1998.

---

40. See Wilbert Shenk, *History of the American Society of Missiology, 1973–2013* (Elkhart, IN: Institute of Mennonite Studies, 2014).

41. See "Who Is the Evangelical Missiological Society?," Evangelical Missiological Society, https://www.emsweb.org/about/us (accessed June 25, 2018).

González, Justo L., and Ondina E. González. *Christianity in Latin America: A History*. Cambridge: Cambridge University Press, 2007.

"History." Samaritan's Purse. https://www.samaritanspurse.org/our-ministry/history/. Accessed June 25, 2018.

"The History of Jesus Film Project." Jesus Film Project. https://www.jesusfilm.org/about/history.html. Accessed June 25, 2018.

Hocking, William Ernest. *Re-thinking Missions: A Laymen's Inquiry after 100 Years*. New York: Harper and Brothers, 1932.

Jenkins, Phillip. *The Next Christendom: The Coming of Global Christianity*. Oxford: Oxford University Press, 2011.

———. "Now That Faith Has Come." Plenary address, Evangelical Theological Society National Meeting, San Diego, 2007.

Latourette, Kenneth S. *A History of the Expansion of Christianity*. Vol. 7. New York: Harper & Brothers, 1937–1945.

Lausanne Covenant. https://www.lausanne.org/content/covenant/lausanne-covenant. Accessed June 25, 2018.

"The Legacy of the Lausanne Movement." Lausanne Movement. https://www.lausanne.org/our-legacy. Accessed June 25, 2018.

Livermore, David A. *Serving with Eyes Wide Open: Doing Short-Term Mission with Cultural Intelligence*. Grand Rapids: Baker, 2006.

Livingstone, Greg. *Planting Churches in Muslim Cities: A Team Approach*. Grand Rapids: Baker Academic, 1993.

Long, Charles Henry. "Allen, Roland." In *Biographical Dictionary of Christian Missions*, edited by Gerald H. Anderson, 12–13. New York: Macmillan Reference USA, 1998.

McGavran, Donald A. *Understanding Church Growth*. Grand Rapids: Eerdmans, 1980.

Moreau, A. Scott, Gary R. Corwin, and Gary B. McGee. *Introducing World Missions: A Biblical, Historical, and Practical Survey*. Grand Rapids: Baker Academic, 2004.

"Our History." World Vision International. https://www.wvi.org/our-history. Accessed June 25, 2018.

Parker, Michael. *The Kingdom of Character: The Student Volunteer Movement for Foreign Missions (1886–1926)*. Lanham, MD: University Press of America, 1998.

Priest, Robert J., ed. *Effective Engagement in Short-Term Missions: Doing It Right!* Pasadena, CA: William Carey Library, 2008.

"Profile: William (Billy) F. Graham, Jr." Billy Graham Evangelistic Association. https://billygraham.org/about/biographies/billy-graham/. Accessed June 25, 2018.

Robert, Dana L. "The Origin of the Student Volunteer Watchword: 'The Evangelization of the World in this Generation.'" *International Bulletin of Missionary Research* 10, no. 4 (October 1986): 146–49.

Roberts, W. Dayton. "The Legacy of R. Kenneth Strachan." *International Bulletin of Missionary Research* 3, no. 1 (1979): 2–6.

Shaw, Mark. *Global Awakening: How Twentieth Century Revivals Triggered a Christian Revolution*. Downers Grove, IL: IVP Academic, 2010.

Shenk, David. "The Legacy of William Wadé Harris." *International Bulletin of Missionary Research* 10, no. 4 (October 1986): 170–76.

Shenk, Wilbert. *History of the American Society of Missiology, 1973–2013*. Elkhart, IN: Institute of Mennonite Studies, 2014.

Smither, Edward L. *Brazilian Evangelical Missions in the Arab World: History, Culture, Practice, and Theology*. Eugene, OR: Pickwick, 2012.

Stanley, Brian. *The Global Diffusion of Evangelicalism: The Age of Billy Graham and John Stott*. Downers Grove, IL: InterVarsity, 2013.

———. *The World Missionary Conference: Edinburgh 1910*. Grand Rapids: Eerdmans, 2009.

Sunquist, Scott W. *The Unexpected Christian Century: The Reversal and Transformation of Global Christianity, 1900–2000*. Grand Rapids: Baker, 2015.

Tucker, Ruth A. *From Jerusalem to Irian Jaya: A Biographical History of Christian Mission*. Grand Rapids: Zondervan, 2004.

"Vision 2025." Wycliffe Global Alliance. http://www.wycliffe.net/vision2025. Accessed June 25, 2018.

"Who Is the Evangelical Missiological Society?" Evangelical Missiological Society. https://www.emsweb.org/about/us. Accessed June 25, 2018.

Wilson, J. Christy. *Today's Tentmakers: Self-Support: An Alternative Model for Worldwide Witness*. Eugene, OR: Wipf & Stock, 2002.

6
Mission from the Majority World (Twenty-First Century)

Following the emergence of Global South Christianity in the latter part of the twentieth century, the demographic of the global mission movement began to shift. Though the United States continued to be the leading mission-sending nation at the beginning of the twenty-first century, the Global South church now sends the majority of the missionaries to the nations. The profile of the missionary is no longer William Carey or David Livingstone but global workers from Korea, Brazil, Nigeria, India, and the Philippines. These include those who self-identify as full-time vocational missionaries as well as laypeople who minister in places where their work and lives have taken them. The latter group we will refer to as diaspora Christians.

After a brief discussion of background issues to twenty-first century global Christianity, this chapter will explore the development of missionary movements from the non-Western world. What does mission look like *from* Asia, Africa, and Latin America? What are the mission approaches, opportunities, and challenges for majority world missionaries and also for diaspora Christians? This final chapter reveals the polycentric nature of twenty-first-century mission—a gospel that flows from everywhere to everyone. While inspiring, it is admittedly a chaotic story to try to capture.[1]

---

1. For more on polycentric mission, see Samuel Escobar, *The New Global Mission: The Gospel from Everywhere to Everyone* (Downers Grove, IL: InterVarsity, 2003); Allen Yeh, *Polycentric Missiology: Twenty-First Century Mission from Everywhere to Everyone* (Downers Grove, IL: InterVarsity, 2016).

THE TWENTY-FIRST-CENTURY WORLD

GLOBALIZATION

Globalization sums up one of the key reasons for the rapid change in the twenty-first-century world. *New York Times* journalist and best-selling author Thomas Friedman notes: "Globalization involves the integration of free markets, nation-states and information technologies to a degree never before witnessed, in a way that is enabling individuals, corporations, and countries to reach around the world further, faster, and cheaper than ever."[2] Friedman points to three distinct eras of globalization:

- 1492–1800, globalization happened on a country level through exploration and imperialism;
- 1820–2000, globalization took place on a company level, as businesses became increasingly transnational;
- 2000–present, globalization occurred on an individual level as people around the world were able to connect, collaborate, and compete with other individuals.

A number of factors have contributed to globalization in a world that Friedman describes as "hot, flat, and crowded."[3] First, global migration— people on the move for study, business, or seeking refuge—makes the world smaller. Second, transportation—particularly quick and affordable air travel—allows individuals and businesses to establish connections around the globe. Third, an increasingly networked global economy shrinks the world even further. The presence of forty thousand transnational companies has forced many agrarian economies to industrialize. Finally, technology, the internet in particular, has allowed companies and individuals to connect and collaborate like never before. Communication platforms such as Skype facilitate international companies conducting real-time meetings across continents. Because of YouTube, an aspiring American hip hop musician such as Chance the Rapper (b. 1993) can

---

2. Cited in Michael Pocock, Gailyn Van Rheenen, and Douglas McConnell, *The Changing Face of World Missions: Engaging Contemporary Issues and Trends* (Grand Rapids: Baker Academic, 2005), 22.

3. See Thomas Friedman, "Three Eras of Globalization," August 22, 2008, https://www.youtube.com/watch?v=lp4znWHvsjU.

produce his own music and even win a Grammy award without ever signing a contract with a record label. Through the same medium, Japanese and Saudi youth can become fans of the artist and then follow or friend him on social media.

Globalization brings numerous benefits to people around the world. Economically, international companies can attract cheaper labor; in turn, consumers pay less for goods. Cheap and frequent international flights help international students to pursue their dreams, businesses to flourish, and local churches to take short-term mission trips each year. Technology and social media also tell the stories of the oppressed and the marginalized. During U2's Zooropa Tour in the mid-1990s, the Irish rock band put a forgotten global conflict into the headlines by broadcasting interviews and scenes from the Balkan War onto the big screen of their concerts. In 2009, Iranians took to the streets to protest corrupt elections, broadcasting it all on Twitter. In addition, many Christian groups continue to leverage technology for global mission. Bible translators are producing Bible apps that allow Scripture to be downloaded in restricted areas where a print Bible cannot be distributed. The Jesus Film can be streamed online from any corner of the globe. Many missionaries leverage social media to begin meaningful gospel conversations.

Of course, globalization also has downsides. While international companies benefit from cheap labor, these laborers, including children, are often exploited in the process. Technology and the ease of travel have also facilitated human trafficking and sex tourism, particularly in Southeast Asia. Internet technology has also aided an ever-growing pornography industry. Islamic extremists have developed savvy recruiting techniques through social media and chat rooms. Finally, a generation of youth texting instead of talking has led to a breakdown of social skills needed for daily relationships and work. It has also resulted in increased anxiety levels and decreased abilities to resist adversity.

GLOBAL MIGRATION

The twenty-first century has continued to witness significant global migration. In 2017, over one million international students were studying in the United States, while half that number were pursuing their education in Canada. Executives and managers within the world's forty thousand transnational companies continued to travel and relocate for work. Finally, others have forsaken the limited employment opportunities in their home countries to work in the Middle East, Europe, and North America. Half of Toronto's six million inhabitants were born outside Canada, including large numbers of Indians, Chinese, and Filipinos who migrated to the city for work.[4]

Students, businesspeople, and workers have all chosen to migrate. However, by 2018, over sixty-five million people (one in 113 people on the planet) have been forcibly displaced by war, famine, and other crises. While more than half have been displaced within their own country, over twenty-two million have crossed national borders and sought refuge in another country. The majority of refugees are fleeing South Sudan, Afghanistan, and Syria. Although refugee and migration issues have been discussed at length in American and European politics, these countries are not leading the way to respond to this crisis. Instead, the top six nations that welcome refugees are actually poorer countries in Asia and Africa—Turkey, Pakistan, Lebanon, Iran, Uganda, and Ethiopia. As of 2016, only two hundred thousand of the twenty-two million refugees have been resettled.[5]

Whether for business, study, work, or seeking refuge, global peoples continue to be on the move. This "diaspora" or "scattering" refers to a "large-scale movement of people from their homeland to settle permanently or temporarily in other countries."[6] While some individuals and groups (e.g., international students in the United States) migrate to a place where they can hear the gospel and begin following Christ, other immigrants (e.g., Korean medical workers in Germany) are already believers and enjoy a witness for Christ in their adopted homeland.

---

4. See "Mapping the SEVIS by the Numbers," Homeland Security, https://studyinthestates .dhs.gov/sevis-by-the-numbers (accessed June 25, 2018); "Facts and Figures," Canadian Bureau for International Education, https://cbie.ca/media/facts-and-figures/ (accessed June 25, 2018).

5. See "Figures at a Glance," UNHCR: The UN Refugee Agency, http://www.unhcr.org/ en-us/figures-at-a-glance.html (accessed June 25, 2018); also Stephan Bauman, Matthew Soerens, and Samir Issam, *Seeking Refuge: On the Shores of the Global Refugee Crisis* (Chicago: Moody, 2016).

6. Tom Houston, Robin Thomson, Ram Gidoomal, and Leiton Chinn, "The New People Next Door," Lausanne Occasional Paper 33 (Lausanne Committee for World Evangelization, 2004), https://www.lausanne.org/wp-content/uploads/2007/06/LOP55_IG26.pdf, 1.

VIOLENCE

In addition to the tyranny on the part of some governments leading to forced displacement, the twenty-first century has been marked by significant violence. Following al-Qaeda's attacks on New York City and Washington, DC, on September 11, 2001, countless cities in Europe, Africa, and Asia have been the targets of Muslim terrorists. Based in northern Nigeria, Boko Haram began terrorizing West Africa in 2002. In 2014, the group kidnapped 276 Nigerian girls from a boarding school, prompting the #BringBackOurGirls campaign. Political vulnerability created by the Syrian civil war in 2011 allowed the emergence of the Islamic State in Iraq and Syria (ISIS). In addition to violently taking over regions of Syria and Iraq, forcing thousands of Arab Christians to flee, the group enslaved women from the Yazidi people, a non-Muslim Iraqi people.[7] African and Middle Eastern Christians have often been targeted by Muslim extremists and terrorists. In many other cases, cross-cultural missionaries have been injured or lost their lives in contexts of violence.[8] Though Westerners have been attacked by al-Qaeda and ISIS, the people most affected by Islamic extremists are actually other Muslims.

Violence, particularly gun violence, continually plagues the United States. In 2017, over fifteen thousand Americans were shot and killed, with another thirty thousand injured. The country experienced 346 mass shootings, including attacks on schools and other public places. Many of America's inner cities have become war zones between rival gangs with access to lethal weapons. Amid this reality of gun violence, Americans remain divided over the application of the Second Amendment.[9]

---

7. See "Who, What, Why: Who are the Yazidis?" BBC News, August 8, 2014, http://www.bbc.com/news/blogs-magazine-monitor-28686607.

8. See Keith E. Eitel, ed., *Missions in Contexts of Violence* (Pasadena, CA: William Carey Library, 2008).

9. See "Past Summary Ledgers," Gun Violence Archive, http://www.gunviolencearchive.org/past-tolls (accessed June 25, 2018).

MISSION FROM ASIA

KOREA

Shortly after the revivals of 1906, which resulted in significant church growth, Korean Presbyterian churches began sending missionaries to neighboring China. Even during the period of Japanese occupation, which lasted until 1955, over eighty Korean missionaries went as global missionaries. By 1980, just under one hundred Koreans were serving as full-time missionaries.

The Korean missionary movement began to explode in the 1980s. In 1988, "Mission Korea"—a student mission conference similar to Urbana in the United States—began to meet every two years and attracted up to five thousand students at each conference. This conference encouraged intercessory prayer movements for global mission and mobilized many Korean young people to commit their lives to serving in mission. As a result, the number of Korean cross-cultural missionaries ballooned to over twenty thousand global workers in 2013, serving with 166 organizations in 171 countries.

Korean missionaries have been sent out by denominational churches—Presbyterian, Methodist, Baptist, and Assemblies of God, among others—and also through mission organizations such as the Global Mission Society. About 90 percent serve through Korean mission structures, while the remainder work with Western or international mission groups. Currently about half of Korean missionaries are ministering in Asia, while 25 percent are serving in the Muslim world. Since the 1990s, Korean mission groups and missionaries have increased their focus on evangelizing and planting churches among unreached people groups.

Because many Korean missionaries are well educated, they are serving as tentmakers—doctors, teachers, and in business—in China as well as in Buddhist and Muslim contexts. Historically, most Korean global workers have emphasized proclamation in their work; however, increasingly others are pursuing holistic mission, including medical work, business as mission, and community development. Some Korean mission leaders have set a goal of sending one hundred thousand missionaries and one million Christian professionals by 2030.[10]

---

10. See Chul Ho Han, "Korean Sending," in *Perspectives on the World Christian Movement: A Reader*, ed. Ralph D. Winter and Steven C. Hawthorne (Pasadena, CA: William Carey Library, 2009), 372–73; Timothy Kiho Park, "Korean Christian World Mission: Missionary Movement of the Korean Church," in *Missions from the Majority World: Progress, Challenges, and Case Studies,*

CHINA

In the 1940s, three Chinese pastors had a vision to send laborers to the rest of the world. Calling it "Back to Jerusalem," their vision was to send missionaries from China westward along the Silk Road toward Jerusalem, evangelizing the peoples of east Asia, central Asia, and the Middle East along the way. During this initial period, they trained itinerant evangelists and sent them out on preaching tours. The new communist regime that came to power in 1949 largely squelched this movement.

In 1976, Chinese church leaders met in Hong Kong to convene the first Chinese Congress on World Evangelization. Their intention was to evaluate the church's role in mission. In 2006, over three thousand Chinese believers attended the seventh congress, which met for the first time on Chinese soil. The delegates reflected on the history of the Chinese church and made a renewed commitment to fulfill the Great Commission. Within China, the church has focused on evangelizing rural areas, urban centers, and the majority Han Chinese. They have also begun to minister to minority peoples such as the Hui and Uyghur peoples. In addition, Chinese church planters have evangelized Chinese expatriate communities in Southeast Asia, Europe, South America, and North America.

With the revival of the "Back to Jerusalem" movement in the 1990s, the Chinese church's mission vision has grown beyond simply reaching their own people in China or abroad. Rather, they are committed to sending one hundred thousand bivocational evangelists and church planters to Muslim, Hindu, and Buddhist peoples between China and Jerusalem.[11]

INDIA

Following India's independence from Britain in 1947, many Protestant mission organizations began to withdraw from the country. In the 1960s, indigenous missionary movements began springing up, filling this vacuum. Most Indian missionaries during this period labored as itinerant

---

ed. Enoch Wan and Michael Pocock (Pasadena, CA: William Carey Library, 2009), 97–120; and Steven Sang-Cheol Moon, *The Korean Missionary Movement: Dynamics and Trends, 1988–2013* (Pasadena, CA: William Carey Library, 2016), xi–36.

11. See "What Is 'Back to Jerusalem'?," Back to Jerusalem, https://backtojerusalem.com/about/ (accessed June 25, 2018); also Enoch Wan, "Chinese Sending," in Winter and Hawthorne, *Perspectives on the World Christian Movement*, 374.

preachers and church planters within the cross-cultural mosaic of the Indian subcontinent.

In 1977, the India Missions Association was founded with five partnering organizations. By 2009, the network included 220 mission agencies and over fifty thousand Indian missionaries. While continuing to focus on evangelism and church planting among minority peoples within India, other missionaries pioneered work in community development, youth ministry, and engaging India's wealthy upper class with the gospel. Most Indian missionaries continue to serve cross-culturally within India; however, others are now going outside the country in mission.[12]

MISSION FROM AFRICA

Once African nations began achieving independence from Europe in the 1950s and 1960s, African indigenous Christians increasingly assumed church leadership roles. In addition, spiritual revivals occurred in Burundi and Zululand in southern Africa. In this environment of renewal, Africans made their first efforts to mobilize for mission in Ghana and Nigeria. In Ghana, the national evangelism committee succeeded in launching eight thousand new churches. Later, mission-sending networks emerged in South Africa and Kenya.

In Nigeria, the Nigerian Evangelical Mission network formed in 1982. By 1986, when ten thousand international missionaries were laboring inside Nigeria, the Nigerian church had sent out five hundred nationals for mission in other places. By 2005, over five thousand Nigerians connected to ninety different organizations were ministering in sixty-five countries around the world, including China, Brazil, and Bolivia. In 2006, this network launched a campaign called Vision 50/15 with a goal to send fifty thousand Nigerians in mission by the year 2021.[13]

---

12. See K. Rajendran, "Indian Sending," in Winter and Hawthorne, *Perspectives on the World Christian Movement*, 373; also India Mission Association, http://www.imaindia.org (accessed June 25, 2018).

13. See Timothy Olonade, "African Sending," in Winter and Hawthorne, *Perspectives on the World Christian Movement*, 371.

MISSION FROM LATIN AMERICA

In 1976, five hundred Latin American student delegates gathered at the University of Paraná in Curitiba, Brazil, for a global mission conference organized by the International Fellowship of Evangelical Students. The conference concluded with a declaration that "the church is a missionary church or it is no church at all."[14] In 1987, COMIBAM (the Ibero-American Missions Conference) met for its first conference in São Paulo. There, mission strategist Luis Bush declared that Latin America had gone from being a mission field to being a mission sender. The thirty-one hundred delegates affirmed the call for the Latin American church to participate in global mission.

By 2009, over ten thousand Latin Americans had been sent in mission, serving with 462 international or Latin American organizations. While many are serving cross-culturally within their own countries or in other parts of the Americas, around 10 percent are serving among unreached peoples in Hindu, Buddhist, and Muslim contexts. Because of historic connections with Arabs in the Iberian Peninsula (Spain and Portugal), Latin Americans have a cultural affinity with Arab-Muslims. Many Latinos began serving in mission among Muslims beginning in the 1980s and 1990s. In 1984, PMI (Muslim Peoples International), the first Latin American mission focused on the Muslim world, was founded.[15]

BRAZIL

Brazilians make up the oldest and largest Latin American mission movement. While Brazil has been sending missionaries to the world since the early twentieth century, global engagement began in earnest during the 1970s, when Brazilians started serving with international mission groups such as Operation Mobilization. In 1975, following revival in a Bible institute in Paraná, Antioch Mission, one of the earliest indigenous Brazilian mission organizations, was founded. The mission gatherings in Curitiba and São Paulo also encouraged a Brazilian mission engagement.

---

14. Edward L. Smither, *Brazilian Evangelical Missions in the Arab World: History, Culture, Practice, and Theology* (Eugene, OR: Pickwick, 2012), 1.

15. See Carlos Scott, "Latin American Sending," in Winter and Hawthorne, *Perspectives on the World Christian Movement*, 375.

The Brazilian missionary movement grew from 595 laborers in 1972 to over five thousand in 2010. Presently, Brazilians are serving with 115 mission organizations, both international and Brazilian. Around 40 percent serve cross-culturally within Brazil or in other parts of Latin America, with an increasing number serving in Africa, Asia, and in the Middle East. By 2010, at least two hundred Brazilians were serving among Arab-Muslims.

In addition to COMIBAM, the Association of Transcultural Missions Agencies (AMTB) functions as a network for forty Brazilian mission organizations. They mobilize Brazilian evangelical churches to greater mission involvement, promote cooperation between organizations, develop materials to educate churches about mission, and provide training for Brazilian missionaries. Since 1990, the AMTB has convened a strategic planning conference every few years.

Since Brazilians are very relational people, many have focused on friendship evangelism. Often, they have built relationships through showing hospitality or conducting soccer camps. These relationships have naturally led to opportunities for discipleship and even church planting. Brazilians also emphasize humanitarian work in mission, including medical ministry, community development projects, and caring for the handicapped. Finally, many Brazilians note that intercessory prayer is a vital part of their work.[16]

WHO ARE MAJORITY WORLD MISSIONARIES?

FULL-TIME VOCATIONAL MISSIONARIES

Majority world missionaries include African, Asian, and Latin American global workers who are sent out as official missionaries from their local churches and possibly through a mission organization. Often formally trained in a theological seminary or mission training institute, they self-identify as missionaries at least in their home countries.

---

16. See Bertil Ekström, "Brazilian Sending," in Winter and Hawthorne, *Perspectives on the World Christian Movement*, 371–72; also Smither, *Brazilian Evangelical Missions in the Arab World*.

DIASPORA BELIEVERS

Peruvian missiologist Samuel Escobar argues that for every Latin American missionary sent out as an official missionary in the twentieth century, another ten Latinos migrated for work. This second group shared their faith, made disciples, planted churches, and participated in mission.[17] Though these immigrants do not self-identify as missionaries or religious workers, they clearly contribute to the task of global mission. Three representative groups of diaspora believers that we will highlight briefly include Koreans, Filipinos, and Iranians.

Koreans

During the Japanese occupation of Korea between 1910 and 1945, many Koreans left their homeland, fleeing oppression. Today, over seven million Koreans live in 180 countries around the world. Korean Christians have established five thousand churches around the world. It is difficult to enter any major population center in the world and not find a Korean congregation. In the United States, many churches have a Korean-language service for first-generation immigrants and an English service for the second generation. Historically, the ministry focus of the Korean diaspora has been rather insulated and focused on the Korean believing community. However, well-educated Korean professionals, including professors, doctors, and diplomats, are increasingly engaging in witness with their neighbors and coworkers in Europe, Latin America, the Middle East, and China.[18]

Filipinos

Because of poverty and the lack of employment opportunities, for nearly half a century the government of the Philippines has actively encouraged its citizens to move abroad for work. Presently, 10 percent of the Filipino population (one hundred million) live and work abroad in 197 countries. Large concentrations of Filipinos work in Saudi Arabia, the Gulf countries, Libya,

---

17. See J. Daniel Salinas, "The Great Commission in Latin America," in *The Great Commission: Evangelicals and the History of World Missions*, ed. Martin I. Klauber and Scott M. Manetsch (Nashville: B&H Academic, 2008), 134–39.

18. See S. Hun Kim and Susie Hershberger, "Korean Diaspora Ministries," in *Scattered and Gathered: A Global Compendium of Diaspora Missiology*, ed. Sadiri Joy Tira and Testsunao Yamamori (Oxford: Regnum, 2016), 408–13.

and Canada. While some work in business, IT, engineering and the medical field, others labor as household servants and in factories.

In 2010, approximately two hundred thousand Filipino evangelical Christians had immigrated abroad. They have established Filipino churches in many nations, including the restricted Gulf states. While these congregations have historically cared for Filipino believers, since 2005 diaspora church leaders have exhorted them toward more deliberate mission engagement.[19]

Iranians

Since the Islamic revolution in Iran in 1979, millions of Iranians have left their homeland. Following an initial wave of immigrants to Turkey, Pakistan, and the United States, Iranians have also settled in Europe, the United Kingdom, and Canada. Because Iranians do not need a visa for neighboring Turkey, this has often been the first stop on their migration highway. Presently, one million Iranians reside in Turkey. They are the most well-educated and financially independent refugees in the world. International mission organizations have been ministering to Iranians in Turkey for decades. Iranians who have come to faith in Christ are now evangelizing other Iranians in Turkey. The fastest-growing churches in Turkey are Iranian congregations. By 2004, approximately 1 percent of the Iranians living abroad (about fifty thousand people) had embraced the gospel. Iranian churches have since been planted in the United States, Canada, the United Kingdom, and Scandinavia. Presently in Sweden some of the most vibrant churches are pastored by Iranian women.[20]

---

19. See Berting Fernando, "Filipino Sending," in Winter and Hawthorne, *Perspectives on the World Christian Movement*, 374–75; also Luis Pantoja, Joy B. Tira Sadiri, and Enoch Wan, eds., *Scattered: The Filipino Global Presence* (Manila: LifeChange, 2004).

20. See Houston et al., "New People Next Door," 52–53.

WHAT DO MAJORITY WORLD
MISSIONARIES DO?

EVANGELISM

Non-Western missionaries have been faithful evangelists. Chinese and Indian missionaries have proclaimed the gospel through itinerant preaching. Brazilians share their faith while showing hospitality and through sports ministry. Korean diaspora believers build relationships with coworkers and communicate their faith. They also invite friends to gospel concerts at Korean churches, where the gospel is presented. In Canada, Filipino diaspora believers are actively involved in strategies such as Evangelism Explosion, sharing the gospel with other internationals as well as European-background Canadians.[21]

Majority world missionaries demonstrate a real burden for reaching Muslims. Latin Americans share the gospel with Arab-Muslims through personal relationships and while showing hospitality. The Chinese church's "Back to Jerusalem" strategy involves a great emphasis on the Muslim world. In the Gulf countries, Filipino diaspora pastors are striving to transform their churches into training centers, equipping Filipino laypeople to evangelize their Muslim neighbors. Iranian diaspora believers remain steadfast in reaching other Iranians. Founded in 1980, Iranian Christians International exists to minister to the eight million Iranian and Persian-speaking Afghans living abroad. The Colorado-based group shares the gospel through relationships, establishes Persian language Bible studies and churches, conducts discipleship conferences, and trains Iranians in evangelizing other Iranians.[22]

CHURCH PLANTING

While sharing the gospel and discipling new believers, majority world believers emphasize church planting. Korean missionaries are focused on planting churches among unreached people groups, while Indians are doing the same cross-culturally within the Indian subcontinent. Chinese, Korean, and Iranian diaspora communities are continually planting new

---

21. See Evangelism Explosion, http://evangelismexplosion.org (accessed June 25, 2018).

22. See "Who Is ICI?," Iranian Christians International, http://www.iranchristians.org (accessed June 25, 2018).

congregations around the world in order to evangelize their own people. In some contexts, Filipino diaspora churches are moving beyond the Filipino community and are now planting multicultural churches.

MINISTER IN WORD AND DEED

In addition to proclaiming the gospel, many majority world missionaries are also addressing real human needs. Koreans, Brazilians, and Indians integrate medical care, business development, and community development in their ministries. Brazilians have led the way in social ministry, including ministry to the poor, to vulnerable women, and to the handicapped. As part of their work among Iranians, Iranian Christians International assists refugees with resettlement, provides trauma counseling, and works as an advocate for the suffering church.

PRAYER

Global South missionaries and believers also emphasize prayer as a part of their mission work. One of the key outcomes of the "Mission Korea" conferences was a global intercessory prayer ministry. Some Brazilian and Latin American missionaries report that intercessory prayer is a central part of their work. This includes praying for healing and deliverance in contexts of spiritual warfare in the Muslim world. Antioch Mission, one of Brazil's first indigenous mission organizations, established a prayer chapel on its mission base. Intercessors have been praying there almost around the clock since the 1980s.

SUMMARY

In evaluating the contribution of majority world missionaries (full-time vocational workers and diaspora Christians) within the bigger picture of twenty-first-century global mission, non-Western missionaries possess certain advantages that their Western counterparts do not have. They also face unique challenges.

ADVANTAGES

Fewer Political Barriers

Global South Christians can often access countries that Western missionaries cannot. Because of diplomatic and trade relations, Brazilian and Korean believers are allowed entry into Iran. Chinese Christians can freely enter North Korea. Non-Western believers are also free of the political "baggage" that Western Christians bring. An American living in North Africa or the Middle East will constantly be confronted with political questions by Muslim friends; however, Argentinian missionaries are asked about things such as World Cup soccer. Also, since Argentina has never sent troops to the Middle East, they do not share a bitter history with people in the region as North Americans do.

Hardship and Suffering

Because many majority world missionaries come from modest economic backgrounds, they are able to identify with the poor in their context. Throughout mission history, barriers have often developed when affluent Western missionaries settled in a poor area and lived at a higher standard of living than their host people. A veteran Brazilian missionary who was serving in north Africa while his own country's economy was collapsing during the late 1980s wrote: "Because of our background of relative poverty and economic crises and inflation, we can identify with [Arab] Muslims. People perceive that and it is possible to bond with Arabs in a deep level of friendship." Another Latin American missionary added: "[Muslims] see us as Latinos, partners and similar. Not as westerners, dominant and indifferent. It seems as we share the same struggles, the same pain."[23]

Majority world Christians are also generally better prepared to endure hardship and suffering in the work of mission because of their backgrounds. For example, Chinese missionaries have already endured much difficulty in their home country; therefore, the challenges of living in the Middle East and central Asia are not as shocking as they might be to someone from North America or Europe.

---

23. Smither, *Brazilian Evangelical Mission in the Arab World*, 90.

Cultural and Spirit World Connections

Majority world believers enjoy effective ministries because of the cultural closeness between their own culture and the host culture. Latin Americans generally adapt well to Arab culture because of similar values of time, family, relationships, and hospitality.

Non-Western believers also seem to adapt well to animistic and folk religious contexts, which include demonic encounters and magic. Because spiritism (belief in spirits that affect human lives) is so prevalent in Brazil, Brazilian workers from across the evangelical spectrum do not seem shocked by spiritual warfare they encounter in folk Muslim contexts (mixing magic and Islam). Many already have experience in deliverance-type ministries before going to the Arab world.

CHALLENGES

Training, Resources, Care

While the younger churches of the non-Western world are embracing global mission with zeal, many have not received appropriate cross-cultural and missiological training. This is especially true for diaspora believers who are not going out as missionaries in an official sense.

Many majority world missionaries also go to the field with a lack of adequate financial resources. While, on one hand, poor missionaries might connect better with the poor on their mission field, on the other hand, lack of resources may result in discouragement, burnout, and the need to return home.

Non-Western missionaries often lack member or missionary care—pastoral care from home church or agencies for missionaries—which might cut short their cross-cultural ministry. This strategy of providing care, counseling, and support is still rather new for Western mission organizations. So it is not a surprise that Latin American, Asian, and African Christians also lack this needed care.

Language Barriers

Some majority world missionaries are unable to partner with other Christian workers in a country because of language barriers. Typically, English is the common language for the mission community in most contexts in the world. This poses challenges for missionaries who speak only

Spanish, Portuguese, or Chinese. Some non-Westerners have chosen to learn English to bridge this barrier. However, this choice requires an investment of time and energy away from learning the national language.

Political Vulnerability

Finally, while non-Western missionaries may not have the political baggage of Western workers, they do lack political leverage and might face more discrimination from local authorities. If a missionary from a powerful Western country is arrested for leading a Bible study, she may receive a warning or, at worst, be expelled from the country. In the same scenario, a Filipino believer might be imprisoned and denied any legal due process. Majority world missionaries certainly labor from a posture of vulnerability.

FURTHER READING

Bauman, Stephan, Matthew Soerens, and Samir Issam. *Seeking Refuge: On the Shores of the Global Refugee Crisis*. Chicago: Moody, 2016.

Eitel, Keith E., ed. *Missions in Contexts of Violence*. Pasadena, CA: William Carey Library, 2008.

Ekström, Bertil. "Brazilian Sending." In *Perspectives on the World Christian Movement: A Reader*, edited by Ralph D. Winter and Steven C. Hawthorne, 371–72. Pasadena, CA: William Carey Library, 2009.

Escobar, Samuel. *The New Global Mission: The Gospel from Everywhere to Everyone*. Downers Grove, IL: InterVarsity, 2003.

Evangelism Explosion. http://evangelismexplosion.org. Accessed June 25, 2018.

"Facts and Figures." Canadian Bureau for International Education. https://cbie.ca/media/facts-and-figures/. Accessed June 25, 2018.

Fernando, Berting. "Filipino Sending." In *Perspectives on the World Christian Movement: A Reader*, edited by Ralph D. Winter and Steven C. Hawthorne, 374–75. Pasadena, CA: William Carey Library, 2009.

"Figures at a Glance." UNHCR: The UN Refugee Agency. http://www.unhcr.org/en-us/figures-at-a-glance.html. Accessed June 25, 2018.

Friedman, Thomas. "Three Eras of Globalization." August 22, 2008. https://www.youtube.com/watch?v=lp4znWHvsjU.

Han, Chul Ho. "Korean Sending." In *Perspectives on the World Christian Movement: A Reader*, edited by Ralph D. Winter and Steven C. Hawthorne, 372–73. Pasadena, CA: William Carey Library, 2009.

Houston, Tom, Robin Thomson, Ram Gidoomal, and Leiton Chinn. "The New People Next Door." Lausanne Occasional Paper 33. Lausanne Committee for World

Evangelization, 2004. https://www.lausanne.org/wp-content/uploads/2007/06/LOP55_IG26.pdf.

India Mission Association. http://www.imaindia.org. Accessed June 25, 2018.

Kim, S. Hun, and Hershberger, Susie. "Korean Diaspora Ministries." In *Scattered and Gathered: A Global Compendium of Diaspora Missiology*, edited by Sadiri Joy Tira and Testsunao Yamamori, 408–13. Oxford: Regnum, 2016.

"Mapping the SEVIS by the Numbers." Homeland Security. https://studyinthestates.dhs.gov/sevis-by-the-numbers. Accessed June 25, 2018.

Moon, Steven Sang-Cheol. *The Korean Missionary Movement: Dynamics and Trends, 1988–2013*. Pasadena, CA: William Carey Library, 2016.

Olonade, Timothy. "African Sending." In *Perspectives on the World Christian Movement: A Reader*, edited by Ralph D. Winter and Steven C. Hawthorne, 371. Pasadena, CA: William Carey Library, 2009.

Pantoja, Luis, Joy B. Tira Sadiri, and Enoch Wan, eds. *Scattered: The Filipino Global Presence*. Manila: LifeChange, 2004.

Park, Timothy Kiho. "Korean Christian World Mission: Missionary Movement of the Korean Church." In *Missions from the Majority World: Progress, Challenges, and Case Studies*, edited by Enoch Wan and Michael Pocock, 97–120. Pasadena, CA: William Carey Library, 2009.

"Past Summary Ledgers." Gun Violence Archive. http://www.gunviolencearchive.org/past-tolls. Accessed June 25, 2018.

Pocock, Michael, Gailyn Van Rheenen, and Douglas McConnell. *The Changing Face of World Missions: Engaging Contemporary Issues and Trends*. Grand Rapids: Baker Academic, 2005.

Rajendran, K. "Indian Sending." In *Perspectives on the World Christian Movement: A Reader*, edited by Ralph D. Winter and Steven C. Hawthorne, 373. Pasadena, CA: William Carey Library, 2009.

Salinas, J. Daniel. "The Great Commission in Latin America." In *The Great Commission: Evangelicals and the History of World Missions*, edited by Martin I. Klauber and Scott M. Manetsch, 134–48. Nashville: B&H Academic, 2008.

Scott, Carlos. "Latin American Sending." In *Perspectives on the World Christian Movement: A Reader*, edited by Ralph D. Winter and Steven C. Hawthorne, 375. Pasadena, CA: William Carey Library, 2009.

Smither, Edward L. *Brazilian Evangelical Missions in the Arab World: History, Culture, Practice, and Theology*. Eugene, OR: Pickwick, 2012.

Wan, Enoch. "Chinese Sending." In *Perspectives on the World Christian Movement: A Reader*, edited by Ralph D. Winter and Steven C. Hawthorne, 374. Pasadena, CA: William Carey Library, 2009.

"What Is 'Back to Jerusalem'?" Back to Jerusalem. https://backtojerusalem.com/about/. Accessed June 25, 2018.

"Who Is ICI?" Iranian Christians International. http://www.iranchristians.org. Accessed June 25, 2018.

"Who, What, Why: Who Are the Yazidis?" BBC News. August 8, 2014. http://www .bbc.com/news/blogs-magazine-monitor-28686607.

Yeh, Allen. *Polycentric Missiology: Twenty-First Century Mission from Everywhere to Everyone*. Downers Grove, IL: Intervarsity, 2016.

Epilogue

God's people imitate God, declaring his glory among the nations and crossing boundaries from faith to nonfaith. That's Christian mission. This book offers a snapshot of this global history, showing how the church has been a missionary people since the first century to the present day. This survey is introductory in nature but invites deeper study on each period, person, region, and approach in it.

Studying mission history allows us to learn from the past as we contemplate the future of mission. Reflecting on mistakes in mission (e.g., the abuse of power, the conflation of empire and mission) gives us the chance to repent and renounce wrong thinking and bad practices. We can move on and not repeat these mistakes. Learning from the innovations and breakthroughs in mission, and the great sacrifices made by missionaries through the ages, should teach us humility. When we engage in mission today, we stand on the shoulders of giants who still have much to teach us. Finally, reflecting on mission history reminds us that this is God's mission. Despite successful innovation and embarrassing failures, God sustains his global church and his kingdom continues.

This raises further questions that ought to be addressed as we move forward in mission. First, *who are the missionaries?* Our survey of the early church showed us that much of the church (bishops, monks, everyday believers) felt a sense of ownership for mission. Twenty-first-century majority world missionaries, especially diaspora believers, witness wherever they live and work. Looking ahead, how does the whole church—every believer from everywhere—winsomely participate in mission?

Second, *how does the whole church collaborate in mission?* Today the majority of believers and missionaries come from the Global South, while the majority of resources (money, theological education resources) remain in North America and Europe. Should Western churches simply send money while the majority world sends laborers? How should the global church work together?

Also, with the growth of indigenous churches and national leaders, how should international missionaries (Western or majority world) relate to and collaborate with national church leaders? How should mission be carried out in parts of the world that are already highly evangelized? What should be the posture of a missionary entering a country where a national church already exists?

Third, given the reality that suffering and hardship will continue, *how does the church on mission address suffering?* How should the church respond when believers go to jail for proclaiming the gospel? How should mission be approached in contexts of violence? What is an appropriate biblical theology of suffering in mission?

Finally, *how do we remain focused on the biblical meaning of Christian mission?* Mission without proclaiming the death, burial, resurrection, and ascension of Christ ceases to be mission. However, what is the relationship between mission in word (proclamation) and deed (caring for human needs)? Is it okay for some groups to focus on evangelism while others work to solve problems related to world hunger, human trafficking, and other social issues?

While these questions require time and attention, we wrestle with them in hope. Indeed, Christ's power and presence undergird his Great Commission to the church.

> Then Jesus came to them and said, "All authority in heaven and on earth has been given to me. Therefore go and make disciples of all nations, baptizing them in the name of the Father and of the Son and of the Holy Spirit, and teaching them to obey everything I have commanded you. And surely I am with you always, to the very end of the age." (Matt 28:18–20)

Christian Mission Index